Enjoy the journey!

Jay Sommer

JOURNEY TO THE GOLDEN DOOR

A Survivor's Tale

by JAY SOMMER

SHENGOLD PUBLISHERS, INC.
New York

ISBN 0-88400-177-6
Library of Congress Catalog Card Number: 94-067009
Copyright © 1994 by Jay Sommer
Published by Shengold Publishers, Inc.
18 West 45th Street
New York, NY 10036
Printed in the United States of America

Table of Contents

PART ONE: EUROPE

PART TWO: THE GOLDEN DOOR

Dedication

To the two women whose love, steadfastness, strength, and vision have nourished my life; my mother Feiga and my wife Shirley.

To my brother Samuel who at the age of fourteen was already endowed with the goodness, grace, and courage of the man he would have become.

And finally, to my son Jason, his wife Bernardine, and my grandchildren Matthias, Danielle, and Benjamin who have been the joy of my life.

Acknowledgments

I wish to express my profound gratitude to my wife for all she has done for me during the writing of this book. With her expert knowledge of English, she has led me (when I was wise enough to let her!) out of more than one verbal quagmire. It was she who provided the title for the book I thought most effective. Her presence and support were a great solace to me as I relived in writing the pain of the past. With her, my return to the places which held unhappy memories became more bearable.

I cannot thank my son Jason enough for taking time out from college teaching and his own writing to read the book in its entirety and to advise me on some matters of style and substance which made the book better than it otherwise would have been. Just as important, he expressed to me his satisfaction with my work.

I am most grateful to my niece Chica (Jessica) Kopp, an illustrator, for her creative efforts. She arrived from California simply to visit with us, but found herself with a job offer, that of designing my book jacket, which she accepted enthusiastically, with results that have pleased us both.

To my brother Harry and his wife Lilly I extend my appreciation for their help in recalling experiences that we shared in the past and that are part of this book. My cousin Sandor's knowledge of Czechoslovakia, Hungary, and the former Soviet Union was of great help to me when I needed authoritative information on these countries.

My special thanks also go to Yanos Lahav who gave my manuscript a last thorough review and improved it greatly by correcting certain historical and biblical references, helping with the transliteration of a number of foreign words, and suggesting changes in usage.

Many thanks go to Eva and Gyuri Kelenyi in Budapest. Eva helped plan my return to Mukachevo and made arrangements for a comfortable stay in the Hungarian capital. She also accompanied my wife and me to the scenes of my early life as did her friend Nina whose family extended their hospitality to us. Volodya, Nina's boyfriend, generously transported us everywhere we wished to go.

I want to thank my friend Ella Mazel for helping in the preparation of the manuscript for presentation to various publishers. I am also indebted to her for painstakingly transcribing onto a computer disk the edited manuscript after its acceptance for publication. In the process, she also made her own valuable editorial contributions. All of this in the face of imminent eye surgery! Lastly, I want to thank my friend Bernie, Ella's husband, himself a publisher, for his practical advice on matters concerning the book's publication.

In the Rose Garden

It is a lovely spring day, and I am at the White House about to receive the 1981 National Teacher of the Year award. The Rose Garden is resplendent. In the audience, surrounded by television equipment and clicking cameras, are my lovely wife, Shirley, and my son, Jason, who made a special trip from Ireland for this occasion. The Secretary of Education, the New York State Commissioner of Education, and many other dignitaries are present as well.

Mrs. Reagan presides over the ceremony, standing in for the President, who is recovering from the recent attempt on his life. Having read about my background as a survivor of the Holocaust, the First Lady speaks movingly about the difficulties I have overcome. She hands me the crystal apple traditionally given to the National Teacher of the Year, and kisses me on the cheek.

I, too, am given the opportunity to say a few words. As I stand in front of the microphone, I am more than ever aware of how lucky I am to be the recipient of an award that seems just as much a tribute to America as it is to me. America is one of the few countries where such miracles are possible, where a young immigrant, without knowing the language, with very little formal education, can eventually be honored in the White House in the presence of his family.

How did all this happen? How did life's vicissitudes take a poor boy from a small Czechoslovakian village to forced-labor camps, to refugee camps, and finally to America? After much reflection I decided that I should tell the story of my wanderings. There were several compelling reasons for this. For one, I am, be it in a small way, a witness to a Holocaust that some claim never happened. I wanted my odyssey to serve as a reminder of Hitler's foul deeds and help ensure that, once the few survivors are no longer here, there would be one more record of it. Furthermore, as a teacher it is incumbent on me to touch on the importance of education in countering the ignorance that can lead to such crimes against humanity.

I also felt that writing about my family, and the tragedies that befell them and the rest of my people, would be a memorial to them. It was equally important to me to evoke some of the names and deeds of the gallant Christians who were instrumental in helping me and other Jews to survive the Holocaust, often at the risk of their own lives. They represented a vestige of light in history's darkest hour.

Although this book may be classified as an autobiography, it is filled with many personalities who are only marginally related to my story but who stand on their own as participants in the panorama of events I describe. There are, however, two people who could be considered as heroine and hero of this book — my mother, whose unique love sustained me during many difficult times, and my brother Samuel, whose fate you will soon learn.

Jay Sommer receiving the Crystal Apple, awarded annually to the National Teacher of the Year.

PART ONE

EUROPE

The three problems of the age—the degradation of man by poverty, the ruin of women by starvation, and the dwarfing of childhood by physical and spiritual night.

Victor Hugo, *Les Miserables*

Chapter 1

Life In A Carpathian Village

My mother, Yitta Feiga (Fanny), was born in Szaplonca in the Carpathian area of Czechoslovakia in 1898. Before World War II Szaplonca had a vibrant Jewish community, with many institutions of learning and a famous lineage of rabbis.

Yitta Feiga and five other children were the product of my grandfather's fruitful second marriage which followed the death of his first wife at a young age. Grandfather Melach, after whom I am partially named, was a very energetic, handsome man, well-respected in Szaplonca by Jew and Gentile. Although observant, he was a modern Jew who believed that the study of Talmud alone was not enough and that hard physical work and participation in secular life were of great importance as well. Everyone in the family spoke Yiddish, but the preferred language in the household was Hungarian. Unlike the wives of Hasidic or Orthodox men, my grandmother did not wear a wig. The young men in the family, like my grandfather, were clean-shaven and without the *payoth* (sidelocks). Nor did they have to wear *zizith* (fringes) or *yarmulkes* (skullcaps). The girls attended social functions in mixed company and were permitted to have rendezvous.

As a young man, Grandpa Melach was apprenticed in a flour mill and became proficient in every phase of the craft. He soon became the foreman of the same mill and made a fine living for his large family. As a consequence, all his children were able to attend both secular and religious schools beyond what was then customary for the children of a Jewish working man. Once the children finished their basic schooling, every one of them, including the girls, had to learn a trade and become self-sufficient.

Fanny was a bright, vivacious, pretty child. She was known as the happy little comedienne who made everyone laugh. She was loved by the entire family, but especially adored by her father who, among other things, admired her for her tomboyish nature. He did not call her

5

Feiga, but always by her diminutive, Feigele (little bird). Fanny was an excellent student; given different circumstances, she could have gone on to the gymnasium (academic high school) as well as to the university.

By the time she was fifteen, Fanny had been helping take care of two younger brothers and was a second mother to her baby sister. Even as a young girl, she was a fine cook and baked the best bread in Szaplonca. At the age of fifteen she was apprenticed to a seamstress, and after two years she was able to sew dresses in the latest styles, as well as garments for the smaller boys. Socially, Fanny was a great success. Before she was eighteen, she had many well-to-do suitors and a few offers of marriage, but none lived up to her romantic expectations. She was waiting for her ideal, a gentle human being who would match her sensitive nature; she did not care if he was rich or poor.

Things were going well for the family until tragedy befell my grandfather. As he was replacing the belt on the shaft that drove the grinding wheels, his left leg was caught in the belt and torn off above the knee. My poor grandfather survived the accident but lost his job as a consequence. The family's savings were soon depleted, and they were forced to give up their comfortable home. Fortunately, all the children had trades, but in order for them to find work they had to move to the city of Mukachevo. In very short order, the children found employment and were able to support their parents and remain together. They no longer enjoyed the bounty that had been available to them when Grandfather was working. They were now living on the edge of poverty—but not at the mercy of charity, which would have been unacceptable to any member of that very proud clan.

It was in Mukachevo that Fanny met the man she believed would make her happy. Shmeel (Samuel) Weis was handsome, and just a few years older than she. The principal quality that attracted her to Samuel was his sensitive nature. After a long romantic courtship, a date was set for marriage. Despite Grandfather's ill fortune, the family still succeeded in finding enough money to give Feigele an appropriate wedding that included an elegant gown in which she looked the picture of the ideal bride. The couple settled in a modest one-room apartment on the edge of town.

Samuel was a fine cobbler who knew not only how to repair shoes but how to make new ones to order. Though it was neither a prestigious trade nor a source of future wealth, it was a way to eke out a steady living. Fanny felt confident that with the combination of Samuel's talents and her own skills as a seamstress the couple would eventually manage to live a good life and be able to afford to raise a family.

But these were difficult times. People were still suffering from the aftereffects of the devastating First World War. Samuel's small shoemaker shop did not do well, and he had a hard time paying the rent. Fanny could not find enough clients for her dressmaking. A year later, they decided to find a location where both would be able to do better. Fanny knew her best chances for earning good money were in a rural setting. After a brief search, a suitable place was found. It was the small village of Kustanovice, tucked away in one of the valleys of the majestic Carpathian Mountains, where on a clear day one could see jagged peaks touching the sky. The thatched huts that dotted the village blended with nature as though they had been there from time immemorial.

Winter in Kustanovice was severe and somber. The snowfalls were often so heavy that it was virtually impossible to leave the huts. Visits between neighbors were rare during those dismal winter months. More frequent visitors were reindeer, stray wolves, mountain goats, and hosts of other animals, all in search of food.

Spring in the Carpathians was very slow in coming. It was not unusual to have 30-degree weather and sizable snowfalls well into late April. However, the Maker rewarded the young couple for their long-suffering patience. Once spring did arrive, nature erupted into soul-touching beauty, obliterating the gloom of the harsh winter as though it had never existed. Most impressive was the endless variety of splendid wildflowers—crocuses that pushed their way through the snow, dandelions that bobbed their yellow heads in the breeze, and bluebells and cornflowers that offered a delightful contrast to the greens and yellows—all of which formed acres and acres of dazzling beauty surrounding the little gray hut.

In this bucolic setting the couple prospered beyond expectations. Fanny's dressmaking business was particularly successful. Her Singer sewing machine was in perpetual motion. The future looked bright for the young people; adding to their happiness was Fanny's pregnancy. In due course she gave birth to a boy whom they named Hershel (Harry). However, their almost idyllic life was doomed not to last. When Harry was two years old, the young father contracted pneumonia and, after a pitifully short time, died. Fanny was left a widow at the age of twenty-four.

As soon as the matchmakers in Mukachevo learned that a potential marriage prospect was available, they descended on Fanny like vultures on wounded prey. Each one presented her with choices of suitors who they assured her would lighten the burdens of her difficult life. Actually, these great finds were, for the most part, themselves beset by misfortune. They were poor wanderers looking for a woman to cook them a decent meal, mend their clothes, and provide them with the warmth of a permanent home. One in Fanny's predicament, however, could not be too particular. Compelled by poverty and solitude, she had to give serious consideration to the possibility of marriage. The more she thought about it, the more she was lured into perceiving matrimony as a way out of the desolate, lonely existence that followed the loss of the husband she had loved. Marriage could also alleviate the fears that came with being alone in a village full of virulently anti-Semitic men who would not hesitate to rape an unprotected Jewish woman. The final argument—that a good man would be a mentor for her orphan boy, a teacher of Torah who is so important in the life of a Jewish child—carried with it all the persuasive powers that were needed to accept the services of Leah the matchmaker, who could not wait to begin her hunt.

Leah, whose name later evoked multiple maledictions from Fanny, set out on her job with diabolical speed and confidence. Once she landed a customer, matching him or her with a suitable consort was simply a matter of time, and so her crude negotiations with a long procession of suitors began. Potentially eligible men were brought to the village until Leah's salesmanship prevailed and the most likely man was selected.

Unfortunately, there was much about Leah's offering that was kept a secret. Moshe Elijahu Sommer was a Hasidic Jew who, like many others of his caste, had accepted anti-Semitism with resignation and learned to live with it. He had also reconciled himself to the grim fact that employment opportunities for a Jew in that part of the world were virtually nonexistent. Having an intense dislike for peddling, the main source of income for many Jews, Moshe Elijahu could find little else to do to earn money. Thus he devoted more time to prayer than to labor. Other than his occasional work as a part-time fisherman he was unemployed with no real economic assets to his name.

The fact that he was twice Fanny's age gave her some pause. Still, he had redeeming features which partially obscured this shortcoming. Most appealing to Fanny was Leah's characterization of Moshe Elijahu as a Talmudic scholar endowed with cantorial talents. He was, according to Leah, one of the most respected men in the Jewish community of Mukachevo. Carrying some weight with Fanny as well was the description of Moshe Elijahu as an attractive man and who was rather young-looking for his age.

Leah's persuasive words and Fanny's hopes for a better life combined to bring about a meeting. On a Sunday afternoon, Moshe Elijahu and Leah the matchmaker made the five-mile walk to Kustanovice. Moshe Elijahu's appearance confirmed Leah's description. He was indeed an attractive man. He was fairly tall with a handsome face and a very impressive beard à la Michelangelo's *Moses*. Considering his poor economic status, he was impeccably dressed in customary Hasidic attire and shiny high black boots that showed a few scuffs from the long muddy road he had just traveled. He proved himself articulate and seemed to substantiate the matchmaker's report of his Talmudic knowledge. He often quoted entire passages from the Bible during his three-hour stay.

As was later revealed by Leah, Moshe Elijahu was captivated by Fanny's good looks, as well as by her intelligence. Fanny was indeed an engaging woman in both appearance and personality. She had deep brown eyes, and a somewhat large nose that might not please a perfectionist but suited her face, which always radiated charm. Moshe Elijahu must have appreciated her wonderful sense of humor and her uniquely sharp wit.

After the necessary small talk was dispensed with, the conversation turned to inquiries of a more serious nature. Several new facts about my father, hitherto not revealed by the matchmaker, were disclosed. Though Fanny knew that Moshe Elijahu was a widower, she had not known that he had seven grown children, one older than herself and six already married. She also learned that her suitor had no permanent residence of his own, but lived alternately with a son and a daughter in Mukachevo. Although these new revelations did not particularly please Fanny, they did not cast enough additional doubts to prevent her from considering marriage.

This first rendezvous ended with the fixing of a second meeting when more details leading to an eventual union would be discussed, and even a possible date for marriage set. Fanny would have preferred a less hasty pace for making these very important decisions. She would have liked some kind of courtship, something that would resemble the romance she had experienced in her first marriage. But her circumstances did not permit such luxuries, and she yielded to Leah whose tactics were aimed solely at hastening the collection of her matchmaking fee.

Two weeks later, Moshe Elijahu embarked on his voyage to Kustanovice in a broken-down carriage that belonged to one of his sons, drawn by a pitiably emaciated old nag. Not only was her gait slow, but one could see every part of the poor beast's bone structure. This time, Moshe Elijahu was accompanied by an entourage, two of his sons and the matchmaker, all of whom suffered terribly from the bitter cold brought on by an unexpected blizzard. As the storm raged, the men displayed their compassion for the poor nag, observing the Biblical dictum not to impose additional suffering on God's creatures. Instead of riding in the carriage, they walked the entire five miles. From time to time they even helped the horse by pushing the carriage along the steep mountain road which traversed the beautiful yet unfriendly birch forest.

On their arrival, Leah recounted the perils of the journey, depicting Moshe Elijahu in the most heroic language. This description gave the usually businesslike conduct of Leah's matchmaking a tinge of the romantic and at the same time placed the suitor in a more favorable light in the eyes of his future bride. Despite the inclement weather and the arduous work on behalf of the poor horse, Moshe Elijahu appeared to be in fine shape and happy to be again in Fanny's company. His two sons, eclipsed by their dominating father, nevertheless, expressed their delight with Fanny's warmth and charm. The tasty meal she had prepared was effusively praised by all the visitors. An atmosphere of familial harmony prevailed which could lead only to the joining of these two lives, a union that hopefully would meet with the approval of the Lord.

Thus fate, circumstances, necessity, and a conniving matchmaker conspired to bring Moshe Elijahu and Fanny together as husband and wife. A date was set for a small religious ceremony to be performed, not by a rabbi, but by a congregational substitute who was often employed by poor folk unable to afford a "regular" wedding.

The question of a dowry, however small, was a matter of prestige even among poor Jewish men. This business was easily settled. Once the marriage was consummated, Moshe Elijahu was to become the co-owner of a household that consisted of two single beds, a table, two chairs, a long bench, an old wardrobe that had seen better days, a Singer sewing machine, and a stove that would often fill the place with more smoke than heat. These were the total contents of the immaculately kept one-room hut that Fanny rented from a Ukrainian peasant. Perhaps the most valuable of Moshe Elijahu's acquisitions, though not strictly speaking part of a dowry, was Fanny's vocation as a seamstress. With this talent, she had been able to earn enough to feed and clothe herself and her child. Young peasant women eager to emulate the latest fashions flocked to her with the choicest patterns and fabrics, which she quickly turned into elegant garments. The young women prized these and wore them when they promenaded in front of the church on Sundays to the admiration of all the men.

The remuneration for Fanny's work came more often in the form of produce than in cash; nevertheless, it was of great value to a family that would otherwise have had to go hungry. Fanny's little enterprise must have been very attractive to Moshe Elijahu. Not only would his basic needs be provided for but, more importantly, he would now have the opportunity to devote more time to his studies and not have to look for a job. As a consequence of all his past rejections, searching for work had become a dreaded pursuit.

Although legal in the eyes of the Jewish community, this ceremony, performed by a congregant, was viewed by Hasidim as drab, lacking in the joys that should accompany a union between two people. This poor man's version of the wedding ceremony held in Mukachevo was followed by a modest party that did not offer enough to satisfy the physical hunger of the guests, but the lack of good food did not dampen the human spirit. The shortage of food was compensated for by the merriment that traditionally accompanies a Jewish wedding no matter how humble the betrothed. Indeed, according to my mother's detailed account of the event, it was a gay occasion animated by song and dance, with a solo clarinetist playing a variety of klezmer music that ran the gamut of musical moods from sadness to abandoned joy. Fanny and Moshe Elijahu displayed their Hasidic dancing talents. Joined by two ends of a handkerchief and urged on by lively hand-clapping, they leaped and whirled to the klezmer's varied rhythms.

Since honeymoons were not yet in fashion for poor folk, Moshe Elijahu and Fanny returned to Kustanovice on the same day that they became husband and wife. No special arrangements were necessary for the transportation of Moshe Elijahu's belongings. Except for his two fishing nets, which were badly in need of repair, the groom's wealth was that of a typically indigent Hasidic Jew: a caftan, a fur hat for the Sabbath, a pair of phylacteries, a prayer shawl, a prayer book, a book on the Talmud, the five books of the Torah bound in one tome, and several items of well-worn clothing. All these were carried by the couple on their way to the hut that had become Moshe Elijahu's new home in a village that had only one other Jewish family in a population of about 300. The other inhabitants of the village were almost exclusively Carpatho-Ukrainian peasants, who invariably treated the Jews with centuries-old anti-Semitic scorn.

Life for the newlyweds began on a hopeful financial footing. With spring quickly approaching, peasant women were standing in line to have measurements taken for their new garments. Moshe Elijahu's contribution to the household was limited to serving reluctantly from time to time as baby-sitter to Harry while Fanny worked, often from six in the morning until midnight. He made only a feeble attempt to find work and contented himself with the earnings from a few days of fishing in the mountain streams that surrounded the village. The few buckets of fish he sold in the town market yielded very little money. The burden of providing for the family and taking care of the household chores fell entirely on Fanny's shoulders. Yet she held on to her optimism, hoping that things would change for the better. It seemed to her then that it was still worthwhile to have exchanged her lonely widowhood for an imperfect marriage. Life rolled on, with no particular event out of the ordinary for a poor Jewish family isolated in a remote village.

Since Moshe Elijahu was still capable of observing the biblical injunction to "be fruitful and multiply," I, Jehudah Melach, came into the world within a year after the marriage. Two years later, my brother Shmuel (Samuel) fought his way into the family despite my mother's attempt to abort the fetus by drinking bitter tea and other concoctions recommended for such purposes. My mother's desperate action was prompted by some unhappy discoveries about my father, among them the fact that he did not really know how to be a parent to his children, besides being unable to provide for his family. Notwithstanding Mother's reluctance to bring another baby into the world, once she saw Samuel's beautiful face, she loved him as tenderly as she did Harry and me. Samuel turned out to be a very happy baby, and grew into a sweet-tempered, loving son.

Mother knew early in her marriage that Moshe Elijahu was a restless, unhappy soul. She did not suspect then that there were other more troubling aspects to his personality. As time passed, it turned out that not only did my father drink heavily, but he suffered from uncontrollable fits of rage that led to physical abuse of his wife and children. Had it not been for Mother, who at great risk to herself managed somehow to protect us, we would most likely have been beaten to a pulp. Despite Mother's intercession, we were still regularly subjected to severe thrashings.

One of my first childhood memories of consequence is of the time, when I was about five, that I witnessed my father's first frightful display of rage and brutality. After being away for several days, Father came home from the city quite drunk and belligerent. Mother tried everything to appease him, but to no avail. In his ravings, he accused her of not taking care of him and even of being unfaithful. At one point his fury reached such an extreme that he went out of the hut, picked up an ax, came back into the house, and started to smash the few pieces of furniture that Mother had worked so hard to acquire. We were all petrified by this outrageous spectacle. Mother had enough presence of mind to send Harry for the gendarmes in the nearest village, about three miles away. Harry revealed to me later that he knew exactly where the gendarmerie was located, since it was not the first time he had to go there. He must have run for his life, for it was not long before two huge officers armed with shotguns arrived on their bicycles, leaving poor Harry behind somewhere in the meadows. By then, most of the furniture had been damaged. My father was standing with a bundle of his belongings, presumably ready to leave us. The officers severely reprimanded him in Czech, which, like most Hasidic Jews, he did not understand. After making sure that he really left the hut, the officer in charge made some notes and said what appeared to be a few comforting words to Mother. Before leaving, he patted me on the head and said, "*Ne plach! Ne plach!* [Don't cry! Don't cry!]."

A few days later, Father returned with his bundle of clothing as if nothing had happened, as though he had no memory of that horrible day. He did remember that Harry and Mother had betrayed him by calling the gendarmes. As a result, each of us, separately, was subjected to a whipping. I could not understand why I too was being punished.

My first serious beating at the age of five left me terribly shaken. I realized that I was no longer just an observer, an exempted bystander, but old enough to be a helpless victim in a drama that was to unfold with great frequency. In order to avoid at least some of these attacks, I had to acquire the cunning of a boy far beyond my actual age and find ways to escape those cruel hands. It was as though I were no longer permitted to remain a child. Father's uncontrolled temper on that fateful morning was an introduction to a way of life in which I learned how to read his moods and anticipate the oncoming furies. Once I was able to recognize when he had too much to drink, I would escape from his presence by roaming in the meadows for hours at a time with my dear friend, my cat Miriam. We would flee the house even in the cold of the winter, when both of us would rather have been in a warm place. In the evenings, when I could not be outside, I went to bed early and huddled under the covers in hope of avoiding his notice.

Whenever Father's attacks were visited on us, Mother tried very hard to comfort us and to minimize in our eyes the import of what had taken place. She even tried to blame evil spirits for his behavior. But the mutilated furniture that could never be repaired and the repeated abuse to which we were subjected were much more convincing evidence of the sad reality than Mother's supernatural explanations. Children learn quickly and comprehend much more than is suspected by adults. I believe I understood intuitively, the way children often interpret their world, that much was amiss with our way of life.

Because this pitiable man who was my father seemed to have no capacity for affection or tenderness, he deprived himself of the joys of loving, and receiving the love of his children and his devoted wife. If, indeed, he had ever possessed those human qualities, they must have vanished before he came to us. I cannot recall one single instance that moved him to demonstrate affection to me or my brothers. If anything, his presence guaranteed an atmosphere of tension and fear.

Fortunately for us, the parental love so sorely lacking in my father's nature we found in great abundance in our gentle mother. In a very real sense, she compensated for many of Father's deficiencies by softening the many mental and physical blows he inflicted on the family. Mother's magic as a nurturer and her ever-present affection gave us hope and the strength to endure. She was the greatest source of whatever happiness we had in our bleak childhood.

Though Mother's formal education ended with the eighth grade—in itself rare for a poor Jewish woman in Eastern Europe in those days— she was knowledgeable in areas one would expect only from someone with much more schooling. She spoke four languages fairly fluently and knew her Bible quite well. She loved mythology, and was a superb storyteller. We could not wait for evening, when, while pedaling the Singer sewing machine, she fascinated us with her wondrous fairy tales. Her repertoire included "Rumpelstiltskin," "Sleeping Beauty," and many other stories about enchanted forests and wicked witches who ultimately paid for their evildoing.

There were variations in Mother's performances. If it wasn't storytelling she entertained us with, it was the singing of Yiddish and Carpatho-Ukrainian songs. Only when Father was away from home could we turn the little hut into a happy place fit for the songs that lifted our spirits or for the fairy tales that transported us to exciting, mysterious lands where Rumpelstiltskin turned straw into gold.

On summer days when the weather was good and Mother could carve out some time from a working day, we took walks through the nearby forest, where we could see a variety of animals—our version of the modern-day visit to the zoo. By far the most thrilling diversion on a sunny day was Mother's companionship while we roamed and ran freely through the endless meadows, gathering wildflowers and learning their names. Mother often joined us in our games and carefree laughter as though she had returned to her own childhood. Our good times with her were not merely a diversion but a means of regeneration, renewing the strength, spiritual and physical, of both mother and children. It was as though those happy times were preparation for the difficult tomorrows to come.

Chapter 2

Two Teachers

Before I was six, Father decreed that it was time for me to be sent away to cheder (Jewish school for boys) for the summer. In fairness to my father, this inhumane practice of sending very young boys to cheder prevailed in many parts of Eastern Europe. If a small village did not have a sufficient number of Jewish families to create a school, the family was obliged to send the male children to neighboring towns or villages that had such places of learning. These schools were populated, for the most part, with students from poor families who could not afford better institutions for their children's Jewish education. To arrange for attendance in these schools, the parents walked from village to village till they found a cheder with affordable tuition for their child. Then they had to beg the people of the community, who were themselves poor, to give the boy food and lodging. In our case, this mission fell entirely to Mother. My father did not participate nor was he concerned as to whether or not the arrangements for his son were good or bad; he simply did not care. Since Mother already had experience in finding lodging for my older brother, she was confident that she could do the same for me.

When the preparations for my Jewish education were under way, I was filled with fear and anxiety. The thought of leaving home and going to those strange places that Harry described with such vivid dislike troubled me greatly. All sorts of suspicions crossed my mind, among them the possibility that I was about to be given away for adoption to another family because of the discord that existed in our household. I was also concerned with my mother's safety. What would happen to her should my father come home drunk and decide to beat her? Who would run for the gendarmes? Who would take care of Samuel while Mother was at work in the fields? These and many other worries moved me to pray to God. I spoke to Him with the hope that He would intercede on my behalf and allow me to remain at home.

Though my prayers were not answered, I did receive much comfort from Mother, who was aware of my concerns. As usual, her gentle magic worked wonders. She managed to allay some of my apprehension and to prepare me for leaving my familiar nest for the first time. So persuasive were her consoling words that I was actually excited about my adventure and eager to begin our journey.

Early on a Sunday morning in May, Mother and I started our four-mile walk to the village of Bukovinka, where Harry had attended cheder for two years. Being fairly sure that one way or another a place would be found for me, Mother packed my belongings in a brown cardboard box, which hopefully no one would suspect was not a suitcase. It contained very few items—a little pillow, a small blanket, made of odd patches of cloth, two shirts, and a pair of shoes in very poor condition. I polished the shoes with the juice of wild blueberries, giving them a shine that enhanced their looks beyond their worth. I wore a pair of blue short pants with a shirt to match, both made from an old bedspread the night before our journey, leaving one of our beds naked but our poverty disguised, a matter of great importance to my proud mother. Despite her limited wardrobe, Mother looked very presentable in a new white dress she had made.

On the way to Bukovinka, Mother and I walked hand in hand. Her strong, calloused grip made me feel secure and more at ease about things to come. Interspersed through our conversation were her reminders about how important it was for me to learn Torah and get an education. She also cautioned me to be well-behaved which was very important, particularly when I was away from home. The Yiddish word *derkherets* (watch your manners) was evoked many times as we crossed the meadows toward our destination. I listened attentively to Mother's admonitions, distracted only by the occasional appearance of some animal chasing down its meal, and by the breathtaking view of the jagged mountain peaks still covered with small patches of snow.

It was a mild spring day. The ground was warm for the most part, and to preserve our shoes we walked barefoot the entire distance, feeling discomfort only when our bare feet touched the frozen earth in areas where the early morning sun did not reach. When we arrived at the edge of the village, we washed our feet in an abandoned trough, put on our shoes, and walked toward the center of the village where the cheder was located. As we neared the building, Mother looked upward, folded her hands in prayer and whispered several times, "*Se zol zein mit mazel, se zol zein mit mazel, Gotinyu* [May we have good luck, my Lord]."

We were greeted by the rabbi and several members of the congregation with whom Mother spent some time discussing tuition arrangements and other matters concerning my stay. I was then taken to Fishel, the rabbi's assistant, who was to test me on the knowledge I had acquired from my father's instruction in prayer and religious customs. Fishel was a sour-faced, ugly young man of about nineteen with a long, misshapen nose and a scrawny, elongated body, altogether a macabre-looking individual. It did not take long to discover that Fishel's unprepossessing appearance was a true reflection of his vicious soul. On the very first incorrect response to a question concerning Jewish ritual, he pulled my ears so hard that my agonized scream could probably be heard in the adjacent class. Regrettably, at that time many varieties of corporal punishment were not only condoned but were deemed proper for the acquisition of knowledge. Fishel's method of examination and his instructional approach were not alien to me. My father, who surpassed his cruelty, had prepared me well for my new despot. Despite Fishel's inhumane treatment, I proved to be worthy of being placed in a grade with children of my own age. This placement relieved me greatly, because I had dreaded the humiliation of being put in a class with younger children.

The next step in providing for my stay in Bukovinka was to find places which would provide me with free meals and lodging. Since no one family could afford to provide meals for a whole week, arrangements had to be made for me to eat each day with different families. To extend charity in this way was an established custom among Jews in Eastern Europe; it was considered a *mitzvah* (a good deed). From past experience, Mother knew exactly where to go; a few hours of walking from household to household yielded the desired results. I was now assured of three meals for every day of the week.

My lodging for the whole week, except Friday, was provided by Zhishe, the village milkman. I was to sleep in a converted tool shed called *dos shtiebel* (the little house), a tiny room that bore a greater resemblance to its former identity than to a *shtiebel*.

Having secured my room and board, Mother made last-minute preparations for my stay and for her departure. Before leaving Bukovinka, she gave a schedule of my eating days to her friend Chave, who was to be a kind of surrogate mother to me. Once more, I had to promise Mother that I would conduct myself in an exemplary way and that I would study Torah diligently. Mother's departure broke my heart. I could not understand why this separation from her was necessary. Luckily, Chave and her three children distracted me with games and talk, and helped me to accept the inevitable.

My *shtiebel* allowed no natural light to come in, other than the few rays that made their way through the cracks of the rickety door. There were no windows except for a square opening facing a stable that housed four milk cows, a horse, and three noisy goats. Fortunately for me, I did not have to sleep there by myself. Zhishe's youngest son, Chaim, who was my age, had for a long time wanted to sleep there but was too afraid to do it alone. He became the roommate and friend with whom I shared the strangeness of my new "bedroom."

The *shtiebel* was furnished with two small cots made of old picket fencing. Between them there were an orange crate that served as a night table and a kerosene lamp that neither Chaim nor I was ever allowed to light for fear that we would set fire to the place. In my honor, the mattress was filled with new straw, but the smell of its former occupant, an old peasant from the village, was still pervasive. As I later learned, he had served as a stable hand for many years before he died. His contact with the horses and cows must have been more frequent than with people because the odor in the bunk had no resemblance to anything human.

The *shtiebel* was used exclusively for sleeping. In the evening, Zhishe's family always gathered in a large room that served as living room, dining room, and kitchen. When supper was over, we all retired to our sleeping places, with one of the sons on the top of the baking oven, a privileged location. Chaim and I could not wait to get back to our private quarters, where we were free to act up. One of our favorite amusements was to imitate the noises made by the animals. Chaim was able to make the best bleating sound, to which one of the goats invariably responded, sending us into exuberant giggles. The *shtiebel* became my favorite hiding place when I wanted amusement or felt dejected. Chaim became my best friend. He made my stay in an unfamiliar place tolerable for two consecutive summer semesters, each of which lasted over three months.

The first day of cheder turned out to be a very lucky one, for on Mondays I was to take my meals in the house of Sima and Mendel, an amiable couple with five children. It was a happy family in which every effort was made to put me at ease and to include me in their circle. Sima was a fine cook; her delicious potato and bean soups, if eaten with a lot of homemade black bread, could keep one satiated till the next meal—that is, if one did not run around too much. For poor Jewish people, soup represented a complete meal. It was only on Saturdays that soup was served as an appetizer before the main dish.

Although most of the people at whose houses I ate were poor, and the food was not much to write home about, their charity was given graciously. Invariably, I was made to feel as though I were part of the family. Friday turned out to be the least nourishing for the body, yet the most nourishing for the spirit. On that day I ate breakfast and lunch at the house of the poorest of my hosts, a shoemaker who, in consenting to give me the two meals, had apologetically informed my mother of the family's limited menu. Almost without exception, it was onion soup into which we would put the dry bread left over from the rest of the week. In addition to finding it hard to swallow, I felt hunger pains almost immediately after I left the table. Yet it was at this little house that I was happiest. The tastelessness of the soup was always mitigated by the kindness of those around me.

Aaron Hersh, the shoemaker, and his quiet wife were sweet, unassuming people. Despite dire poverty they rarely complained. He was grateful for what he had, always hopeful that some day soon, luck would come his way. He was a truly pious man. Whenever I heard him pray, I imagined that God was nearby, listening to his every word. Unlike my father, Aaron Hersh was an affectionate man who was consistently good to his family and to me. He always found time to engage us in play or in conversation. The high point of the day came in the afternoon (there was no cheder on Friday), when we all went swimming and fishing in the nearby river. In spite of torn nets, we almost always returned with a catch sufficient for the family to have the traditional Sabbath appetizer of gefilte fish. Unfortunately, my half-day stay did not permit me to enjoy the fish I had such fun catching. My departure was always preceded by a hug from Aaron Hersh and some pleasant words from his wife. I was now on my way to the place I most dreaded.

Friday night, Sabbath eve, and Sabbath, I was supplied with meals and lodging by the Lampert family in the village adjacent to Bukovinka. The Lamperts were rich, and lived in a very large house with two servants and an old stable-man who also served as the carriage driver for the family. Aaron Shlome had acquired most of his fortune making whiskey and other alcoholic beverages. Unlike Aaron Hersh, he rarely acknowledged my presence, and his children, who were much older than I, were also aloof. As for Mrs. Lampert, I do not recall her ever saying a word to me in the twelve Sabbaths that I was there.

No matter how rich or how poor, for Jewish people Friday night meals are supposed to be festive and, if possible, abundant. It is traditionally a night of joy, when peace reigns over the entire household. But those Sabbaths that I spent with the Lampert family were neither joyful nor peaceful for me. Rather, they were a succession of humiliations inflicted by insensitive people on a homesick boy. While the Lamperts were eating in an elegant dining room, I was having my solitary meal in the kitchen. As the maids ran in and out, the gay laughter of the family came through the open doors. I wanted to participate in the laughter and sing the Sabbath songs I loved so much. On those Friday evenings, I would gladly have exchanged the abundant food at the Lamperts' for the meager onion soup at the shoemaker's house.

Since the Friday evening meals were a long, drawn-out affair, and Bukovinka was too far for me to return to my tool shed, I was supposed to stay overnight with the Lamperts. Adjacent to their home was a synagogue belonging to the family. Hasidic Jews from the nearby villages, including my father, attended prayer services in that synagogue on Saturday mornings and on the high holidays. After my first meal at the Lamperts, one of the maids led me to the synagogue which I had been in many times before, but never as a lodger. She showed me to an army cot that was to serve as my bed, turned down the kerosene lamp to a low flicker, and left. As she closed the door behind her, I was seized by terror. After all, this was the first time in the six years of my life that I was to sleep without anyone near me. There was something accusatory about that synagogue that conjured up in me all the sins for which I had not repented. A host of Biblical events, mostly the kind that evoked God's wrath, haunted me. I felt as though God were right there to carry out the punishment for all my wrongdoings. As a result, many dreadful hours would pass before I finally slept.

It was only the heartening words of my mother, who came to visit me that week, that enabled me to endure two or three more Fridays sleeping in the synagogue. She explained to me that it was really a good thing, because the Torah that was stored there protected me from evil. Mother's soothing wisdom lasted only a short time and I chose, for the rest of the semester, to walk the three miles on a lonely road back to my tool shed and my friend Chaim. Though walking back to Bukovinka in the pitch dark was a frightening ordeal for a six-year-old, it was preferable to sleeping in the spooky synagogue.

It was under these trying conditions that I acquired some knowledge of Jewish liturgy and ritual. By the end of the semester, I was able to recite most of the daily prayers and understand some small portions of the Torah that were read in the synagogue during the Sabbath services. Fishel, my teacher, did not mellow with the passage of time. His cruelty to the children persisted to the end. I am sure that my academic achievement had little to do with his pedagogical methods, because like all children, I possessed a natural love for learning and a spontaneous curiosity which sadistic teachers cannot extinguish.

The three months went by quickly and I looked forward with great anticipation to my return because Mother told me on her last visit that she had enrolled me in the first grade at the regular school in Kustanovice. At the end of August, a thinner but happier Melach walked hand in hand with her back to our hut. Miriam greeted me with affectionate purrs. My brother Harry, back from his Jewish school, was glad to see me, and Samuel, who was now four years old and very handsome, was wild with joy at the return of his playmates. My homecoming was celebrated with a special meal, and the hut was filled with the sound of children's hilarity. What made the occasion more joyous was the fact that my father was not there and was not likely to return for at least a week. Although my mother never encouraged us to express the slightest hostility toward Father, by now there prevailed a tacit understanding that we were all better off when Moshe Elijahu was not with us.

I had about three weeks' vacation before I was to start first grade. The idea that I could attend school, return to my own home, be with my family, and eat my mother's cooking elated me. The nourishing milk products that were given to Mother in payment for her dressmaking made up for some of the hungry days in Bukovinka.

The school I was to attend conducted classes not in Czech but in Ruthenian, one of the Slavic languages spoken in Eastern Czechoslovakia, mostly by the peasants living in small villages, but by some Jews as well. Except for my father, everyone in our household spoke Ruthenian well. During the few weeks before I was to start school, Harry taught me most of the alphabet, to the point where I could read and write simple syllables. Mother tended to all the other preparations for this important event. Though she did not show it, I am sure she was quite nervous about my schooling. I was, after all, about to enter a world that was alien to me, a society with which I had had little prior contact, since Jewish children rarely played or socialized with Christian children in that part of the world.

It was standard practice for Jewish families to shelter their offspring as long as possible from the hostile world waiting in ambush ready to strike, often without any reason or provocation. Most of the Gentile children had in fact been well indoctrinated in hatred and slander. To them I was a *zhid*, a stinking Jew. I am sure that almost every peasant child had been told at one time or another that the Jews killed Christ and therefore deserved to be punished. As a consequence, there were many occasions when I came home with a nose bloodied by gangs of bullies my age and older while jeering adults stood by without lifting a finger on my behalf. I soon understood why, when I complained about not having friends to play with, Mother suggested that I play with Miriam and with Samuel because, unlike those "bad boys," they would never hurt me.

On the Sunday before I was to enter school, Mother's advice to me was to avoid a fight at any cost, to ignore the name-calling no matter how insulting, and, if that did not work, to run. My clothes were mended and cleaned, and with a few minor exceptions I was going to look like most of the rest of the children. One of the visible differences between me and the Christian children was that all my life I was obliged to wear a yarmulke (skullcap). But this practice, strictly observed by Orthodox Jews, was not permitted in Ruthenian schools. Fortunately, my father was not aware of our dilemma and we were able to resolve this problem without violent arguments. Under no circumstances would my father have agreed to his son's going with his head uncovered. Besides, he was not at all happy with the fact that Mother had arranged for the children to enter a non-Jewish school in the first place. Unlike my mother, my father did not understand the value and the importance of a secular education. We decided that I was to wear the skullcap on the way to school and hide it once I was there, hoping that God would forgive us for this one small transgression. The more difficult problem to resolve was the prominent earlocks that clearly identified me as a Jew, making it difficult to blend with the rest of the children and giving the bullies a visible target. Quite a bit of work went into training the earlocks to stay hidden behind my ears, but it paid off—only the most observant child would have noticed that my hairstyle was different from what was current among the rest of the boys.

It was a sunny September morning when Mother walked me halfway to the school located at the edge of the village near a Greek Orthodox church. After some reassuring words and a few hugs, she ran back to free Harry from baby-sitting for Samuel so that he could go to his school in a different part of the village. Once I entered the schoolyard, my fears about being harassed subsided. The school at that moment became a kind of sanctuary, a refuge where I felt safe. The joyful voices of the children made me feel secure and at ease. Before the bell rang to start classes, I was invited by three boys to join in a soccer game that used a sock stuffed with rags for a ball. The four of us beat the other team, and I distinguished myself by scoring two of the goals, thus gaining three potential friends.

Soon the town crier appeared in the schoolyard beating a small drum that hung from his neck, and the children gathered around him. The old drummer pulled a paper from his pocket and read off the room for each grade. The children, almost without exception, ran toward their classes as though free candy were waiting for them there. I too was very eager to get to mine. At the entrance stood my teacher, Mrs. Zupan, greeting every child as he or she entered, affectionately touching each head as the children passed by.

The class started with a Greek Orthodox prayer that made me feel nervous and ill-at-ease. I did not know how to act when I saw the rest of the children crossing themselves as they turned toward the icon representing the sad and pallid face of Christ on the cross. Yet there was something very moving in hearing a chorus of solemn voices reciting the "Our Father." This was followed by a warm welcome and words of high expectations for the new school year. Attendance was taken. As their names were called, the children stood and waited for Mrs. Zupan to wave her hand to signal that they could sit down. My name, too, was called. This was the first time I heard the Czech equivalent of my Jewish name, Melach, pronounced "Martin" as it appeared on my birth certificate. I was no longer just Yehudah Melach; I felt very good about being called Martin. It was as though this Czech name gave me an added dimension, a sense of belonging to yet another world outside of my Jewish circle.

Mrs. Zupan distributed notebooks, pencils, and a brand new primer. The book had an attractive, fresh scent, and a chorus of long and short sniffs was heard throughout the classroom. I was particularly pleased with it because right there on the first page was the alphabet I had already learned from Harry. Mrs. Zupan followed teaching the alphabet to the class with a simple arithmetic lesson.

The morning concluded with learning and singing some songs from our region that I had sung with my mother many times before. Without exception, Mrs. Zupan complimented all the children for their diligent work and rewarded them with an outdoor lunch, a large ham sandwich and a glass of milk. Of course, because of Jewish dietary laws, I could not eat the forbidden ham—though I was tempted because I found the idea of giving Mrs. Zupan the reason for my refusal extremely embarrassing. Luckily, she did not need any explanations. Within five minutes, I was presented with a huge cottage cheese sandwich, prepared by the caring hands of this teacher who I will remember till my dying day.

Mrs. Zupan had a reputation in Kustanovice for being an excellent teacher as well as a great beauty, and I'm sure her extraordinary characteristics as a teacher were appreciated by every child who ever had the privilege of being in her class. But to me her most precious qualities were her unwavering compassion and empathy for children. How rare it was in our village to find a human being who comprehended what it was like to be a child of the only Jewish family living in hostile surroundings. I could not help but compare Mrs. Zupan, who inspired in me the love for learning, with Fishel, my first Hebrew teacher, whose cruelty had generated so much fear that learning became a dreadful chore.

My good fortune in having Mrs. Zupan for my teacher lasted for two school years. Unhappily, I was not as lucky with some hateful classmates who often gave me a hard time on the way home, calling me insulting names and throwing rocks at me. But for every bully there were a few sensitive, decent children who did not lose their natural humanity and who offered their friendship, and one of them, her affection. That special person was my little friend Anya, who didn't live too far from me. Though Anya's father was not overjoyed by his daughter's associating with a Jew, he allowed her from time to time to come to our hut, where we played and studied together. For the last two years that my family remained in the village, Anya continued to be my best and most loyal friend. My mother adored her and treated her as though she were the daughter she would like to have had if the circumstances of her marriage had been different.

Life at home continued to be just as difficult as it was before. My pathetic father could not find work and resorted to begging, as did many poor Jews who had practically no access to jobs. His problem with excessive drinking continued and so did his violent outbursts. He stayed away more often, but when he did come home, the beatings of Mother and children persisted. To make matters more difficult, the winter that year was even more severe than usual for that part of the Carpathians. In past winters we had been able to get firewood from the peasants for cash or for work Mother did. Now my mother was obliged to trudge through the heavy snows, often in sub-zero temperatures, to forage for fallen branches in the surrounding meadows. Both Harry and I had to participate in this most unfitting work for children, each of us carrying large bundles of wood that would be heavy even for a strong male.

When that source was exhausted it was necessary to go to the forest, an even more unpleasant and trying task, particularly on the rare occasions when I had to accompany my irascible father. He would leave me in an isolated place to guard the wood we had collected, while he went deeper into the forest to search for more. Frightened at being alone, I would call out to him, for which he harshly reprimanded me because this sound might betray our presence to the forest rangers.

The soggy wood refused to burn without using straw from our homemade mattresses for kindling. By the middle of the winter, most of the straw was gone. To avoid sleeping on practically bare planks, we covered them with torn blankets and with the clothing we wore during the day. Even using the dry straw as kindling, our stove provided us with more smoke than warmth.

The winter, as though aware of the suffering it had inflicted on us, gave way to an unusually early and warm spring. The snow melted quickly, and before all of it had vanished, a long line of forsythia appeared in full bloom in front of our hut. The dandelions emerged in great profusion, covering the meadows with a huge yellow blanket. The two hens and the one handsome rooster, who had been saved from the butcher's knife because of their fertility, came down from the attic to enjoy the warm sun. They were soon followed by their offspring, who enlivened our courtyard with their incessant chirping.

Though the arrival of spring made life more bearable, it did nothing to alleviate the hardships of poverty. Perhaps as a consequence of a new wave of anti-Semitism in our area, or for other reasons that I didn't know, Mother's dressmaking business was slow and hardly sufficient to feed three growing children. She had to find new ways to supplement our income. The only real option available to her was to hire herself out as a farmhand and work in the fields in neighboring villages. To get work, she had to hide her Jewish identity since most peasant farmers believed in the slanderous notion that Jews were weak and indolent, incapable of doing hard work. They held to this belief despite the fact that there were Jewish families throughout the Carpathian region who engaged in tenant farming, timber cutting, lumbering, and other hard physical labor.

By working long hours in the fields, Mother managed to earn enough money to feed us, but this meant that we children were frequently left alone. I can still hear Mother's early morning gentle reminders as she issued instructions for the day while we were still half asleep—when to feed Samuel, to lock the door and not to give entrance to Gypsies, who were numerous in the area. Mother was able to endure two summers of working in the fields and two more cold winters in Kustanovice, during which life with Father became more and more impossible. In the past, he had been willing to do occasional shopping for food in the city, but now he refused to do so. That responsibility fell on Harry and me. It broke Mother's heart that Harry, at the age of eleven, and I, only eight, had to carry loads fit for men. Moreover, as if the burden of carrying heavy baskets on our backs was not enough, we had to contend with freezing weather, inadequate clothing, fear of the eerie forest and vicious dogs who sensed our arrival. The hardships we children suffered and the difficult circumstances of living in that godforsaken village ultimately compelled Mother to find some way out of that miserable life.

It was at the urging of Uncle Joseph, Mother's older brother, who was very close to us and had always been supportive, that she decided to move back to Mukachevo, where Joseph lived with his family. We hoped not only that our economic conditions would improve but that we might find a way of ridding ourselves of my father. Thus the search for lodging in Mukachevo began.

After two months or so, Mother found a place that suited her meager budget, a dank one-room basement with no running water, only a pump in the courtyard. Scrubbing and painting, Mother readied the grim basement to receive us. Preparations were made for our move to Mukachevo on a fall Sunday just a few weeks before the High Holy Days.

The last Sabbath day in Kustanovice was spent in great excitement and anticipation. Mother could hardly wait for Sunday morning to come. Father, too, appeared animated and happy about the prospect of moving to the city. I suppose just the fact that he would no longer have to make the dreaded trip through the forest between Mukachevo and the village must have been a source of great satisfaction to him. His good mood brought on a temporary change in him, one of the few times I ever saw him in such a cheerful frame of mind.

Early Saturday morning the entire family set out for the synagogue where I had spent several frightful nights while I attended cheder. It was a lovely day. The mountains and the meadows below were covered with dazzling fall colors, making our long walk less tedious than usual. At the synagogue we were greeted by many well-wishers, for the word was out that the family was moving and that this was the last Sabbath day we would be attending services there. Most of my schoolmates envied me my good fortune. They looked at our leaving for the city as a kind of liberation from the monotony of a village existence. They too would have liked to experience the excitement of embarking on a new way of life.

Most of the congregation knew that Father drank heavily, a habit rare and improper in a Hasidic Jew. Because of this, he had always been viewed as a buffoon, a target for mockery and practical jokes, always to my intense embarrassment. This Sabbath day was different. Father was honored with a call to the Torah and was invited to conduct part of the service. My brothers and I were each blessed by the rabbi, who enjoined us to continue to observe the Sabbath day and to do our daily prayers with devotion.

On the way home from the synagogue, Father was in a particularly jovial mood and as he walked he hummed some melodies from the Sabbath liturgy. With his black caftan fluttering in the wind, he looked as though he were about to take off and fly. Surprisingly, on this occasion, he did not reprimand us for either walking too slowly or running too far ahead. Mother was also cheerful, holding Samuel by the hand and calling our attention to the flowers that surrounded us. From time to time we all walked in single file and in step. Had any passersby seen us, they would surely have concluded that this was a happy family without a care in the world.

On Sunday morning my father's son Leib arrived with horse and carriage to take our belongings to the city. While the adults were preparing for our departure, I asked my mother's permission to say good-bye to Anya. This had to be done in secret, for my father knew nothing about her nor would he ever have permitted my friendship with her. Anya lived on top of a steep hill on a very large farm surrounded by golden wheat fields and a vineyard, where I had had many good meals of huge muscatel grapes. I ran all the way and met Anya and her parents just as they returned home from Sunday morning church services. Anya was particularly pretty in her Sunday dress and appeared very happy to see me. Though her father maintained his usual distance, her mother was affectionate as always. After treating me to some delicious Russian babka cake, they walked me to the dirt road, where Anya's mother embraced me warmly. Anya hugged me shyly. When I said my final good-bye I saw Anya's tears, and as I ran down the hill I heard her thin voice crying, "Don't forget to write!" Thus I left behind my dearest childhood friend, who had shielded me several times from the harassment of the village bullies and with whom I had spent many happy hours.

On the way home I cried also. I kept thinking about Anya and about her affectionate embrace, consoling myself with the hope that someday soon I would have the opportunity to see her again. Unfortunately, that was not to be. But I believe that her kind heart remained the same and that her mind was never poisoned by the anti-Semites of our village who had found it very strange, if not repellent, that Anya and I should have been so close.

When I arrived home the carriage was already loaded with our possessions, except for the few dishes from which the family was having its last meal in Kustanovice. Then Samuel, with Miriam in his lap, was seated on the driver's box. The rest of us, including Leib, who was holding the reins from the side, were obliged to walk. Leib ordered the horse to pull, but the poor animal could not get started on the muddy road with a load meant for two horses. Not until the entire family pitched in were we able to get on our way. I heard my mother whisper several times her usual entreaty to the Lord, "*Se zol zein in a mazel-dike shoo* [May it be in a lucky hour]."

As we passed through the village, several peasants stopped us to say good-bye, but there were others who jeered. One old peasant woman crossed herself, either praying for our safe travel or because she was pleased that the last Jewish family was leaving Kustanovice. When we passed my school, I felt especially sad to leave my dear Mrs. Zupan, whose affection and kindness had made my life more tolerable the past two years. When we reached the outskirts, I took one last look at the magnificent Carpathian cliffs and at the white birches perched on the precipices. I wanted to imprint all that beauty on my mind so I could remember it forever.

Chapter 3

A Dwarfed Childhood

On the way to the city we had to cross the forest on a very steep downhill road. The poor horse must have suffered terribly holding back the carriage. By the time we got to Mukachevo, all of us were exhausted from either pushing the carriage or holding it back. Uncle Joseph and his wife were waiting for us with a big pot of cabbage soup and a small bottle of homemade whiskey to celebrate our arrival. The horse, too, was rewarded for her hard work with a generous portion of oats and several buckets of fresh water. We unloaded our few belongings and set about trying to convert the gloomy, barren basement into a friendlier, more welcoming place.

There were a number of inconveniences that Mother did not anticipate when she rented the basement. The "modern" outhouse which we shared with three other families, was so far from the basement that it was virtually impossible to use it during the cold winter evenings. When the rains were heavy, particularly in the spring, the place would invariably flood, creating an unpleasant smell of mildew. The large oven that occupied one corner of the room looked fairly good from the outside, but Mother soon discovered that she could not bake in it and that only the top of it was usable. Its main function seemed to have been to hide the hundreds of roaches who revealed their presence at night.

I was immediately aware of the sharp contrast between our new lodging and the little hut in the village. The hut, although extremely modest, possessed a special charm for me. Even when I was confined during the bad weather, looking through the tiny windows, I could see miles of lush meadow with its profusion of trees and flowers. From the two basement windows of our new home, however, the only visible signs of life were the legs of passersby walking along the cobblestone courtyard.

Nevertheless, there was an advantage to my new world. In contrast to Kustanovice, I had a chance to play and make friends with many different children, among them boys just like me who spoke Yiddish and had earlocks that looked like mine. I also befriended Czech children who, like Anya, did not display the hatred of Jews I had experienced in Kustanovice. I still missed my dear friend and wished that she could be with us.

Mukachevo was remarkable for its ethnic and cultural diversity. Until the First World War, it was a Hungarian city with a large Czech population. In 1919, although it became part of the newly-formed country of Czechoslovakia, it retained its Hungarian majority. In addition, over 40 percent of its residents, about 15,000, were Jews and of these at least half participated actively in the predominantly Hungarian cultural life of the city. But the Hasidic and other highly Orthodox Jews isolated themselves, for the most part, from that world. In fact, the Mukachevo of their world was famous for its rabbis, who were hailed for their Talmudic scholarship and their rich Hasidic and religious traditions. In Mukachevo, there were about thirty synagogues as well as hundreds of Jewish institutions of learning, both religious and secular.

It was also a vibrant commercial center, with colorful markets where peasants came to sell their produce. They, in turn, bought their necessities in shops which were owned mostly by Jewish merchants. There were several boulevards lined with elegant stores and restaurants. On Sunday afternoons and evenings, well-dressed men and Czech Officers in their handsome uniforms flirted with young women as they promenaded on the main boulevard.

Soon after our arrival in Mukachevo, Mother enrolled my brothers and me in Czech schools as well as in Yiddish cheders. Although my knowledge of Czech was quite limited because the school I had attended was Carpatho-Ukrainian, I very soon caught up with the rest of the children, completing third grade with excellent marks. Here, too, I preferred the secular to the religious Yiddish school. My Czech teacher was a lot like Mrs. Zupan, though she was not as affectionate with the children. My Yiddish teacher, on the other hand, was just as sadistic as Fishel, my Bukovinka nemesis.

Except for a few faithful clients who came from Kustanovice, Mother could not find dressmaking work in the city, so she continued to work in the fields and vineyards. In the winter, she hired out to do cleaning and laundry, working from early morning till late evening. She would often come home with swollen, red hands irritated by the caustic soaps and by the cold water of the river where the clothes were rinsed. Still, since her earnings were barely enough to feed the family, Harry and I were obliged to work. When school was out, we both got summer jobs as ball boys in a private tennis club.

In Czechoslovakia most clubs used ball boys for regular as well as for tournament play. Privileged young men and women who could barely hit a ball had access to ball boys. In those days being a ball boy was a very difficult job and we had to be at work by five o'clock in the morning. We were responsible for preparing the courts, which entailed watering, rolling, and painting the lines, often twice a day. Then came retrieving balls, with a short break for lunch which usually consisted of bread and the juicy pink mulberries we picked from the trees surrounding the courts. We came home exhausted at about nine in the evening with a few Czech kroner that Mother was very happy to have.

By now my father, having given up his occasional fishing and even the idea of finding work, resorted almost entirely to begging, which made the rest of the family cringe in shame. Although many poor Jews lived on handouts, my father's panhandling made Mother very unhappy. Poverty, she thought, had to be confronted, challenged, subdued, and kept as much as possible from public view. She believed that as long as a human being had the ability to work he should not rely on charity. She certainly lived by that credo and, as it turned out, also died by it. Mother's lesson of hard work was taught to us children very early in life and so, as young as we were, we were ashamed of father's means of subsistence. I remember vividly and painfully my concern that one day a schoolmate or a neighbor might find out our deplorable secret.

When we had lived in the isolated village, Mother could not help but endure Father's brutalities. But, now that we were to some degree protected not only by Uncle Joseph but even by one of Father's sons, Mother was determined to free us from this tyrant who made our lives so miserable. My father's departure from our lives was precipitated unexpectedly one day when, after verbally abusing my mother, he lifted his walking cane to strike her. Harry, out of fear that Mother would be badly hurt, stepped in and punched my father in the mouth, knocking out of one of his front teeth. My father was stunned. Poor Harry, who always was and still is, a very gentle human being, recalls how petrified he was when he saw what he had done. He ran away to a friend's house and did not return for several days. That blow resulted in more benefit than harm. Now that Father realized he could no longer dominate us physically, he moved out of the house. Shortly afterwards, my parents were divorced and we experienced a hitherto unknown sense of freedom.

Despite our continuing hardships, compared to the past we were now a fairly happy family. Mother's humor and gaiety returned, and there was much laughter in that poverty-ridden household. Our new-found liberty gave us strength, and we were actually able to mock our poverty.

My father's departure brought yet other improvements in our way of life that I personally enjoyed very much. I had never been happy with his strict Hasidism nor with some of the religious practices that had been forced on us. My failure to observe many restrictions despite Father's constant admonitions had made me feel perpetually guilty. Though I found much comfort and beauty in some aspects of religious life, many requirements of Father's orthodoxy made no sense to me. I was unhappy with the skullcap and the earlocks that had invited so much trouble from the bullies and detested being dragged every Sabbath eve to the town's ritual bath, where I had to bathe in dirty water with crowds of people I didn't know. Perhaps most confusing and frustrating to me was Father's strict prohibition against playing soccer or indulging in any other sports, be it on the Sabbath or on weekdays. The violation of this interdiction cost Harry, Samuel, and me many merciless beatings. As soon as Father was gone, my earlocks disappeared and my former hairdo was replaced by Mother's artistry with a nice stylish haircut, parted on the side, as was worn by both assimilated Jewish boys and non-Jewish children my age. I could now play any game I wanted and relate to Mother the thrills I experienced on a given day. My soccer teammates could visit me freely, and instead of having to hide my soccer shirt I could enjoy wearing it any time.

The family of course continued some of the traditional religious practices. Mother kept a kosher kitchen, and we observed the Sabbath and all the other holidays. I continued my daily prayers, this time with the feeling that I was praying to a more benevolent God than before, a God whose primary function was not so much to punish me for my evildoing as to help me survive the hard times. Since Mother heartily approved of both my change of appearance and my new religious feeling, it was easy to make the transformation. And as though to show her solidarity with my display of independence, Mother abandoned the wig traditionally worn by the wife of a Hasidic Jew and let her rich brown hair grow to full length.

A final word about my father. He had inflicted so much suffering on the family that the pain will persist to the end of my life. From childhood on, I have examined and reexamined my feelings toward this difficult, unhappy man, trying to find a way to reconcile those sad memories, to put them in perspective. When I was very young, I wanted to sit on his lap, to love him and to be loved by him, but his cruelties destroyed that potential love. Ultimately, I neither loved nor hated him. Rather, I pitied him for his shortcomings as a father, for his insensitivity, for being such a miserable soul. I came to see him as the proverbial wandering Jew who never found his place in the sun. Therefore I resolved long ago that I should not be judge or juror, neither justify nor condemn his behavior—that would be yet another burden I prefer not to carry. Perhaps, one must have compassion for this troubled soul who was himself the victim of a world that deprived him of a livelihood because he was a Jew. Perhaps if anti-Semitism had not been so rampant, if the opportunities open to other men had been available to him, his entire life might have turned out to be very different. After the divorce, I often saw him wandering through the streets of Mukachevo, and it moved me to see him more and more broken with the passage of time.

Just before I left for Budapest, we met by chance outside our synagogue. I took the opportunity to tell him that I had no feelings of anger toward him and that I was sorry that fate had not been kinder to both of us. It was hard to know whether he understood what I was saying and whether he felt any remorse. His silence revealed nothing. Perhaps he wanted, but simply didn't know how, to tell me that he was sorry and that he actually loved me in his own way. As sad as the memory of that day is, I am glad I had the chance to express regret for what happened between us rather than to blame him for a past that was too late to change. It was the last time I was to see him.

My father died in poverty of natural causes a few months later, at the time when Hitler's henchmen in Poland were slaughtering thousands of Jewish men, women, and children as a prelude to their destruction of the rest of Europe's Jewry. In retrospect, for what it is worth, I am consoled by the fact that he escaped being dragged to places like Auschwitz, where our people were subjected to unimaginable horrors and suffering. I was working in Budapest by then and did not learn of his death in time to go to the funeral. But to this day, as is the Jewish custom, I say Kaddish (prayers for the dead) in his memory every year.

With Father no longer present in our lives, we understood that a lot of healing would have to occur to overcome our grim emotional past. In order to defy poverty, in order to survive, we three brothers had to hold each other's hands, so to speak, to protect each other and to lighten Mother's burden as much as possible. With an extraordinary display of maturity and character, my brother Harry, who was going on fifteen, took Father's place as the "man" of the family. His devotion to Mother and to his younger brothers made our lives infinitely more tolerable.

Harry became an apprentice with my Uncle Shlomo, a well-known tailor trained in high-fashion English sartorial style. Although my uncle was, for the most part, indifferent to our family's plight, he took Harry under his wing and in his own severe way went about making a good craftsman of him. Indeed, after three years with Solomon, Harry became a fine tailor. Apprentices in those days, however, received no pay—all Harry made was some small change in tips when he delivered the finished garments. At best, Harry's earnings for a week paid for only one day's worth of bread for the family. And while Mother worked fairly steadily, her earnings were still not enough to sustain us. Thus new sacrifices had to be made.

In my two years of attending school in Mukachevo I had almost completed four grades. But now I was obliged to leave school and go to work in order to help keep our heads above water. Naturally, I was very unhappy because I really liked school, but I didn't want to make it even harder on Mother by letting her know how disappointed I was.

Though she suffered in silence, I knew how painful it was for her to accept our situation. Since we had no alternative, however, we consoled ourselves with the hope that soon our lot would improve and I would be able to return to school.

Thus, at the age of ten, I began my career as a full-time worker. For the next two summers, I continued as a ball boy, which now seemed easy compared to the jobs I had during the rest of the year. When the tennis season was over, I went to the center of town, where early in the morning young men and boys my age stood in line to be hired by the day for a number of different jobs. Most of the available work had to do with the transporting by horse and carriage of lumber, bricks, and other building materials to construction sites. The job I got was loading and unloading the carriages. In most cases, the owners took advantage of children and paid them half what adults were getting for the same work. Nevertheless, I didn't mind; as long as I could present Mother with my earnings at the end of each day, I was content.

When the heavy snows came and loading jobs were not available, Samuel and I got work shoveling snow and cutting firewood. I became so proficient at wood cutting that I was hired by a lumberyard to cut and deliver firewood in quantity. Starting very early in the morning, I faced a huge circular saw that terrified me just looking at it. The motor's loud rumbling noise combined with the shrillness of the blade against the wood was so deafening I could hear no other earthly sound. And since this work was done outdoors in freezing temperatures without the proper clothing, I suffered terribly from the penetrating cold.

I had to fill each of about twenty baskets with forty pounds of the cut wood and load them onto a cart. The cart had two wheels with worn-out tires that had originally belonged to a small van, and a long platform that was supported at the rear by two legs. In the front, where I pulled the cart by a leather strap, there was a crossbar I had to press down on in order to raise the legs so I could set the vehicle in motion. When I distributed the wood to customers, I had to climb as many as five stories with one of those baskets on my back. My occasional tips made this job more lucrative than any I had had before, but it was so strenuous that at end of the day I could barely straighten up and walk erect.

Besides the physical hardship of the job, I had to bear the additional burden of shame. As luck would have it, the lumberyard was located directly across the street from my former school, and as I made my deliveries I was constantly in view of children who were either on their way to school or already playing in the schoolyard. Some of these boys and girls were my neighbors, my former classmates, friends with whom I had played. I did not want them to see me shabbily-dressed, half frozen, a beast of burden pulling a cart. Many times, when I saw them, I left the cart and hid in a courtyard, until they were gone. How I envied those warmly-dressed children; how I wished I could join them on the way to school and study with them in their warm classroom.

Along with the hardships and struggles the entire family faced on a daily basis, there were, nevertheless, moments of serenity and even happiness. The Sabbath was by far the most tranquil and enjoyable day, even for a poor family like ours for whom it was difficult to scrape together the few decent meals traditionally served on this day. The preparations for the Sabbath began early Friday morning with Mother's baking of challah, the special white bread made with braided dough on top. The aroma of the freshly baked loaf perfumed the house for the entire day. In the afternoon came the cooking, the washing of clothing, and the house cleaning. By sundown all work stopped, and everything in the house had a festive appearance, a new face. Even the everyday clothing we worked in all week, once washed and mended, took on a holiday look. Mother lit candles and made her prayers over them; Harry, Samuel, and I chanted the prayers that usher in the Sabbath. The softly-lit basement assumed an aura of peace. It was as though everything in that room obeyed God's commandment to rest on the Sabbath day. The delicious Friday night meal, in whose preparation I often participated, though hardly abundant, compensated for the sparse meals, often just a bit of soup, we went to bed with the rest of the week. While we were eating, we laughed and reminisced about the hardships of the week, and praised each other for how well we managed to cope with adversity.

After supper we sang Sabbath songs as well as other tunes that were popular at the time. Mother had a fine soprano voice and always sang, even when she was doing hard work. We boys had inherited her love for singing as well as some of her talent for it. The eve of the Sabbath as well as the Sabbath day itself were the perfect times to rejoice and sing. Samuel was also gifted with a fine voice, and he loved to entertain us with solo performances that we applauded with great fanfare.

Mother was now surrounded by friends, and on Saturday afternoons our home became a refuge for working men and women who came to amuse themselves a bit, to forget some of their troubles. The basement was invariably filled to overflowing. There were animated Yiddish, Hungarian, and Czech conversations as well as singing and dancing to the music of a poorly-played accordion. Among our steady visitors was Morris Breindel, a young man who was a fine dancer and who loved to teach dancing. He had many eager pupils, I among them. By the age of ten, I had learned how to dance and was fairly good at it, so much so that some five years later I was able to earn money by teaching ballroom dancing. Among the precious memories that will never fade from my mind is having danced with my mother, who was herself a graceful dancer. I danced with some of the young women as well. I was particularly popular with those who could not find adult male partners, although because of my short stature they could see only the top of my head, and I, some part of their stomachs.

Uncle Joseph was a frequent visitor on the Sabbath day. This shy man and Mother were very close. He didn't like crowds, so if we had guests when he came, he would wait until they were gone and he could have Mother all to himself. Then they would reminisce about their childhood, tell each other their troubles, and console each other; I can still hear them laughing and telling each other amusing anecdotes. Uncle Joseph was always very affectionate to his nephews and, poor as he was, he rarely came to the house without some gift, often candy, for us.

Saturday was the day for play, a day when we were able to reclaim our childhood for a while. Samuel and I both had a passion for soccer. Nothing else existed while we were playing. Rain or shine, we were on the field, barefoot most of the time so as to preserve the one pair of shoes each of us had. We always played on the same team and took great pride in our frequent victories. At bedtime we discussed in detail every goal we had scored and every well-executed pass we had made, reliving each moment of triumph and excitement.

Samuel and I had yet another source of enjoyment in our free time, our shared love for animals which gave us great pleasure. Mother was not too happy about our courtyard shelter which was home to half a dozen homing pigeons, several kittens that had arrived as a consequence of Miriam's late-night roaming, a puppy, and his multilingual mother whom Uncle Joseph named Polyglot because she understood Czech, Yiddish, and Hungarian. She was able to perform tricks on commands in any of these three languages, and she protected us from neighborhood bullies as well. When it came to taking care of our menagerie, there was, of course, a division of labor. Samuel was in charge of feeding the pigeons and training them to return home from far distances. I continued to train Polyglot to earn her daily bread by entertaining the neighbors, whom I also encouraged to save their leftovers for our extended animal family.

It was through these diversions that we managed to sustain a normal childhood, to some degree, despite the fact that most of the time we were obliged to assume responsibilities that should not have been part of a child's life. Because of our mutual joys and shared sorrows, Samuel and I became very close. We hardly ever fought which was my good fortune because, although I was two years older and quite strong for my age, Samuel was taller and much stronger than I. In any case, he was a very peaceable and even-tempered boy who never started fights. However, whenever we had to defend ourselves against the tough kids who roamed our neighborhood, I had little to worry about with Samuel there.

Two years went by and my dream of returning to school did not materialize. Worse than that, poverty claimed yet another dropout. Samuel, too, had to quit school and go to work after fourth grade. Because Mother was determined that I should learn a trade, I was to become a mechanic's apprentice in the bicycle shop of the landlord from whom we rented the basement. This meant, of course, that my contribution to the family income was ended, except for what I earned on the tennis courts on weekends. Meanwhile, Harry still had half a year to go before he would finish his apprenticeship and begin to draw a salary, albeit a meager one. Thus it fell it was Samuel's lot to replace my earnings. Because of his unusual strength and maturity for a ten-year-old, he had no difficulty in getting work with carriage owners.

Both Mother and I were very pleased with my prospective apprenticeship. It meant I would eventually be able to earn a decent living and someday perhaps even have my own repair shop. I considered myself very lucky, for there were literally hundreds of boys my age and older who would have been very happy to be in my shoes. The contractual arrangements were simple. I was to work for three years for 50 Hungarian pengös a month. (By now our part of Czechoslovakia was back in Hungarian hands which had no particular effect on our economic situation.) This sum was hardly enough to buy my daily lunch.

The final preparation for my new job entailed shopping for work overalls, which turned out to be a problem and, at the same time, a source of amusement for the entire family. Since I was only about five feet tall, we couldn't find overalls small enough for me, so we bought what was available. At least half of the leg had to be cut down and major alterations performed on top before I could wear them without inspiring laughter. Yet despite the imperfect fit, I was very proud to wear them, for they were proof of the fact that I had made a giant step toward manhood. More important, I was now a prospective mechanic, a future member of a group of young men who were respected in Mukachevo. In those days a person with a craft was considered a professional and enjoyed great prestige. I was thrilled with my new life, despite Mother's warning that it would be difficult and at times even humiliating. But I was determined to face almost any hardship to acquire a trade.

The very first day on the job, I became aware that, as the youngest and smallest member of the establishment, I was expected to obey everyone's command without fail. Even the apprentice who had started only a half year before took unfair advantage and ordered me to do some of the menial jobs we were supposed to share. The responsibility for keeping the store and the shop clean now fell totally on me. For almost an entire year, I was the only one of five workers who was obliged to fix flat tires on bicycles as well as on motorbikes. This messy and hateful job was particularly unpleasant during the winter months, since it was always done outdoors no matter how cold it got.

My fortunes changed when a new apprentice was hired. Once I was liberated from fixing flat tires, life became more bearable. In my second year, I was permitted to do all the operations in the process of bicycle building as well as every kind of repair. My favorite job was spot welding. The very act of putting on the protective gear made me feel important. Every time that helmet covered my head I grew taller in prestige as well as in height. I was no longer just a flat-tire fixer but a real craftsman, almost an equal of my colleagues.

Along with my newly-acquired pride came the companionship of young boys and girls I befriended in apprentice school and in the town's main square, where young employees gathered to socialize during their lunch break. Through them, I learned of various social gatherings, including Saturday evening dances at the Young Workmen's Circle, that were attended mostly by teenagers of working families like mine. I felt more at ease knowing that at those dances I would meet young people with whom I had much in common, including poverty.

It was at the ballroom that I met Lilly, some months older than I. She was very pretty, with long auburn hair, shining hazel eyes, and a mouth that was always poised for a smile. Lilly was neatly dressed, her figure graceful and slender. She was extremely popular with the boys, and I too would have liked very much to dance with her. I had no trouble asking other girls, but whenever I started in Lilly's direction my timidity stopped me. It took about three Saturday nights before I could muster enough courage to approach her. When she actually said yes to my request I was even more nervous than before. But once the music started playing a tango, I gathered enough poise to dance with ease and, as much as possible, on my toes, holding myself erect so as to make up for the small difference in our height produced by her high heels. I found it extremely easy to dance with Lilly. She allowed me to lead and she seemed to float as we danced.

The minute the tango was over, our exchange of compliments was effusive and prolonged. During the intermission that followed, I walked Lilly to her table and was invited to sit with her and her girlfriends. In response to her friendly questions, I took the opportunity to impress her with the fact that very soon I was to become a full-fledged bicycle mechanic. I also told her about my eagerness to finish my apprenticeship and make life easier for my mother.

During the course of our conversation, I learned that Lilly worked for a photographer and aspired to become a fashion model some day. After the break, I was particularly happy that during "lady's choice" Lilly asked me to dance with her. When the session was over, my offer to walk her and her friend home was readily accepted. When we got to her house, on the edge of town, I simply thanked Lilly for a nice evening and said good night. As I walked away, I was hoping to hear Lilly's voice say, "Come to visit me next Saturday," or "I'll see you at the dance next week." Unfortunately, she uttered no such words. I was, nevertheless, ecstatic over my success. In spite of my lack of self-assurance and my limited social experience, I had attracted a pretty, popular girl. Everything about the evening pointed to the possibility that Lilly wanted to see me again soon. I was, to say the least, impressed by her charm and her good looks. How delightful it was to think I might already have found my very first special friend, about whom I could give free rein to all kinds of agreeable fantasies.

That night I was so happy I couldn't sleep much for thinking of Lilly and of how well we had danced together. The rest of the working week I spent every lunchtime in the main square, hoping to meet Lilly, but without success. After work on Friday I tried the photography shop in the hope I might see her there, but it was already closed. Saturday I could hardly wait for evening to come so I could go to the dance. I was among the first arrivals, watching as the musicians set up their instruments. But though the dance hall was quickly filled with young people, Lilly did not appear. I danced with other girls but not very happily, for none of them danced as well as Lilly, nor did they possess her charm.

The disappointment of not seeing Lilly at the dance was quite hard to take. Mother and Harry, my advisers in matters of romance, tried to comfort me and exhorted me not to give up hope. They were both sure there was a good reason for Lilly's absence. I made a few more visits to the center of town and to the photography shop during my lunch hour but with no success. I couldn't call her, since telephones were not yet a part of the households of working people. Thus the only thing left for me was to wait and hope for some miracle to happen—and it did. I received a letter from Lilly with the explanation that she had been home for over a week with a bad cold. More important, she invited me to a small party at her home the following Saturday afternoon. She also told me again how much she had enjoyed dancing with me, and complimented me on my personality. Remembering our conversation at the dance, she even wrote about how impressed she was with my devotion to my family.

I was not the only one who was ecstatic over the receipt of that letter. Harry and Mother each read it out loud, sharing my excitement and happiness. I was particularly pleased by Mother's approval and help in my attempt to enter this unfamiliar social world. "This Lilly must be a very fine person," she said, and there was quite a bit of good-natured teasing and joking about my impending "romance." Mother wanted to know whether Lilly would bring a rich dowry to the marriage, and Harry reminded me that it would not be proper for me to get married before him. Samuel took the whole matter more seriously. He wanted to know whether these new events, unfolding so unexpectedly, would impede our activities. Would we still be able to fly the pigeons together, play soccer, and roam in the neighboring meadows with Polyglot?

There remained four more long days to Saturday's party. I was filled with excitement and anticipation. But what would I wear to that party? How would I conceal at least some of my poverty? I literally did not possess a suit of clothing other than what was appropriate for work. Mother understood how self-conscious and unhappy I was at the idea of going out in company wearing Harry's clothing, which was at least two sizes too big for me. On and off, she talked about buying me a suit, but there were always more urgent things to spend our money on. After much agonizing, Mother concluded, with her heart rather than with her pocketbook, that a sacrifice had to be made on my behalf. After all, this was my first invitation to a party by a young lady. Since it was springtime, just a pair of trousers, even if they were secondhand, would suffice; the rest of the attire she would manage with her sewing skills. Harry volunteered part of the money he was saving to buy new shoes, and Samuel offered to sell one of his precious pigeons. Once enough money was scraped together in this fashion, we went straight to old Chane Pesil's secondhand clothing stand at the open market. The transaction began. After showing us several pairs of trousers, she said she also had a special on an entire suit in my size that she had just purchased. It was available at the price we would have had to pay for just trousers alone.

The reason for this unusual bargain was that the suit had belonged to a young man from a very well-to-do Orthodox family. When his aged father died, a cut was made in the lapel of the suit jacket he wore at the burial ceremony. This "rending" of the clothing of family members is a strictly observed traditional symbol of the mourner's grief. We were really lucky, because the suit was practically new and the cut was made on the line of a pinstripe, where it could be repaired so as to be virtually undetectable. In addition, Chane Pesil evoked the Biblical "legend" that whoever wore this clothing would live an even longer life than the deceased. We bought the garment, not because of Chane Pesil's supernatural claims, but because Mother knew it was good value for the money, considering that a new one would have cost about ten times as much.

I was very satisfied with my almost-new suit, but wished I had not been there when Chane Pesil related its history. The thought that I was going to wear a garment connected with someone's death left a bad taste in my mouth. Despite Chane Pesil's assurance that I was going to live a long life, I would have preferred to associate my first suit with happier occasions. Nevertheless, both the trousers and the jacket fit me so well, and Harry mended it so skillfully, that I was often asked who the tailor was who had done such a fine job.

Mother surprised me with a pullover to go with my new outfit and, to be sure that Samuel didn't feel left out in this flurry of shopping, she presented him with an identical pullover and a pair of blue denim shorts she had made for him. Rather than waiting for Saturday afternoon, Samuel and I wore our new clothing on Friday night to usher in the Sabbath. Both of us looked elegant in our new outfits. Harry was obviously happy for us and proud of his workmanship. Bursting with pride Mother looked at all three of her well-dressed sons as if she could hardly believe what she saw. This Sabbath meal, more than others, was filled with laughter and animated conversation.

The Saturday afternoon for which I was impatiently waiting finally arrived. Although my appointment was for three o'clock, and it was only a forty-minute walk to Lilly's house, I left at two, but not before I received my final inspection from Mother, who nodded approvingly and exclaimed, "Yehudah Melach, *dee zeist ois vie a printz* [You look like a prince.]." On this flattering note, I dashed out of the basement. My hurrying steps cut the distance to Lilly's house considerably. I arrived so early that I spent an anxious half hour sitting behind a huge willow tree.

Lilly's house was located on the outskirts of Mukachevo, perched on a hill from which you could see the entire city. It was surrounded by meadows, where large herds of cows were grazing, attended by young peasant boys. The courtyard was guarded by a ferocious dog on a long chain, and his loud barking brought Lilly's father to the gate before I could knock.

A handsome, soft-spoken man with very kind eyes, Mr. Jakobovits reminded me very much of Uncle Joseph. He was clean-shaven, with a small mustache, and it was obvious from what he wore that he was in every respect a "modern" Jew, having little in common with the traditionally Orthodox folk of our town and even less in common with my father, who would never have been seen in anything but his Hasidic regalia.

Mr. Jakobovits greeted me warmly, and led me to the combination living room/bedroom where Lilly and three of her girlfriends were already gathered. I felt relieved, because all along I had been concerned about what I would say to her if I should find her alone. Lilly greeted me with a friendly smile and introduced me to her friends and to her mother. As I shook hands with everyone, I felt uncomfortable because I was the only boy in the company of four females. Fortunately, within a few minutes, Mr. Jakobovits and his two handsome sons came in from the kitchen, followed soon after by the rest of the guests—three young men, older and considerably taller than I, and two girls. It was obvious from their greetings that they all knew one another.

The room was filled with happy chatter and young laughter. Lilly was attentive to me, making sure that, as a newcomer to the group, I should not feel left out. After a short time, the furniture was pushed to the side and Lilly asked me to wind up the phonograph as well as choose the first record to start the afternoon's dancing. With everyone waiting for everyone else to be first, Lilly took me by the hand and led me to the middle of the floor. The others, including Lilly's parents, followed. My nervousness was well-disguised, and the afternoon of my very first party was a huge success.

Lilly's parents were most gracious to me, particularly her father, who engaged me in conversation. He seemed genuinely interested in what I had to say, and invited me to stay for dinner. This first afternoon and evening I spent at Lilly's house made a deep impression on me; it meant more to me than just dancing with my favorite partner, meeting new people, having a good time, and being treated to a meal. Observing the warmth of that loving family made me happy and sad at the same time, happy to be sharing it and sad at the thought of all I had missed. Mr. Jakobovits' affection for his daughter was obvious; he treated her as though she were a fragile object which must be handled delicately. The mutual love displayed not only between husband and wife, but between Mr. Jakobovits and his two sons moved me greatly. The conversation at the dinner table between the father and his children filled me with longing for a relationship I had never had. Once my father had left us, however, our family table too was the scene of lively, fun-loving interchange between Mother and her children.

That afternoon initiated a friendship that was to last for over a year. Lilly's house became almost a second home to me, a place where I always felt welcome. Lilly, in turn, was a frequent visitor in our house and was very fond of my mother, who adored her. Once Lilly came into my existence, my passion for playing soccer did subside somewhat, which made Samuel a bit unhappy and led to a lot of ribbing from my friends. Whenever possible, Lilly and I met in the town square on our lunch breaks and we spent many precious hours together. With her I could share my aspirations and my dreams, as well as the pain that attended my difficult circumstances. Our friendship was unique, based as it was on the kind of tender puppy love that today seems to have gone out of fashion.

As my apprenticeship neared its end, I had to prepare for the mechanic's examination that would earn me a journeyman's certificate. So much hope was riding on this! The successful completion of my training would enable me to get a decent job and save my mother from doing laundry in unhealthy steam-filled basements. By now she was in very poor health. She had contracted tuberculosis, for which there was no cure at the time, and was in and out of the hospital as a result. My earnings as a mechanic might also eventually make it possible for us to get out of that dark lodging of ours and find living quarters more fit for human habitation.

Naturally, the urgency of my passing the examination made me very nervous. Though I had attended a trade school once a week during my apprenticeship, it didn't compensate for the math and other subjects I had missed by dropping out of regular school so early. This proved to be a huge disadvantage, an obstacle I could overcome only through exceedingly hard work. Fortunately, I was well-disciplined and had learned with Mother's help how to study on my own. So, for the three months before the test, I pored over mechanical blueprints and all sorts of other technical material I needed to know.

The dreaded day for the first part of the examination arrived sooner than I would have liked. In front of a panel of four master mechanics, I had to demonstrate skills in spot welding, working with a lathe, using fine measurements, and assembling a bicycle wheel from scratch. I knew from the work I had been doing that I was a good mechanic, so I was not surprised that, despite my trembling hands, I passed this part with flying colors. It was during the written part, where I had to do computations and write a simple business letter, that the Lord must have come to my aid, for though I was sure I had not made it, a very tense four days later I was notified that I had satisfactorily completed the test and that my journeyman's papers were ready to be picked up. The entire family celebrated my success and I was showered with compliments on my achievement.

Chapter 4

The Toll Of Poverty

In general, once an apprentice had finished his three-year term, he was offered an extremely low starting salary as a journeyman. If passing the examination had presented me with a difficult challenge, facing my boss to negotiate my pay was even more difficult. In the three years I had been with him, he had never given me a kind or consoling word. In fact, he had often abused me verbally and, a couple of times, punched me in the face. Although there were laws on the books that were supposed to protect apprentices, they were more often ignored than obeyed. It was universally known that if you undertook apprenticeship you were going to be working for virtually nothing and suffer all sorts of exploitation.

Since I had nothing to lose but an unpaid job, I mustered enough courage to humbly ask my boss what kind of salary he was prepared to pay me now. His immediate reaction was anger. He accused me of insolence and said he would let me know whenever he was good and ready to do so. A week went by before I learned the bad news. Although he knew very well that I was an excellent worker and that we were desperately poor, he nevertheless made me such a humiliating offer that I did not even deign to respond to it. I possessed enough pride and composure to go to the back of the shop, gather my belongings, and walk out without saying a word. It was only when I left the place that I permitted myself an emotional outburst. How was I to break the bad news to my mother? How could I assure her that somehow I would find employment and rescue her from the work that was robbing her of her health?

Mother could not hide her deep disappointment, but rather than despair she offered me soothing words and suggested that I try my luck at the other bicycle mechanic's shop in town. My attempt was at least a partial success. Mr. Schonfeld gave me a temporary job that was to last about six weeks, while the busy season was still on. I suspect I got the work for the sad face I displayed while asking for employment rather than because Mr. Schonfeld needed another mechanic.

Now my contribution, together with the earnings of Harry and Samuel, would bring enough money into the household for Mother to stop working. One of the great satisfactions of getting my temporary job was to go to my mother's clients and inform them that she was no longer available to do their dirty laundry. Within a few weeks, we were also able to get out of that miserable basement of ours. This was particularly important because Mother's condition had worsened, and she was experiencing great difficulty in breathing.

We found a flat in the Yiddishe Gass (Jewish Street), an area populated mainly by poor Jewish families. Our modest apartment consisted of one large room and a very small one that must once have been a kitchen, since there was a big, non-functioning oven in it. Still, it was large enough to accommodate a bed, thus providing Mother for the first time with a room of her own. In contrast with the damp and the dark of our former quarters, the new flat was dry and bright. In addition, the outhouse was considerably closer to the building, a tremendous advantage in the cold months. Thanks to these new surroundings, Mother started feeling somewhat better and her coughing spells were considerably alleviated.

Besides working in Schonfeld's shop, I took on private jobs, fixing bicycles and tricycles for small businesses that appreciated my reasonably priced services. Our courtyard was often filled with items to be repaired. Anticipating the coming of fall, when business would naturally slow down and extra work would no longer be available, I toiled furiously, often sixteen hours a day.

Our combined earnings were so good that, in preparation for the High Holy Days, about four weeks away, we were able to buy a new pair of shoes that Mother needed, as well as material for her to make a dress for herself. We also bought new clothes for ourselves in traditional preparation for these festivities. Compared with former days, financially speaking, the family was riding high. Samuel was doing well driving a horse and carriage, and Harry was able to carry a good deal of our economic burden with his tailoring. The only sad circumstance that hung over us was Mother's illness;

yet we still hoped that she would become well enough to enjoy her new freedom.

Ten days before Rosh Hashanah, we bought a goose that Mother fed with oil-soaked corn to be sure that once the holidays arrived we would have enough meat. The day before Rosh Hashanah, I took the fattened goose to the ritual slaughterer, a procedure that has been strictly observed by Jews since the giving of the Torah. I have always had a feeling that when the Lord handed Moses the tablets, he may have overlooked the fact that some of the rules of the Torah were particularly hard on poor people. It was bad enough that we had to pay the slaughterer for a job we could very well have done ourselves; in addition, we faced the possibility that the bird might be declared "not kosher." As bad fortune would have it, that was exactly what happened to our goose after it had already been deprived of life. The dead bird was found to have a small blood clot on the food pouch. The slaughterer summarily and without any apparent remorse declared that the goose was not kosher and that it could under no circumstances be eaten by a Jew. In such cases, the only option was to sell the fowl to a non-Jew, usually at a third of the cost, assuming a customer could be found. The bad news was devastating. On the way home, it occurred to me that, since the ritual slaughterer did not much care about our fate or whether we would have a decent meal for the Holy Days, and since he was not likely to divulge to anyone the fate of the goose, I could keep the verdict a secret. The only other consideration was for me to ask the Lord's forgiveness for this almost-justifiable violation of His law. So, on the eve of Rosh Hashanah, we had a festive meal that featured as the pièce de résistance our nonkosher goose, which was enjoyed not only by the family but by a local beggar Mother had invited for dinner, as had been her custom even when we did not enjoy such abundance. Although a pang of guilt passed through me at the first bite, to this day I believe that the Almighty overlooked the whole matter, forgave me, and perhaps even commended me for my good sense.

The following day, the first day of Rosh Hashanah, we put on our good clothes to go to the synagogue. In her new dress, Mother looked elegant, her pallid face well-disguised by makeup. Despite her poor health, she looked very pretty. Who could have imagined that this was to be the last time Mother would attend services? Only ten days later, on Yom Kippur, she was too weak to climb to the fifth floor seats reserved for poor women.

The High Holy Days came to an end and, with them, my temporary job. All along, I had been hoping that by some miracle business would remain good and I would be able to stay on for a longer period. Nevertheless, losing my job was not a calamity, for by now I had built up a small clientele as a private entrepreneur. To supplement this income, I undertook other, less prestigious jobs. From time to time, I would work with Samuel transporting lumber and bricks to the areas surrounding Mukachevo. Although Samuel lifted heavy lumber and other objects with amazing ease and facility, I found the work enormously hard, since I had not done such physical work for the past three years. The only positive thing about the job was that I was once more spending time with my younger brother whom I loved.

On Mondays and Wednesdays, when the peasants from the surrounding villages came to market to sell their livestock, a friend and I hired ourselves out to the Jewish butchers to drive the cattle to the kosher slaughterhouse four miles from the marketplace. The disoriented and frightened bullocks, calves, and cows that we tied together with heavy ropes must have sensed they were going to their deaths, for sometimes it took us four or five hours to get them to their destination. Among all my difficult jobs, this was the most repugnant. I had always loved animals and found it hard to deal with the notion that it was all right to kill them to satisfy our hunger. Their plaintive mooing sometimes touched me as I thought of their fate. As much as we needed the money, I could not be involved in bringing these creatures to their deaths. I gave up this distasteful work and found other means to supplement our income.

Although my next job was a lot harder physically than driving cattle, at least it did not induce dreams about dead animals hanging on hooks in the slaughterhouse. This time I worked for a junkyard which collected iron and rubber scraps for sale to smelting plants for recycling. Once again I was in front of a cart, pulling it for long distances to outlying villages where abandoned scraps were most likely to be found, free for the taking, or bought literally for pennies. The iron rim of a wheel, pieces of broken-down threshing machines, sections of abandoned plows, and horseshoes, which I always found in great abundance—these were my stock in trade. Rubber items were particularly valuable—the soles of castaway shoes, torn boots, and tires from all kinds of vehicles. To find a discarded automobile tire on a farm or on the side of the road was rare, but once that good fortune came your way, it was an especially lucrative day for a scrap collector. My journeys to the villages often took me away from home for three and even four days, obliging me to spend some lonely nights in dreary haylofts that farmers allowed me to use despite the objections of their barking dogs. However, these longer periods on the road enabled me to come back with good loads. With all its hardships, the work had the advantage that no one in those villages knew me. This made it easier to suffer the humiliation of being once again in front of a cart.

Meanwhile, on weekends, to further enhance my income, I taught ballroom dancing with Lilly as my assistant. It goes without saying that my clientele did not come from the upper classes of our town. They were, for the most part, young men who made their living in ways similar to mine. Of my five students, two were cabdrivers who, even on the Sabbath day, carried with them the odors of their horses. One was a butcher who must have worn the same shoes all the time because they carried the scent that pervades a butcher shop. The other two were motorcycle mechanics, whose profession was revealed only by their greased-stained fingernails and mercifully not by any foul smells.

The winter of 1941 was quickly approaching. By now Mother's health had declined to such a degree that she was bedridden for a good part of the day. After her last discharge from the hospital, the diagnosis, revealed only to her children, was that one lung had totally deteriorated and she had only a very short time to live. This was devastating news because we had hoped we could somehow keep her alive for a few more years now that she no longer had to work. We informed Uncle Joseph about the doctor's fateful assessment of Mother's condition. For the four weeks during which she was slowly dying, her brother came to visit her almost every day. We were also fortunate that Mother's friends took turns caring for her throughout the time she was ailing, which made it possible for us to go on working. Because I did so much work at home, I was there most of the time to comfort her, as much as one can comfort a dying person who knows her fate. And there was rarely a Saturday that Lilly did not come to console Mother and help with the household chores.

I will never forget December 1, 1941, the last day of her life. Mother, after two consecutive days in bed, suddenly got up and insisted on preparing her own lunch. She claimed she was feeling so much better that she wanted me to take her out for a walk. Providence had granted her a few more hours of strength and lucidity for what was to be our last conversation. She told me how much she loved us and how she wished that she could be there on our wedding days as well as when great successes and good fortune would come our way. She urged me to go back to school as soon as possible and be sure that Samuel did the same, so that we would not have to slave all our lives. Mother's last appeal was that we not forget to say Kaddish and attend memorial services on her behalf. All this was said with angelic calm and with a faint smile that gave me the impression she was not really going to die, but was merely going away on a trip from which she would soon return.

When we came back from our short outing, Mother looked very pale. She lay down and slept for a while. When she awakened, she looked somewhat confused. She closed her eyes again, showing few signs of life. When Harry called to her, she raised her head slightly and said, *"Ich leib noch* [I am still alive]." Those were her last words to us and the friends sitting around the bed, for in less than a half hour we heard her last breath, which sounded like a deep sigh of relief. She was forty-three years old.

The following morning, the Burial Society sent four pallbearers who took Mother's body to a small, dingy room at the cemetery for burial preparation. For poor people, there were no funeral homes, no gatherings with eulogies and farewell speeches. Everything was done without formality and so perfunctorily that one had the impression they were not really buried with the proper dignity; they were simply covered with dirt. It took the man from the Burial Society just two or three minutes to say the few prescribed prayers. According to Jewish Orthodox tradition, there are supposed to be ten men present when a burial takes place. In Mother's case, that custom was overlooked, and the hurried ritual proceeded with only eight males. As we were saying Kaddish, the gravediggers were already fast at work heaping earth on the modest casket. Hardly had we finished the Kaddish prayers than the man presiding over the funeral headed back to the office of the Burial Society. Harry, Samuel, and I returned home from the cemetery to sit Shiva (a week of mourning for the immediate family of the deceased). We were joined by Mother's youngest sister, Leah. Uncle Joseph came nearly every night to comfort us, but could not afford to go for a whole week without working and providing for his own family. As is the custom during Shiva, neighbors came to visit and prepared food for us.

Mother's death had a devastating effect on all of us. I felt as though God had abandoned us. I searched for some solace, some justification for the wrongs heaped on this truly heroic woman who had suffered so much throughout her life. Why was fate so harsh? Why was poverty so potent an adversary? Why was it that just when we were prepared to make her life easier and perhaps even enjoyable, she was taken from us so abruptly? There were no answers to my questions. I did, however, find some consolation in contemplating the kind of woman she was. We were privileged to have had as a mother one imbued with a generous and gallant soul, an inborn nobility. She was a model for us to reach towards. She inspired in us a love for learning. Despite the many hardships we suffered, she managed to sustain in us a love for life and for people. She taught us how to laugh at times when circumstances gave us reason to cry. She gave us the strength with which we were able to overcome many adversities, including the tragedy of her death. For all these things and for other innumerable legacies, she has our eternal love. Some say that there is a Heaven, and I tend to believe there is. In that case, she is no doubt there, still watching over us.

While we were sitting Shiva, we had a chance to talk about how we were going to keep the family together as long as possible. We knew that such a plan would have pleased Mother. During her illness, a young woman who did not have any family became attached to her and stayed with us on and off. When Mother died, Miriam was more than willing to move in with us and take care of the household. This meant that we were able to stay together at least for a time. After all, Samuel with his many years of experience as a bread earner, was still only fifteen years old.

Of the three brothers, I was the most unhappy living in Mukachevo, particularly after my boss's insulting offer when I finished my apprenticeship. However, with Mother's illness and the difficult economic circumstances at home, I had had no choice but to stay and suffer all the hardships and humiliations associated with my various demeaning jobs. Now that Mother was no longer with us, and my earnings were no longer of such great importance to the family, I was, albeit reluctantly, seriously thinking of leaving for Budapest, where I was fairly certain I could find work in my vocation. It took three months before I could tear myself away from my brothers and from Lilly, whom I knew I was going to miss terribly. Harry played a very important part in helping me make this extremely difficult decision, and gave me the confidence I needed so badly.

In the spring of 1942, I packed my few shirts and my worn suit in a paper bag, ready to leave. In his subtle way, Harry suggested that traveling to Budapest with a paper bag would not do. He was concerned that without a suitcase I would be looked on as an itinerant beggar and would not be able to get decent lodging. We quickly ran to town to buy a small suitcase, the price of which considerably depleted the cash I was to take to Budapest. I now had enough money, after my fare, to take care of accommodations and a minimum amount of food for about a week.

The time for my departure arrived. We all shed tears before I left the house, and again as I waved good-bye to Samuel and Harry. It turned out to be much more difficult than I had imagined to leave behind not only the remnant of the small family I loved so much, but Lilly, who for the last year had been such a loyal and devoted friend.

For the first few months, our friendship had gone as far as holding hands affectionately or my braiding her pretty curls as we sat in her garden. With the passage of time, I mustered enough courage to place a furtive kiss on her cheek. Later, I was more daring in depositing kisses on her cheek, but never in public. Now, on the eve of my departure for Budapest, Lilly, in the last moment of our farewell, lightly kissed me on my lips, which I accepted clumsily, blushing profusely. It was the first such kiss I had ever received from a girl.

I will always remember with affection and nostalgia Lilly's lovely smile, her gentle manners, and the pride I felt when I walked with her on the boulevard. Lilly's tenderness and her unique feminine empathy were perfectly suited for the kind of relationship all young boys should experience before they enter the adult world. There were few people in my youth with whom I had shared so much of my early life. Though this precious friendship ended with promises to exchange letters, and hopes of seeing each other again, this was the last time I saw her.

The night train to Budapest arrived at seven o'clock the following morning. As I walked at random through the city, dazed by its beauty, I chanced upon a little bicycle shop, looking as though it had been placed there by Providence especially for me. The shop was still closed. I parked myself on the steps and waited for the owner to appear, in the hope that I might get some work right there and then. As I sat there, frightened by the realization that I had left Mukachevo, I silently prayed to God and to Mother to intercede on my behalf. Since I was already in my overalls, which by now fit much better than four years ago when I had started my apprenticeship, I was prepared to start work immediately, should good fortune come my way.

To this day, I believe that both the Lord and Mother heard my prayer. Ten minutes after the arrival of the store manager, I was hired on a one-month trial basis. Not only was I very happy to be back in my profession, but the salary wasn't bad. It was adequate to pay the rent for the least expensive accommodations available in Budapest and for simple meals at a luncheonette. The only problem was that, this being Monday, I would have to wait until Friday before I could see the paycheck and celebrate my new job with a decent meal.

The store manager, a friendly man, was very unlike my previous boss. He was very considerate of me, realizing that I was nervous as I started my first few repairs. All in all, I had a successful day and was able to do well at a variety of tasks. Due to my lack of money, my first meal in Budapest was a modest lunch consisting of a pound of sweet Tokay grapes and half a pound of bread. But since I hadn't eaten after leaving Mukachevo, the grapes tasted like nectar.

In the evening I found a very small, shabby room in the house of an elderly lady. While she was renting the room, she seemed amiable enough. However, once I had paid for my first week's lodging, she proceeded to tell me, in a very dictatorial tone, about all the restrictions that came with it. I was not permitted to come home after eleven o'clock, nor could I invite any friends to the house or bring food into the room, among many other prohibitions, all of which made me feel as though I were under house arrest.

Budapest was a very lonely place for a small-town boy going on seventeen. Once I finished my work for the day, there was no one I could talk to, certainly not my unsympathetic landlady. I often thought how wonderful it would be if Lilly were to appear suddenly—then I would surely be lonely no longer. Naturally, the thought of going back home to my family and to Lilly often occurred to me. But since it was not a viable option, I simply lived with my loneliness as I had done so many times in the past, starting with cheder in Bukovinka. In time I did make some acquaintances. I discovered a small luncheonette where young men and women from the Carpathian area came to eat and to socialize. Although this helped mitigate my isolation, it did not help me forget that just months ago I had lost my dear mother and left behind my brothers and my closest friend.

The one-month trial period passed quickly. My boss praised my good work and gave me the good news that my job was now permanent. He also promised that I would soon be promoted to the larger shop that the family owned where I would be working almost exclusively on the construction of new bicycles and tricycles. Though I was pleased and even flattered, I was apprehensive about the change. Since I had had little experience in this aspect of the work, I was worried about proving my competence on the new job. There was also the fact that I was content with the smallness of the place and with my co-workers, for they represented the greater part of my social life. Thus, I hoped that my transfer would not come too soon.

But it did come much sooner than I expected. My fears about my ability to do the work didn't last long, however, for my welding skills, in which I had always excelled, turned out to be more than adequate. New bicycle and tricycle frames came off my jig with great rapidity. My fellow workers were friendly and, for a while, even the supervisor of the shop, Mr. Szécsényi, who was a rather surly character, treated me well. Within less than a month, I received a raise that allowed me to move to more cheerful lodgings. It was, in fact, Mr. Szécsényi who found me a decent room in the building where he lived and where his wife was the concierge.

Unfortunately, Mr. Szécsényi's friendly disposition toward me came to an end when he learned that I was Jewish. While this change in him didn't have a profound effect on my job, it created quite a few unpleasant moments that were hard to tolerate. His brand of anti-Semitism was of a covert type, cowardly in expression. When he dealt with me in front of other people he concealed his animosity, but when we were alone, he would use derisive language, always accompanied by a hypocritical smile to hide the cruelty behind it. Instead of calling me by my first name it was always, "Hey, little Jew." He harbored this hatred despite the fact that for over thirty years he had been earning his livelihood in a firm owned by a Jew. I asked him several times to call me by my name, but to no avail.

Mr. Szécsényi's attitude was in keeping with the anti-Semitism that was rampant in Hungary by 1942. The Hungarians had become loyal allies of Nazi Germany, supporting her with a huge army. That year, under the leadership of Miklos Kallay, the Hungarian government participated in discussions concerning Hitler's Final Solution. As was later learned, thousands of Hungary's Jews were already in forced labor camps, where they were brutally mistreated and sometimes killed. As tragic as these events were, life went on, for no one in his right mind could believe that Hitler would be able to carry out his diabolical plan for mass murder.

I was not greatly surprised by Szécsényi's hatred, for I had had all those years of preparation for dealing with the Szécsényis of the world. He was no different from the ignorant peasant boys who had often beaten me up on the way home from school. Mother had taught us how to bear up under adversity, and Szécsényi did not possess the power to undo Mother's teaching nor to weaken my endurance. But being able to live with anti-Semitism did not make it any less painful. One simply had to go on, to do the things that had to be done, to have ideals and to dream one's future, despite the obstacles that often seemed insurmountable. After all, I had secured a fairly good job that afforded me a living; and not less important, I had regained some of my lost pride by doing well at the kind of work I had trained very hard to master.

About six months had now passed since I had left Mukachevo, and the one thing that still made me unhappy was being away from my family and from Lilly. Though I learned through correspondence that Lilly had replaced me with one of my friends, I was still very eager to see her. And as the Yom Kippur holidays approached, I knew I would feel particularly lonely without my brothers. I became obsessed by the desire to go back for a short visit and share with them my successes as well as some of my preoccupations. But to realize this dream I had to live very frugally. For at least six weeks, by having only two meals a day, I managed to save enough money to buy my first new suit and return home in style. I also bought a handsome felt hat, a pair of shoes that made a proud noise as I walked in them, and a suitcase made of real leather, filled with gifts for everyone.

My six months of employment entitled me to a week's vacation with pay, and I had no problem arranging it with my employer. A week before my departure for Mukachevo, I wrote to my brothers and to Lilly announcing my homecoming. On a Sunday late in August I arrived at the station dressed to the hilt. To make my entrance into town more memorable and to thumb my nose at my former poverty, I rode in a carriage to the Yiddishe Gass where my brothers and Miriam still lived.

Since very few carriages ever came through the run-down Yiddishe Gass, many curious eyes turned in my direction to witness this rare event. My elegant garb so totally disguised my persona that not even my closest acquaintances recognized me. On my arrival at the house, my brothers were already waiting for me and, with them, Miriam and several curious neighbors who examined me from head to toe, marveling at my new height as well as my distinguished appearance. But to my great disappointment, Lilly was not there.

Our meeting was filled with the happy tears without which the reunion of a Jewish family would not be complete. In the seven months of my absence, Samuel had grown amazingly tall. He had totally lost his boyish features and looked more like an adult than a teenager going on sixteen. He was robust and very muscular. In retrospect, I think he resembled Michelangelo's famous sculpture of David. Miriam had prepared a special meal, and questions were thrown at me right and left at the dinner table. Everyone wanted to know about life in Budapest and how I had managed to be so successful in such a short time.

The eight days in Mukachevo went by very fast, and conversations lasted well into the night. I learned about everything that had happened during my absence—who had died, who had gotten married, who had been drafted into forced-labor camps by the Hungarian army, and who had managed to run to the Soviet side in order to escape the camps or arrest by the Hungarian fascists. The Yom Kippur holidays were always the best occasion to visit with the friends and distant relatives one did not have a chance to see during the year. On Rosh Hashanah, when all of us went to the synagogue—the first time without Mother—I was surrounded by old acquaintances and by those seeking advice on how to escape to Budapest and make their fortunes.

During my stay, the family gave a party in my honor. Many of my friends and former dance pupils were there, but not the one that I would have given anything to see again. Lilly, for some unknown reason, never did come to our house. To ease my disappointment, I made a number of excuses for her non-appearance, but I never found out why she did not come. However, the love and joy with which I was received by my family and friends during those eight days more than made up for Lilly's absence, and made me dread my inevitable separation from them.

On Sunday morning, the day of my departure, an entourage of six people accompanied me on the two-mile walk to the railroad station. Though I would have preferred riding in style as I had arrived, I yielded when Harry pointed out that the extravagance of two carriages would leave me virtually broke. Being surrounded by all these affectionate people was more important than showing off. As I leaned out of the railroad car window to wave my final good-bye, several thoughts went through my mind: How many of these beloved people would I see again? What would become of young Samuel, who was particularly upset by my departure? How could I adjust to living without them when I was alone once more in Budapest?

When I returned to the shop Monday morning, my workmates greeted me warmly, and even Mr. Szécsényi managed to turn on a forced grin and say he had missed me. More exciting was the news that I had been promoted during my absence. From now on, I would be participating in every operation rather than being confined to welding. I was sure this wasn't due to Mr. Szécsényi's intercession on my

Jay at the age of seventeen, in Budapest, after his visit to Mukachevo.

behalf, but to the fact that the owner of the shop, Mr. Feifer, had heard of my good work.

As for my social life in Budapest, I remained as lonely as ever. During my vacation, Uncle Joseph had suggested I look up an aunt in Budapest in the hope that visiting her from time to time would relieve my solitude. From her cold reception on the telephone, however, I got the impression that Aunt Margit was afraid I had come to her with a request for money. In her early fifties and recently widowed, she lived with her twenty-year-old daughter in a spacious apartment that could have accommodated a large family. It provided all the comforts and amenities of middle-class living. When I came to see her, I was immediately struck by the strong resemblance she bore to my mother. But they had totally different personalities. In contrast to my mother's charm, Aunt Margit's face seemed to convey permanent anger. It was as though she had never possessed the ability to laugh or even to smile.

The reason for her bitterness was clarified when I learned her story. Some twenty years earlier, she had been disowned by my grandparents because she married a Gentile tailor, and with the passage of time all contact had been lost between her and the rest of the family. Since I knew that my mother had not been among those family members who had condemned her, it was very painful to see the equanimity with which she took the news of Mother's recent death and the troubled life that had preceded it. It seemed to me that a total stranger would have reacted with greater sympathy to Mother's tragedy than her own sister did.

I visited Aunt Margit a few more times just to see the features that so resembled my mother's, still hoping as well that I had been mistaken in my previous assessment. But she never displayed any warmth toward me, nor did she seem to understand what her affection would have meant to a boy living alone in Budapest.

A few months after my visit to Mukachevo, I received a letter from home with bad news. Harry was one of thousands of young men from the Carpathian area who had been drafted into forced-labor camps, often referred to as labor units. He was obliged to report within ten days. These units were deceptively touted as being a patriotic service in the war the Germans and Hungarians were waging against Russia. The real intent, as we later learned, was to gather young Jews under the Nazi thumb, use their labor and when they were no longer of use to the fascists kill them off. The "draftees" were issued genuine Hungarian army hats, taught marching drills and patriotic songs, and otherwise led to believe that they were actually soldiers. Most of them were engaged in road construction, dredging rivers, loading and unloading freight in railroad yards, and building airports all over Hungary. In 1942, they were sent by the thousands to the Russian front to comb minefields, build fortifications, and dispose of dead German and Hungarian soldiers.

By the spring of 1944, some 42,000 Jewish men had already lost their lives on the Russian front. So intent were the Germans on the murder of the Jewish people that even while they were retreating, they made every effort to transport survivors of the labor units to the death camps. Often this was done even when it jeopardized their war effort. Those who were still dispersed in Hungary did not fare much better than their brethren; the atrocities perpetrated on them were simply delayed. Eventually, they too were dispatched to Auschwitz and other

German camps where, with very few exceptions, they were killed with the rest of the Jewish men, women, and children. This fate awaited Harry after he was "drafted."

In October 1942 Harry had been summoned to the historic city of Mohács, but I heard no news of him until the following spring when I received a crumpled postcard. Though the writing was partially obliterated, I was able to decipher that he was in a small town near Debrecen, lying ill in an infirmary. Since it wasn't far from Budapest, I made plans to visit him. Being very concerned about his health, and suspecting that the illness was due to the lack of good food, I spent all I could to bring him a package that would supplement the poor diet fed to the inmates.

I arrived by train on a Friday night and found Harry's camp only with great difficulty. At the entrance, I was stopped by Hungarian soldiers. I identified myself and told them I had come to visit my sick brother. One of the guards, a sergeant, pointed to the package and asked me what I had inside. After I enumerated the contents, he rudely ordered me to hand it over to him. When I did, he started to beat me with the butt of his rifle. Frightened out of my wits, I ran for dear life. In my flight I could hear a chorus of anti-Semitic jeers and obscenities. As an additional cruelty, I learned later the guards gave Harry a detailed description of their assault on me. Actually, Harry was not seriously ill. Having routinely slept on bare straw, he had developed a skin infection which, by the time I came to see him, had cleared up.

The few bruises were not as hard to take as was my deep disappointment at not seeing my brother and my frustration at not being able to revenge myself on those animals. However, as in the past, there was really nothing I could do but bemoan my fate while continuing to maintain hope for better things to come.

Chapter 5

Hitler's Scourge

Life in Budapest was getting better. With periodic salary increases, I could finally permit myself the luxury of a social life. From time to time, I even invited a girl to go to a dance with me—hoping she would come well-fed and not want to go to dinner, which was rather costly in a city like Budapest. More important, I could now seriously consider the possibility of going back to school for some evening courses, though they were quite expensive. I had been determined to return to school ever since I was forced to leave at such a young age. I was haunted by a sense of shame and degradation that had been particularly painful during my apprenticeship when I was competing with students who had completed their basic education. Except for the threat posed by Hitler, which I hoped would subside, my chances for going back to school looked good. I started to put away money on the assumption that in the spring semester of 1944 my dream would finally be realized. Just planning to resume my formal education made me very happy. I couldn't wait for the day when I would attend my first class.

However, it was not to be. Once more, my aspirations were dashed. In March of 1944 Hitler occupied Hungary and, soon after, the rest of the young Jewish men were "drafted" into forced-labor camps scattered throughout the country. No sooner had I finished three weeks of evening classes than a draft notice summoned me to a transit labor camp in a small village called Jolsva on the Slovak-Hungarian border.

With the summons came a list of necessaries such as blankets, two pairs of boots, and clothing for both winter and summer weather. Luckily, Mr. Feifer, my employer, generously provided me with many items of clothing I could not have bought with the kind of money I had. He also put me in touch with a doctor, a member of his family, who was being sent to Jolsva, leaving behind his wife and two children. I was to help him to carry some of his equipment, in return for which he would be of some service to me. Other than the fact that I had the chance of being in the company of an intelligent adult, this arrangement yielded me no particular advantages. My traveling companion brought far too many things, making our trip unnecessarily burdensome, since most of what we carried turned out to be of no use in camp. The poor doctor hadn't foreseen that a pickaxe and shovel, rather than medical instruments, were going to be his working tools.

We were put onto a freight train that was lined with hay which was bad enough, but not to be compared with the transports heading for Auschwitz and other extermination camps. At Jolsva, we were obliged to walk with our belongings about three miles up a mountain road to where a Hungarian army post had been converted into a labor camp. We were received by about half a dozen Hungarian sergeants who assured us, in speeches interspersed with ferocious swearing, that life was going to be rough. They outlined all the rules we would have to obey strictly. After standing in line for an hour, we were assigned to barracks whose floors were lined with straw. Each inmate was permitted to create his own little bed, occupying just enough space for one person to sleep. My traveling companion invited me to choose a spot adjacent to his. I was rather proud that he introduced me to our bunkmates as his friend, and felt reassured that, should some illness befall me, he would be able to cure me.

After we arranged our belongings, we were summoned for a lineup, where we were each given a mess kit, a loaf of black bread meant to last three days, and a hat that displayed the Hungarian crown on its front. This was accompanied by a patriotic speech delivered by a captain. In a friendly and persuasive manner, he told us the crown meant that we were indeed soldiers in the Hungarian army and that with our labor, we would help defeat the enemies of the Hungarian people. A few naive listeners undoubtedly bought the captain's feigned benevolence and overlooked not only the reception we had gotten from the sergeants but the facts, by now well-known, concerning the tragic fate of other Hungarian Jews in forced-labor camps. However, the majority of us knew better than to believe the patriotic bilge and the other lies.

Since Jolsva was mainly a transit camp from which labor units were eventually sent to various permanent work sites, the work we were called on to perform there was not too difficult for me—though it must have been arduous for those who were not accustomed to physical labor. I was part of a thirty-man detail using pickaxe and shovel to dig a foundation for a huge bunker which was being built for the protection of the town folk. More difficult to suffer than the physical work were the pranks played on us after the working day. Aside from senseless marching drills and roll calls, it was not unusual for the guards to come into the barracks in the middle of the night, chase all of us out in our underwear, throw out our belongings, and watch with great amusement as we scrambled in the dark for our clothing. In addition to these group harassments, minor and major assaults were perpetrated on selected individuals. I fell victim to a beating the very first week. One evening, as I was walking near the mess hall, I was grabbed by three soldiers, dragged into the kitchen, beaten by all three, pelted with tomatoes, and then thrown out into the courtyard. Random attacks like these were part of the daily diet. We had to learn to live with them because there was no way out. Fighting back, as I attempted on one occasion, risked severe and costly consequences. Yet there were among us some truly heroic boys and men who, when it was a question of principle, were prepared to suffer harsh punishment and defy their oppressors. My dear friend Imre Neimann was one such courageous man.

Imre was a very handsome, bright young man from a fine upper-class, assimilated Jewish family. When his university education was interrupted by the draft, he left behind in Budapest his childhood sweetheart and fiancée, Ilona. Though she was Catholic, neither set of parents objected to their relationship. In fact, Ilona's mother was very fond of Imre and hoped that the couple would be married some day. However, Ilona's uncle, a priest and an ardent anti-Semite, made several trips to our camp, demanding that the commander extract from Imre a formal written statement to send to Ilona stating that he was prepared to give her up. The commander tried a variety of punishments—depriving Imre of his food ration, assigning him to excruciatingly hard work, and threatening to do harm to his family. When this didn't work, poor Imre was subjected to such a beating that when they brought him back, half dead, he was unrecognizable; his handsome, aristocratic face had been turned into a black and blue balloon, and his hands looked like inflated red rubber gloves. We recognized him only because he had been placed on his own pile of straw.

Imre's horrendous experience was duplicated the next day. This time the victim was a young man who, with equal courage, had refused to send a letter denouncing his Jewish mother for having married his father, a Hungarian of German descent who was no longer alive. He, too, was beaten beyond recognition. Although I don't remember his name, I do recall very vividly not only his plaintive moans as he lay there in terrible pain, but his many appeals to Jesus Christ. This poor soul had been brought up as a Catholic—but, under Nazi law, he was considered a Jew on the principle that a child born to parents with any Jewish blood was himself a Jew.

The priest, in Imre's case, probably rationalized his deeds on a religious basis to absolve himself of his sin. But what kind of explanation could the camp commander give to justify his inhuman cruelty toward these two young men, and undoubtedly to hundreds of others? Was he "just carrying out orders," as so many Nazis claimed when they committed their atrocities? The cruelty of our major seems to point to the tragic fact that the Hungarian Jews were subject to the same hate, the same horrors as their German brethren. The Hungarian Nazis did not merely cooperate with Hitler—rather, they were full partners in Hitler's villainy and in the eventual deaths of most of Hungary's Jewish men, women, and children.

It must be said that the beatings and other reprehensible acts at Jolsva were a far cry from the extreme suffering that Jews were by then enduring in Polish ghettos, in other labor camps, and in German concentration camps. In Jolsva we actually had the luxury of a day off on Sundays. Those who were brave enough, and had an irresistible yearning to be free for a few hours, would steal into town—knowing that they were guaranteed ten or more lashes if caught—a reasonable trade-off for those who felt suffocated by their confinement. I was caught only once in four of my excursions.

Unlike other forced-labor camps, ours allowed us to receive mail. The occasional letter from home, as well as parcels of food and clothing sent by relatives who were not yet dragged into ghettos, made life more bearable. Also, there was at least a semblance of concern for men who became sick. An infirmary with several beds gave the seriously-ill the opportunity to leave their dreary barracks and get out of a day's hard work. Even the food was not too bad, compared to the starvation diet in other Nazi camps.

Meanwhile, though I didn't know it at the time, my brother Harry had been on the Russian front for over a year, digging trenches and combing minefields for the German and Hungarian armies. Nor did he know that I was already in a forced-labor camp. A postcard he sent to my Budapest address was miraculously forwarded to Jolsva. He wrote that he badly needed a decent pair of boots because he was practically barefoot and the weather on the Russian front was bitterly cold. I had two pairs of boots, one, brand new courtesy of Mr. Feifer, which I was saving, literally, for a rainy day, the other, an old pair that had already seen many rainy days and was full of holes. Without hesitation, I decided to send the new ones to my brother. Suspecting that Harry's rations were as meager as mine, I sneaked into the village, where I purchased two hard-skinned Hungarian salamis. I stuffed one into each boot, made a good sturdy package, and mailed it to him. Only after the war did I learn that Harry had indeed received the strong-smelling parcel. We have had many good laughs about the "salami-boots" that retained their garlicky odor for as long as he wore them. Harry is convinced to this day that they made his life easier because the stench was so powerful that the sergeant, who used to push his fellow inmates around, would never come near him.

When rumors about our leaving Jolsva started circulating around the camp, there were numerous theories about where we were going, most of them boding ill for our future. The voices of the few optimists were heard less frequently. Naturally, opinions and conjectures about our destination were based on rumor rather than on fact since none of us had an authentic source of information. The Hungarians as well as the Germans who were in charge of the destruction of the Jews made sure that the planning was carried out in great secrecy so as to engender as much fear and therefore as much obedience as possible. This secrecy was maintained to the very end.

To counteract our anxiety, we banded together, as people tend to do in time of trouble. All sorts of friendships and loyalties were formed among the three hundred men in our unit. It was interesting to see how, within the four weeks that we were in camp, the inmates found kindred spirits and formed their own little fraternities. The university students, to whom I was drawn, together with a variety of artists, formed their own social unit. In a half-clandestine way, they organized poetry readings, lectures on art, musical concerts, and other cultural activities. A young baritone from the Budapest Opera performed for us, and a gifted young pianist played as best he could on a poorly-tuned old piano that belonged to the camp caretaker. Naturally, the Orthodox men didn't want anything to do with the impious students and intellectuals—they formed their own cohesive group, held secret religious services every day, and tried to persuade the nonbelievers to mend their ways and attend at least the Sabbath services. There were, of course, a variety of other solidarities. People who came from the same town tended to band together, as well as did those of the same profession. There were also the loners, who fraternized with no one. Once the obligatory day's work was done, they isolated themselves in their own separate worlds.

When the time came for our departure, we learned that we were to be divided among seven different transports, but had no way of knowing whether they were going to the same place. As we were herded onto the trucks, there were desperate struggles to try to stay together with one's friends. However, many were separated from their friends when particular transports were filled. I was among the fortunate ones. Imre and I, who had become close friends, succeeded in getting on the same truck, along with my doctor companion and some others from our barracks. In each other's company we felt a little less apprehensive about our new journey into the unknown.

We were driven to the train where once more we were loaded onto freight cars, still with no idea where we were being taken. Again, in our uneasiness, all kinds of theories were advanced as to our destination. The further we were into the trip, the worse the scenario became. About four hours after our departure, we stopped in a small village, where we were allowed to use the toilet facilities and fill our canteens with water. A railroad worker there told us surreptitiously that we were traveling in the direction of Budapest. Two hours later we were deposited at a military airfield which seemed far removed from civilization though it turned out to be only a hundred kilometers from the city. But the authorities were not prepared for our arrival, and for the first two nights we were obliged to sleep in the open, near a cemetery. As if suffering the cold of the early spring nights was not bad enough, I had to sleep almost on top of a grave, giving me a chill of yet another kind.

Our unit had been brought here to rebuild and enlarge the landing strips. The work was very difficult and strictly supervised, much worse than at Jolsva, where we could rest on and off because the soldiers who accompanied us paid little attention to what we were doing. Here, the guards watched our every move and yelled furiously if we slowed down. In the 12-hour work day, a certain number of acres of topsoil had to be removed and gravel spread so it was ready for the rolling and laying of the hardtop. Some of the boys who were not used to hard physical work suffered enormous fatigue; many had painful blisters. Fortunately, at this point we could still claim illness and visit the makeshift infirmary. If one of us was in really bad shape he might be lucky enough to be excused from work for a day.

This project lasted for about two weeks, after which we were moved to a succession of other locations to repair airfields and roads, or rebuild old bridges. In the span of about four weeks, we must have worked in six different places, but other than the fact that we were somewhere within a hundred-mile radius of Budapest, we rarely knew the name of the village or town near which our camp was located. Our peregrinations ended when, in May of 1944, we were shipped to the town of Csepel, an industrial suburb of Budapest. Although we didn't know what awaited us there, everyone was relieved that, for now, we were not being taken to Auschwitz or some other concentration camp. Those who came from Budapest were particularly heartened, hoping for an eventual twenty four hour furlough which was still possible at the time, depending on the mood of the unit officer and the subtle promise of a bribe.

The town of Csepel was an island, the site of the largest manufacturing plant in Hungary which was also known as Csepel. Before the war, the factory had produced a variety of hard goods, among them very fine bicycles. It had belonged to a Jewish family, from whom it was confiscated on the eve of the war. As soon as the war began, it had been converted for the manufacture of military hardware to assist Hitler's assaults. There was a huge smelting system in which iron scrap of all sizes was turned into raw materials to be used in the making of bombs and other weapons. There was a separate section for fabricating explosives, and another for the assembly of finished products.

When our transport arrived, it was immediately obvious that Csepel was a well-guarded military installation. It was hardly possible to walk anywhere in the plant without seeing soldiers armed with rifles. Lodgings for our unit, and for others that kept arriving every day, were situated inside the plant on the periphery of the property. The poorly constructed underground chambers, apparently built originally as air raid shelters, resembled jail cells rather than living quarters. There was no furniture other than double bunk beds. Into each of these "rooms," measuring about twenty feet square, were jammed about fifty people. Adjacent to the "dorm" was another cell, small and poorly lit, which contained three washbasins and primitive toilet facilities—the kind where, in order to relieve yourself, you had to squat. There were no doors separating these areas, so whatever bit of air and natural light we had filtered through from the entryway. Dismal and stuffy as it was, the one advantage of living there was that it did indeed serve to some extent as a shelter from the constant bombings. However, while the thin walls and the five-inch rooftop might protect us from shrapnel, they weren't likely to survive a direct hit or even an explosion in the vicinity.

Other than the fact that one could have some contact with the outside world through the regular workers at the plant, Csepel was a gloomy and depressing place. Within the confines of those high concrete walls, topped by barbed wire, everything smelled of industrial fumes that contaminated the air we had to breathe twenty-four hours a day. It was a dark, somber world, where the humans were rendered subservient to the machinery that crowded every structure in Csepel. Almost everything the eye could see was either black or brown, as though other colors did not exist—black smoke rising from the furnaces, black and brown bombshells that were filled with brown explosives, brown machine guns, black metal-stamping presses. Even the people working at their various tasks looked as though they had just emerged from coal mines. Although we arrived in Csepel in the springtime, there were virtually no blossoms or greenery of any kind. Here and there, a tuft of grass or a seedling emerging from the cracks in the cement assured one that nature was not totally subdued by the u-biquitous concrete.

Our transport arrived in Csepel on a Sunday afternoon, and by Monday morning everyone had a job assignment. My group was placed in a detail of about sixty men who loaded iron scrap from a dump onto freight wagons called gondolas, then pushed the gondolas on rails to the smelting area, where we unloaded them. Here, again, we were guarded by Hungarian soldiers. We worked ten hours a day, only the work was considerably harder than our pickaxe-and-shovel labor at the airfield. Since there was no machinery to help us, it often took ten or even more persons to lift heavy objects like the shell of an old motor or a heavy locomotive wheel. Some of us could have been seriously maimed had it not been for the great concern that we as a group had for each other. Every one of those Jewish men and boys showed admirable toughness and character. They would under no cir-cumstances make work easier for themselves at the expense of a fel-low.

One particular soul who best personified this loyalty and concern was a dear, dear man whom we affectionately called Gunga Din—so named because he was our water carrier and literally saved us from dehydration. Even more difficult to bear than the very poor food and the hard work in Csepel was the intense heat under the burning sun. The heat was especially hard to endure in the area of the smelter ovens, where the temperature reached 120 degrees or more. To help us survive, Providence sent Gunga Din. All day, this fragile little man ran back and forth between the work site and the water pump, which was at least a half mile away, without stopping for a moment's rest. Gunga Din rarely ever walked erect; he was always bent forward from the weight of the heavy pails filled with fresh water. He would hand us the ladle of water with a faint benevolent smile, as though the water he brought us were a special meal prepared by him exclusively for each of his fellow-workers. Gunga Din was about forty years old when he was taken to Csepel from Budapest, where he left behind a wife and children who were later confined in a ghetto there. I learned at the end of the war that our dear water carrier was later sent to Auschwitz, where he did not survive. Had it ever been possible, I would have liked to visit his wife—in the unlikely event that she and her children were still alive—to tell her about her husband's selflessness and the eternal affection I have for him.

After four weeks of this back-breaking work, I was lucky enough to be transferred to a different job. Because my dossier indicated that I knew spot welding, I was assigned for an unspecified period to a group whose job was to cut old rails being taken to the smeltery. Except for the intense heat, I certainly preferred working with the cutting torch to loading scrap. And as it turned out, I didn't even have to be separated from my friends, since the cutting took place right at the loading site. But the real bonus came from the fact that I now had the chance to work with Hungarian welders, some of whom were decent and generous. One particular fellow became aware that the food we were given was substandard, to say the least, our menu consisting most frequently of a watery soup that had virtually no nutritional value. This good-hearted man, at great risk to himself, brought us sandwiches and other foods almost daily.

As far as the difficulty of the work in Csepel was concerned, most of us were able to cope. Ironically, what made our lives excruciatingly difficult and frightening was the relentless round-the-clock bombings. At night, when the British bombed, we were more or less protected in our living quarters. During the day, when the Americans took over, many Jewish boys lost their lives—sometimes a dozen or more on a given day. There were, of course, well-built bunkers to protect the regular workers and our captors, and on rare occasions some of us sneaked into them. But most of the time we were obliged to run for cover to the river while the bombs were already dropping. It was at such times that some Jewish boys were killed by the falling bombs or shrapnel, while others were cut down by the machine guns of pilots who didn't know they were helping Hitler. There were among us a number of men who reacted with hysteria to the bombings, particularly at night, when the attacks tended to be most intense. The suffering caused by those dreadful bombings has left those of us who survived Hitler's scourge with permanent scars. All through the years that followed, I have had recurring dreams about those shrieking sirens. To this day, when I hear the sound of an ambulance or fire engine, my heart begins to pound.

The round-the-clock bombings, in addition to the hard work, made our existence in Csepel a hell on earth. There prevailed among us a collective despair; even the songs we used to sing in the evening to cheer ourselves up became depressingly sad. Adding to our hopelessness was the fact that, through a variety of sources, we became acutely aware of what was happening in the outside world to the Jews at large and to our families. We knew, for example, that by the middle of the summer of 1944 most Hungarian Jews were either in overcrowded ghettos, without adequate food or medical supplies, or already in Auschwitz and other camps where Adolf Eichmann's Final Solution was being carried out relentlessly. We learned later that brave men like Raoul Wallenberg were making desperate efforts to save the Jews of Budapest, to little avail. Those noble efforts were being thwarted by the overwhelming Nazi determination to obliterate the Jews.

There was rarely a day in Csepel when we would not receive some news about the atrocities in Budapest and other parts of Hungary. Not only did factory workers sympathetic to our plight give us detailed descriptions of what they heard was going on, but as new forced-labor workers kept coming in, they brought with them incredible horror stories. That was how I received bad news about my family. A childhood friend from Mukachevo, who had just arrived in Csepel, related to me the awful sequence of events that had befallen the Jews of Carpatho-Ruthenia. He told me that, by the end of April, all the Jews of that area had been forced into ghettos, among them my brother Samuel and many other members of my extended family. Within a month or so, they were on their way to concentration camps. The news left me so stunned and despondent that I couldn't even cry. It was a tragic fact that the better the news regarding the Allied war effort, the worse matters became for Jews everywhere. The triumph in Normandy on D-Day, and other victories in Europe, only meant that the Nazis sped up their efforts to eliminate as many Jews as possible.

All these events confirmed in us a feeling that we too were doomed to a disastrous end. We had been safe so far only because our slave labor was more valuable to the Nazis than our deaths. At the end of July rumors began to circulate that we were very soon to be transported to a concentration camp. The majority seemed resigned to our impending doom while still hoping for some miracle, as has been the case with Jews from time immemorial. Since there was really very little we could do about our situation, hope was just about all that was left for us. One could say that in Csepel there prevailed among us a kind of terrified resignation, a *que sera* mentality, which left our fate in the hands of Providence. However, there were a few who were not going to go like lambs to the slaughter. These more daring souls began to think and talk about taking steps to save themselves.

Fleeing from our oppressors was the most talked-about option because a few boys had indeed managed to get away and find refuge in Budapest. In most cases, they were from families who had connections with Christians willing to risk hiding a Jew, a brave and precarious undertaking. While a few Christians did this for money, most did this godly deed for humanitarian reasons.

Escape was difficult and dangerous, treated by the fascists as a very serious offense. Nevertheless, within a period of three or four weeks, there were so many escapes from Csepel and neighboring camps that the Hungarians adopted much more stringent measures. There was a nationwide announcement that those who returned within a specified number of days would be pardoned. Anyone caught after the deadline faced death. Some did come back, but when the officials realized that many escapees had not returned, they initiated a manhunt.

Among the few who were caught, was Jancsi, part of my group, who was on his way back but missed the deadline by a few hours. On Sunday, the camp commander ordered all the inmates of Csepel to line up facing a cement wall that surrounded the factory. We knew that we were summoned to witness the punishment of a captured fellow worker, but we did not realize that it was Jancsi, nor did we know what his fate was going to be.

Within a few minutes of the lineup, Jancsi appeared, accompanied by two guards, hands tied behind his back and barely able to walk. He seemed dazed and confused as though he did not know what was happening to him. Quickly, the two Hungarian soldiers tied a black kerchief over his eyes and led him to the wall. Four Hungarian soldiers carrying rifles moved to a distance of some ten paces from Jancsi at the wall. Nothing was said. With a wave of his hand, the camp commander gave the order to fire. Within seconds a barrage of bullets was discharged. We watched in horror as Jancsi's limp body fell to the ground. Almost in one voice we cried out *"Istenem* [Oh my God]!" a wail that could be heard by the entire town of Csepel, had anyone listened.

The murder sent a shock wave through the camp. However, it did not produce the effect desired by the Nazis, for there were still a few of us who were prepared to pay with their lives for even the remote possibility of freedom.

The brutality of the camp authorities was demonstrated in yet other ways. The already inferior food became even worse and the behavior of our guards more belligerent. Punishments were meted out with great frequency for the least infraction of the absurd rules. The castigations came in a variety of forms. One could often see some of our boys with hands and feet tied to a broomstick, or suspended from a tree with hands tied in the back and feet barely touching the ground. For what they considered a more serious violation, whipping was the usual punishment. This, for some incomprehensible reason, was often administered by the major in charge of our camp, assisted by his orderly.

Among many others, I was once the recipient of the major's attentions. My crime was that I had bought a small crate of marmalade in the village grocery near where we were digging trenches. On our return to camp, the sergeant confiscated my purchase and reported me to his superior officer. On a Sunday afternoon, I was taken by a soldier to the commandant's office to receive my punishment. Though I had seen him several times before, he looked much larger at close range, and I was intimidated by his imposing figure and stern, official-looking face. The dreaded moment for my lashing came. I was stripped practically naked. Just before I was to receive my first lash, I looked into the major's eyes to see whether I might find in them some humanity or compassion; there was none. All I saw was an expression of cold indifference and savage satisfaction. It still seems strange to me that this man, whose chest was covered with medals, among them several for bravery, should find gratification in beating a boy less than half his size.

Another beating I suffered while in Csepel occurred when a high-ranking officer came to inspect our camp. At a lineup, our visitor kicked me about because he didn't like the way I was standing at attention. This was one of my most distressing experiences at Csepel, not so much because of the physical punishment, but because it was degrading to be beaten in front of my fellow inmates. As I was being battered, I saw the frustrated expressions on the faces of my friends, who had no choice but to watch helplessly as the sadist did his ugly work. Had he not been protected by at least ten guards, I'm sure they would have come to my rescue, disregarding the grave consequences that would certainly have ensued. I was glad no one tried; I did not want others to endanger themselves on my behalf. In the final analysis, their intercession would have made no difference.

This most recent humiliation in front of my friends, the general hopelessness, and the impending probability that we would be shipped to a German concentration camp where I would be put to death made me realize that relying on miracles would not save me. Along with those who did not want to go to the slaughter without resistance, I too began to think seriously of escape. It turned out that Imre, who was clandestinely in touch with his mother, had all along been making plans in which he had hoped to include me should I decide to take the risk. His mother, who was still living in a Budapest ghetto, was trying to arrange a hiding place for the family where she could have Imre join them. Perhaps, after all, we were not doomed.

Because making arrangements for escape was a very risky matter for both Imre and his family, contact had to be interrupted at one point and no progress was made for several weeks. Unexpectedly, good fortune came our way when we were both transferred to a work detail of Hungarian electricians. The assignment of our group was to restore the high voltage power lines in the outskirts of Budapest after they were knocked down by the incessant Allied bombings. This new job was physically taxing and exceedingly dangerous. In the four weeks we were on this detail, one Hungarian worker was burned to death and many others were injured. However, it had several important advantages. For one, we were able to leave the dreary plant every day and see a bit of nature, of which we were almost totally deprived in Csepel. More important for Imre's plans, we were not guarded by our sergeants during the work day. Once the truck left the camp, we were under the supervision of the foreman in charge of the electricians. Several times, Imre was able to get to a telephone to discuss arrangements for our escape. It would have been relatively easy to run off then, but two considerations held us back. First of all, the details of our hiding place were not yet finalized. More important, we were worried that the Hungarians with whom we worked would be in danger of severe punishment. As luck would have it, the job ended a week before the day that was designated for our departure, and we were once more confined within the Csepel complex. Now we had to wait still another week before we could carry out our plans to get to Imre's house from which we would be taken to the home of a blind college professor who was going to shelter twenty people.

It was easier to make the decision to escape than to act on it. Once we faced the reality of taking the final step, there were many agonizing doubts. For one, the vivid memory of the recent execution gave both of us pause. I had yet another reason to be concerned about this dangerous move—my chances of being able to hide out with the family were not altogether a certainty. What would happen if there wasn't room for me in the hiding place? Added to this concern, I felt guilty at escaping and abandoning my friends who did not have a place to run to or the blind courage to do so. I was particularly heartbroken to leave behind Gunga Din of whom I had grown very fond, for our poor water carrier appeared to be distressingly emaciated and helpless.

A few days before the attempt, we made our final plans and preparations. We had to be ready to get on one of the trucks that took Hungarian employees out of Csepel to bus stops or to the railroad station. The idea was to look as much as possible like regular workers so as not to arouse any suspicions. For this we needed identification badges, without which no one could leave camp, and the kind of lunch boxes that Hungarians carried to work with them. Our only recourse was to steal these items from the lockers of a couple of workers, knowing that they could easily replace them without getting into trouble. We attended to many other details, including washing the left-hand sleeves of our jackets repeatedly to get rid of the stripe left by the yellow band we Jews were required to wear.

The last night at Csepel was a sad one as we said good-bye to some of our friends. All this was done in great secrecy—not that we didn't trust our fellow-inmates, but out of fear that someone might inadvertently say something that would undo us. Fear had became the dominating force in everything that concerned our escape, perhaps more so in my case than in Imre's, especially in the last phase of the preparations. Not a night passed that I didn't have terrifyingly vivid dreams about being caught and executed, dreams in which I had the sensation of a bullet entering my heart and felt myself dying.

Chapter 6

On The Run

My last working day in Csepel was on a Monday in the middle of August 1944. It still seems to me the longest day of my life. Waiting for that six o'clock factory horn to announce the end of the shift was like waiting for eternity. The day was filled with conflicting emotions, ranging from hopes for success and survival to the certainty of disaster. Finally, as we pushed our last gondola to the smeltery, the factory horn sounded. Our time had come. Imre and I exchanged a furtive look as if to say, "This is it." We walked for a while with our working group; then, at an opportune moment when we were sure we were unobserved, we separated from them as inconspicuously as possible, took off our yellow bands, put on our identification badges, and mingled with the crowd heading for the gates.

Imre, not realizing that I was far behind him, jumped onto a crowded truck which was already in motion. Only by running desperately did I manage to climb into the same one, barely controlling my feeling of panic. Although I knew Imre's address in Budapest, without him I would have had no idea where to get off. The prospect of going into Budapest on my own would probably have changed my mind about the whole idea of escape.

On the truck we held our breath, but none of the workers recognized us and we were in the clear. At the first trolley station, we got off with some others and took the streetcar into the city—fearful at every moment of the tap on the shoulder that would mean the difference between freedom and almost certain death.

Miraculously, we made our way without incident to Imre's mother's apartment building. In no time, we were rushed to our temporary hiding place—a small crawl space under the staircase that was used for the storage of roof tiles. The blankets we were given we spread over the bits of broken tile that littered the floor, to sleep on at night and sit on during the day, since there was no room to stand. In addition, we had to move very cautiously because, with the slightest shift, the tile fragments made a noise that could betray our presence. It was only late at night that we were able to emerge from our total darkness and go up to the apartment to use the toilet facilities and replenish our food supplies.

Our concealment had lasted for about a week when I was given the dreadful news. My worst fear had became a reality. Weeping and distraught, Imre told me that there was no room for me at the professor's house. Although I thought I had mentally prepared myself for this eventuality, I was stunned. I had no doubt that Imre had tried his best, and have never questioned his loyalty and affection, but obviously there was absolutely nothing he could do. Within an hour, Imre, his two sisters, and his mother were taken to their sanctuary.

I was left with very few options. I could remain in the crawl space for a day or two until my food supplies were exhausted; then I had to come up with a plan to save my life. Frightened and lonely, I had a good cry which cleared my head and helped to rid me of my inner turmoil. I started to think more lucidly about what to do.

I remembered that, when I worked in Budapest as a mechanic, I had become acquainted with a printer whose shop was not far from mine. We were friendly, and often had lunch together in a neighborhood cafeteria or at his workplace while we chatted. Although I had never really gotten to know him well, I did know that he had served on the Russian front in 1941 with the Hungarian army and was very proud of his accomplishments as a soldier, having killed many "Russkies," as he called the Russians.

As I searched for some way out of my predicament, it occurred to me that in order to try to hide my identity I would need falsified documents with a plausible Hungarian name. Who better than a well-disposed printer for such a purpose. Before leaving Imre's building, I decided that I would be Balogh László, seventeen years old. I also concocted a story to explain my presence in Budapest, just in case I was stopped before I had any papers. My reason would be that my fictitious father, a former Hungarian soldier wounded in the war against the Russians, was afraid to remain in the area of Mukachevo. This fear was actually well-founded, since Hungarian soldiers who had served on the Russian front were petrified of the Russian army, for good reason. Since the Russians were fast approaching, it had been supposedly decided that the family flee to safer ground and hopefully reunite once victory came our way. Therefore, my story continued, I had determined to seek my fortune in Budapest, since I was a mechanic who also had a great deal of experience farming and taking care of livestock. Even with this fabrication, I knew full well that should I be caught by the German or Hungarian fascists and properly examined, my story would not be worth a farthing.

My new identity well memorized, I emerged apprehensively from my crawl space ready to go to the printing shop. I carried a small bundle containing a threadbare sweater, a shirt, a pair of socks, and briefs. It was a brilliantly sunny August day. Having been confined to almost total darkness for a whole week, I had to squint for a long time before I could fully open my eyes. Among the crowds milling about the streets were large numbers of German SS walking in pairs, and my heart pounded every time I passed them. I felt totally isolated, a terrified being, an alien walking among people leading a normal life, Hungarian men and women strolled along as happily as they had before Hitler had come to Hungary only five months earlier. Perhaps some of them didn't know, or didn't care that just a few streets away there was a large synagogue into which hundreds of Jewish men, women, and children had been crammed before being sent to Auschwitz.

The printing shop was situated in a basement. Ferenc recognized me when I entered, and said in a loud voice, "Hello, Micky [my Hungarian name], what are you doing here?" His words sounded to me more like an accusation than a welcome. "Aren't you supposed to be in some camp or other?" he asked in the same unfriendly tone. I was glad he was alone so that I could come to the point very quickly and explain the reason for my visit. He suddenly became restless and abrupt. Saying he was very busy, he asked what name and age I wanted on the identification papers. Unwise as it sounds, I felt I had no choice but to trust him despite his hostile reception. He told me to come back the following morning, but I left feeling pretty doubtful about whether he would indeed have the documents for me.

It was almost noon when I came out of the printing shop. I started walking very quickly, looking back several times to see if I was being followed. I went to a nearby park, consumed my last bit of salami and bread, and washed it down with fresh water from a fountain. Not knowing what else to do, I walked aimlessly through the streets of Budapest until an impulse propelled me in the direction of the shop where I had worked in what now seemed another lifetime. It was as though I wanted to believe that everything was all right, that I was still a working mechanic rather than a fugitive in grave danger. Across the street from the shop, I found a spot from which I could see one of my former colleagues working with a welding torch, my favorite job. At the large office window, I saw Mr. Szécsényi sitting in the chair where the Jewish owner, Mr. Feifer, used to sit. The store had apparently been confiscated, and Mr. Feifer was now most likely waiting in the ghetto or already at Auschwitz.

After spending an hour watching the activities of the shop in which I would have loved to be working, I left and continued wandering the streets. Exhausted and hungry, I began to think of where I could safely spend the night. All sorts of possibilities ran through my mind, most of them impractical or dangerous. I thought of hiding in the sewers, something I had seen in a movie about Paris, but then I thought of the rats that would be there and immediately abandoned that idea. I also thought of locking myself in one of the underground toilets, but that didn't appear safe enough. I decided my best bet was to try the place where I had been living at the time of my departure for labor camp. My landlady who had appeared sympathetic and even seemed upset when I was summoned to Jolsva would perhaps allow me to stay over for one night. It was already dusk when I got there. I had to be sure that neither Szécsényi nor his wife, the concierge, would see me, for that would definitely spell trouble.

I succeeded in getting to the third floor, where my former landlady occupied a three-bedroom apartment, without being noticed by any of the neighbors who might have recognized me. At the sight of me, the landlady exclaimed, "Jesus Maria, you are alive?" I could tell from her face that she was quite taken aback by my appearance—it hadn't occurred to me that my recent experiences had wrought such great changes. As I had with Ferenc, I gave her a brief account of my situation, but unlike his unresponsive reaction, hers was compassionate; she even wept as I spoke. She offered me food, which I gobbled up gratefully and in great haste, as had become my habit, as if it might be taken from me before I finished it all.

As to whether I could stay overnight with her, she was very reluctant and even afraid to give me an answer; she said she would let me if Mr. Szécsényi agreed to it. As far as I could see, this reduced my chances to zero. I could only pray that this hateful man had mellowed in the five months since he had last seen me. It didn't take long, though, to find out I was mistaken. As soon as he saw me, he flew into a rage, screaming anti-Semitic insults. The dumbfounded landlady never had a chance to finish her plea on my behalf. Mr. Szécsényi obviously understood right away what it was all about and made it quite plain that if I didn't clear out immediately he would denounce me to the authorities.

It was already around ten o'clock, a dangerous time for a luckless Jewish escapee to be in the city without identification. As I was leaving the building, I noticed an open window that led to the basement. Whoever had left it that way would never know what a blessed favor he had done me. I climbed through and found myself in a dark boiler room that was not only pleasantly warm but even had a spot where I could sleep fairly comfortably. It was certainly an improvement on the damp crawl space in Imre's building and preferable to sleeping in the sewers with the rats. Fortunately, though the basement also served as an air raid shelter, no one had reason to come down there that night. Even if they had, my refuge was so well-concealed that only a bloodhound would have found me. Considering Mr. Szécsényi's outbursts and threats to report me, the boiler room might not have seemed the safest place to spend the night, but my choice turned out to be a good one after all. Having found some torn blankets, I was able to fix up a cozy sleeping place—better than the wooden cot in the tool shed at Bukavinka and the pile of straw at Jolsva.

Since I was physically exhausted and emotionally drained, sleep came easily that night. As if to reassure me, Providence sent my mother in a dream. I had not dreamed of her in a long time. She was covering me with the little patched blanket that she had made for me when I went away to cheder, and she whispered softly her oft-repeated words of comfort, *"Zorg zich nisht, Gott it unz helfen* [Don't worry, the Almighty will help us]." When I awoke in the morning, I heard myself repeating Mother's soothing words.

The tolling of the church bells across the street informed me that it was eight o'clock. I was sure that Mr. Szécsényi had left the house by now. Since climbing out of the window might arouse suspicion, I waited for the right moment to leave through the gates. As I made my way to the printing shop, I passed several sidewalk cafes. It was painful to see people eating huge breakfasts while I was terribly hungry. But without a penny to my name, all I could do was pray that I would get my new identity document and find a job quickly. Despite my empty stomach I walked briskly, again looking constantly over my shoulder in fear that someone might be following me. At the printer's, I was careful not to go right down to the basement, but passed it a few times to make sure Ferenc was alone. Just when I thought it was safe, and was about to go in, I took one more look and was horrified to see two German soldiers with rifles on their shoulders speaking to my supposed benefactor. I did what any frightened fugitive would do— turned around and ran for dear life as far as my breath and my legs would permit. When I no longer had the strength to run, I sat down on a bench in a small park a good distance away. Feeling safe for the moment, I was able to recover my equilibrium. I have no way of knowing for sure that Ferenc had betrayed me, but I strongly suspect that the Germans were waiting for me and that this had been a close call.

My next thought was to go to the outskirts of Budapest. I sometimes used to take a trolley on Sundays to a rural, agricultural area where farmers cultivated a variety of produce and raised horses. If I got there safely, I might find someone who would believe my story and give me a job without asking for identification papers. With no money even for trolley fare, I had no choice but to walk for some two hours to my destination.

The long walk further aggravated my hunger; I was starved. Stopping to rest, I saw across the road a herd of horses grazing in a large field that surrounded several castle-like buildings. Nearby was a fire station, in front of which a fireman was polishing his truck. Since he looked friendly, I gathered up my courage and asked about the imposing structures. He told me they belonged to an agricultural school which had closed because of the war.

I thanked him, and was about to leave, when my pathetic appearance perhaps made him stop me and ask me a lot of questions about where I was going and what I was looking for. This gave me my first chance to practice using my new identity and to advertise my availability as a farm hand. I was very pleased with the poise and ease with which I narrated my story, and felt comfortable with my new persona. "So you can do farm work," said the affable fireman. "As a matter of fact, László, I believe the agricultural school is in need of some one like you who can take care of animals. Let me call the foreman and tell him about you." In a moment he was repeating my tale almost verbatim, but even more dramatically than I had. The foreman, Mr. Kovács, seemed eager to see me, and I was told to go to his office in an hour.

My amiable fireman introduced himself and the rest of the four-man crew. Várady Gyula was about fifty years old and bore a resemblance to the image of Jesus Christ one usually sees on the cross or in paintings. His face was pale and long, with sunken blue eyes that looked at me with sympathy. Apparently guessing that I was hungry, Mr. Várady offered me a sandwich, probably part of his lunch, and I ate it with gusto and gratitude. When the time came for my interview with my new employer, I thanked Mr. Várady for his kindness, and agreed to visit him as soon as I had some free time.

On the way to the foreman's house I reviewed my story a few times and even prepared answers to questions he might ask. The interview with Mr. Kovács went well, but unlike Mr. Várady he appeared cold and very businesslike—he showed little personal interest in me and stuck strictly to the subject of the job. I was to help an old man who had been in his employ for many years. The work entailed grooming eighteen horses, feeding six pigs, bringing in the hay from the fields, and transporting manure to our fields from a nearby funeral home that had about thirty horses. In return I was to receive food and lodging and occasional pocket money. But before I could start, I would have to get identification documents. Since his son was a police officer, he offered to take me to the precinct, where he thought they would provide me with papers on the basis of my story. My heart stood still. This seemingly routine procedure conjured up all sorts of potential calamities. What if one of the officers decided to have me undress and discovered that I was circumcised? What if they interrogated me and found an inconsistency in my story? These and other thoughts flashed through my mind as the foreman made his proposal. Somehow, however, I kept my composure and convinced myself that my luck would continue to hold.

Béla, the man I was to work under, was summoned to the office and the foreman introduced us in his curt manner. Béla, probably in his late sixties, was a sinister-looking man, with a very wrinkled face. The boss told him what my responsibilities were going to be and dismissed us abruptly. On the way to his cottage, Béla asked me many questions about my family and my past, even testing my knowledge of the area around Mukachevo—all in a hostile, suspicious tone, accompanying every question with the raising of his protruding, bushy eyebrows. Once we were in the dingy cottage, he showed me to a tiny room adjacent to his.

The fact that I would have a separate place to sleep eliminated at least one of my many fears of being found out. During the Hitler era, circumcision was one of the principal ways by which Jews were most easily identified. Not to have to undress in front of Béla was a real boon. The room contained a small army cot and a beautifully carved wardrobe that looked like a valuable antique. I had little need for it as far as my clothing was concerned—the small bundle of belongings with which I had emerged from the crawl space could have been accommodated in a less sumptuous place. But I enjoyed the wardrobe for its aesthetic features, and it was a distraction in my lonely moments when, lying on my cot, I would examine its decorations, seeing in them exotic animals, bearded old men, gnarled trees, and other shapes from nature.

Béla took me to the stable to show me where I was to feed and groom the horses, milk the cows, and clean eighteen stalls every day. Then he led me to the pigpen, where I was introduced to the half-dozen charges I would be feeding three times a day. Finally we got to the equipment room. I was pretty nervous when Béla showed me a complex harness and asked me to prepare the two draft horses so we could ride over to the funeral home. I was relieved that, other than two leather straps for which I could find no attachments, I managed well enough. The hardest part came when those huge animals refused to bow their heads to my outstretched arms straining to put their headgear on. Not until Béla emitted a loud Hungarian curse, partly to reprimand me for my lack of command and partly to admonish the horses, did I succeed in accomplishing the task.

Béla's stern enumeration of my assignments made it clear that I was in for some tough work. But that wasn't my major worry at the moment. Rather, it was the foreman's emphatic demand that I obtain my identification papers. The idea of going to the police station struck terror in my heart. It seemed tantamount to setting and stepping into my own trap. I delayed going for as long as possible, convinced it would be my downfall.

Three agonizing days and nights had passed when the foreman's son, dressed in handsome police regalia, paid me a visit. Although his uniform inspired fear in me, as uniforms always did, his benign demeanor was reassuring. It was apparent from the start of our conversation that he had already heard part of my story from his father. He wanted an amplified version, but his questions did not have the investigative tone I would have expected of a policeman. His reactions to my replies were mild and sympathetic. It crossed my mind that he suspected I was Jewish, and I prayed that if this were indeed the case, he would not betray me.

Finally he said that he thought I wouldn't have too much trouble obtaining the document. In fact, he volunteered to bring me the registration form. All I would have to do was fill it out and bring it to the station to be stamped. He brought it the next day as promised but, as truly benevolent as this man seemed to be, I had learned not to be too trusting and was still filled with great trepidation when the time came to bring it to police headquarters. Just when I was about to leave, to my amazement, my benefactor appeared and said he would take care of getting the paper for me. And so he did, returning about an hour later. As he handed me the document he explained awkwardly that it wasn't necessary for me to tell anyone he had helped me. I understood what he was trying to say, and concluded that Providence or my mother in Heaven had once more interceded on my behalf by sending this good and decent man to extricate me from a desperate situation.

My speech and appearance in themselves were not likely to give me away, and now I could prove officially that I was Balog László, a seventeen year old Gentile boy from the town of Mukachevo running away from the oncoming Russian army. With this new identity, I had a reasonable chance of emerging from this horrendous situation alive, and seeing the downfall of Hitler.

The days at the agricultural school passed very slowly. Most of my work I did alone, without other people around; on the rare occasions that Béla accompanied me to the funeral home, he displayed dislike rather than friendship toward me. Except for occasional visits with Mr. Várady at the firehouse, I had no companionship. In my extreme loneliness, especially on those cold dreary winter evenings, I sometimes wished I was back in Csepel with my friends, my fellow Jews, even if my prospects for survival were far worse there. Having no one to talk to in my isolation, I would often unburden myself to the horses while I groomed and fed them in the warm stables. My favorite confidante was the draft mare I named Táltos, from a fairy tale my mother had told me about a very loyal horse. I had the distinct feeling that whenever I talked to Táltos, she actually listened and understood my plight. She seemed to me to possess more humanity than many of the humans with whom I had to deal.

Loneliness was only one of the trials I had to bear. It was rare to have a day of hard work only, one without encountering some sort of disaster or fearing an impending one. If it was not the incessant pounding of the Russian artillery that made me spend frightful sleepless nights, then it was the frequent visits by German and Hungarian officers who came to the farm to requisition horses and produce. One day a German lieutenant started a conversation with me and sternly "suggested" I join the army, assuring me that I would make a fine soldier. As he was leaving he promised to be back soon to see that I honored his suggestion. Fortunately, he never returned, but I remained in a constant state of anxiety about what would happen to me if he did.

There was an even more immediate physical threat that resulted from the double life I was leading. As though it weren't enough to live in perpetual fear of the Nazis, the British too made their contribution to my misery. Low-flying reconnaissance planes often showered the field with machine-gun bullets when I was bringing in the hay. One day, a plane flying practically over my head encircled the wagon with bullets, cutting a deep furrow around us and so maddening the horses that they ran over the fields totally out of control with me hanging on for dear life. Obviously, the pilot was just showing off his sharpshooting skills, and having fun at my expense because if he had meant to cut me down he could have done it very easily.

Another time, a single stray bomb hit not far from the cottage and covered me with a mound of debris, leaving me terrified, with many cuts and bruises. Fortunately, I didn't have to be taken to the hospital where I would have surely been undressed and my secret discovered.

Perhaps the most unexpected and dangerous incident took place about two months after I had started work. Béla and I were bringing hay to the funeral home from our fields. After I loaded the wagon, we sat near each other on top of the hay. Midway to the funeral home, I heard a thin voice desperately calling my real Hungarian name several times, "Micky, Micky." Forgetting my assumed identity for the moment, I turned around and saw a young man running after us. Béla noticed my instinctive reaction and looked at me with his suspicious, scornful eyes, raising his beetling eyebrows even higher than usual. I did all I could to act as though nothing had happened, urging the horses to go faster in order to leave our pursuer as far behind as possible. Of course, I had recognized the poor man; he was one of the inmates from Csepel, an escapee like me. I wished that I could have exchanged at least a few words with my fellow fugitive who was no doubt as lonely in his concealment as I was in mine. Had we met at a more opportune time, we could have had the great relief of being free and open with another human being.

This episode—which lasted just a few seconds—caused me great anguish for the rest of my stay on the farm. Despite my attempt to cover it up, my blunder must have aroused serious doubts in Béla about my identity. When we arrived home, his inquisition began: "Who was that young man calling your name?" "Why didn't you stop the horses?" "Are you sure you told the boss the truth?"—and many other such questions, always menacingly. I told him that Micky was the nickname I was occasionally called by, but that I had no idea who the young man was. Béla threatened that unless I took on a good deal more of the work he was responsible for, he would tell the foreman what had happened. He started to push me around, and sometimes deprived me of part of my meals, filling his plate with twice the amount that was due him. In short, I lived in constant fear, literally held hostage to this hateful man. Luck was with me in one respect; apparently, he never suspected I was Jewish. Had it even remotely occurred to him, I would have been in great trouble. But judging from the way he questioned me, he seemed to think I had committed some minor crime, or was trying to avoid volunteering for the German or the Hungarian army as patriotic men of my age were expected to do. In fact, when he was particularly angry with me, he would scream, "Why don't you join the army? You would probably be of greater use there than you are here!"

It was now the beginning of November. I had several ways of figuring out that the Allied Forces were doing well. For example, though the Hungarian newspapers were controlled by the fascists and gave distorted reports about German losses, it was clear to me that every time they referred to a "tactical retreat" it meant that the Russians had occupied more Hungarian and German territory. Furthermore, the workers at the funeral home spoke with great concern about the rapid advances the Russians were making daily. A final indication of the impending fascist defeat was the successful bombardment that had by now virtually paralyzed the Hungarian war industry. I heard at the funeral home that Csepel was leveled and almost inoperable.

One of the carriage drivers predicted that at the rate the Russians were advancing, Budapest would be taken by late December or mid-January. Although most of his colleagues scoffed at him, he was actually on target. Early in December, the Russians were close enough to Budapest for us to hear the artillery around the clock. The bombing on the outskirts was so intense that transportation was halted and the city was coming to a standstill. With the beginning of the new year, street-to-street and house-to-house combat was fierce all along the periphery of Budapest. Despite enormous resistance, by mid-January the Russians had occupied practically the whole city, and within a few weeks they subdued the few Germans who had barricaded themselves in the Royal Castle in Buda.

Chapter 7

Liberation

A few days after the Russians took Budapest, I was liberated. The fighting around the agricultural school was heavy, and several people on the farm lost their lives. I found myself stuck in the stable alone for over six hours—petrified not only by the combat but by the horses, who were going crazy from the deafening noises of the explosions all around us. The stable, in fact, took several direct hits and one of the projectiles landed just a few yards from me. Around noon, the shooting subsided into the distance and I heard screaming—in Russian.

When I emerged from the stable, two Asiatic-looking soldiers, who reeked of alcohol, kicked, punched, and hit me with their rifle butts as they pushed me to the courtyard, where the director of the school, the foreman, his son, and various men and women employees were already assembled. All were relieved of their watches, and several men were knocked to the ground while the soldiers shouted obscenities at them. My protestations in Russian didn't help me at all. I was still hesitant to reveal my true identity, lest the Germans recapture the place. However, when the two drunken Uzbek soldiers came at me with their bayonets, I became so frightened that I yelled out, "*Ya Yevrey! Ya Yevrey is lagera!* [I am a Jew, I am a Jew from camp!]," but it didn't deter the two savages. I really thought my end was near, that I was going to get a bullet in the head.

My salvation this time came from an officer who had overheard my exclamation, came over to us, and sharply reprimanded the Uzbeks. "Idiots," he shouted, "don't you know what a *Yevrey* is? I am a *Yevrey*! Let him be." Captain Gregory Yakovlevich Weinstein quietly asked me, "*Du bist take a yid?* [You are really a Jew?], and led me away from the others. Those friendly Yiddish words will be forever engraved in my memory.

As the captain and I were walking away from the courtyard, we passed my benefactor, the handsome police officer, who looked at me with a benevolent smile as if to say, "I knew all the time that you were a Jew."

I told Captain Weinstein, in Yiddish of course, of the young policeman's kindness, praying that it would not become necessary for me to intercede on his behalf. But everyone except the director of the school, who was allegedly involved in Nazi activities, was immediately released. It did occur to me that this would have been a good chance to scare the wits out of my archenemy, Béla, but I refrained— just happy to be alive and free.

Captain Weinstein spent about twenty minutes listening to part of my story, trying to comfort me by reminding me every now and then that I was lucky to have emerged alive from the German hell. He told me some of his own experiences with anti-Semitism and how difficult it had been for him, as a Jew, to earn his rank in the Russian army. He was, nevertheless, very proud to be a Russian soldier, particularly now when the battle was raging against the vilest of Jewish murderers. As we said good-bye, Captain Weinstein pulled out a little bundle of German and Hungarian paper currency and stuck it in my trousers pocket.

I went back to the cottage to fetch my few items of clothing. Despite the fact that it was still dangerous to be on the streets, I was eager to make my way to Budapest in the hope of learning something about my family and finding Imre. Before taking off, though, I stopped at the foreman's house to thank his son for his part in my survival. The young policeman seemed to take delight in the role he had played. Not so his father, who was still cold, and who apparently resented my deception. His wife, on the other hand, invited me to join the family in a bite to eat. When I told her that I was in a hurry to get to Budapest, she wrapped some food in a bag and insisted I take it.

Just as I was about to leave, we heard shooting right outside the building. It turned out that a half-dozen German soldiers had emerged from a hiding place and begun to shoot at the Russians. We all rushed to the basement where we crouched until they were subdued. During the half-hour skirmish, a young soldier kicked in the basement window, yelled in poor Russian, "*Yest rusky soldat?* [Are there Russian soldiers here?]," and fired a barrage of bullets that whistled by us. We remained silent. Thankfully he didn't come down to continue his search, or once again my life might, ironically, have ended on the day of my liberation.

When all seemed quiet, we came up from the basement. Near the window lay the dead body of a handsome blond German soldier, no more than seventeen years old, who, like many of his kind, had been persuaded to give his life to an infamous cause. The young policeman and his mother wished me well. I was finally on my way to Budapest, eager to leave behind me a place where for four months I had lived in constant fear.

It was an extremely cold, windy day, and the fields were covered with high drifts of snow. As a result of the heavy military traffic, however, the snow on the roads was well packed, making my ten-mile walk to the city a little easier. Other than the few civilians who were emerging from their refuges to return to their homes, the outskirts of Budapest were populated mainly by Russian soldiers and their German prisoners. The Germans looked bedraggled, pitiable, and forlorn. Gone was the image of the invincible soldier so handsomely portrayed on the placards hanging on kiosks. Defeat had given birth to a new look, one of weakness rather than bravery.

The ditches and the fields on the way to Budapest were strewn with the frozen remains of horses, and with the bodies of soldiers who appeared to have fallen just days ago. I was sickened and moved to tears by this macabre sight, unable, in my feelings of compassion, to distinguish between German and Russian. Somehow the deaths of all these men were equally lamentable to my eyes. I was so absorbed by the destruction surrounding me that I lost awareness of the passage of time, the fatigue of the two-hour walk, and the penetrating cold. Suddenly, I found myself at the gates of Budapest.

In spite of what I had seen on the way, I could not have imagined that Budapest, this once gay and bustling city, could turn into the desolation that unfolded before me. Here too, under the freshly fallen film of snow, lay dead German soldiers and a few civilians whose bodies had not been claimed by anyone. The parks that were once filled with the sound of children at play were now deserted and silent. Many of the imposing buildings and monuments were riddled by machine-gun bullets and a few were still smoldering. The five magnificent bridges connecting Buda with Pest had been blown up by the Germans as they retreated, just a few days before I got there.

The streets here, just as in the suburbs, were occupied mostly by the Russians. Since at this point they no longer had to fight, they busied themselves mainly with looting homes and accosting women. The most popular items the soldiers helped themselves to were watches, bicycles, and fur coats—their "*Davay chasy* [Give me your watch]!" must have been the first Russian words Hungarians learned.

On one of the main squares, called Oktogon, I witnessed the arrest of fascists and German collaborators who were hanged on the spot. More than likely, many among them deserved punishment, but probably not this way. It was especially horrifying to see that some of the spectators appeared to be entertained by the gruesome sight. As I looked on confusedly at these executions, I wondered at man's capacity for cruelty and seeming indifference to taking life.

It was getting dark, and I realized that I had no place to sleep that night. The streets, with the exception of a few Russian soldiers, were by now deserted. I thought of looking for Imre at the home of his rescuer, or finding my way into the Szacsanyi basement, but I was far from these neighborhoods, the streets were dangerous, and there was no transportation. My only chance seemed to be to throw myself on the mercy of strangers.

Freezing and exhausted, I went from gate to gate ringing bells and knocking on doors, but no one would respond. Evidently the beleaguered Hungarian families, particularly those with young women, were so scared of the Russians that they had barricaded themselves in their apartments.

Just when I was about to give up all hope, I heard a commotion and a woman's screams coming from an open courtyard. I ran in the direction of the voices. On the second floor, a drunken Russian soldier had grabbed a girl of about twenty while her parents and some of the neighbors were trying to fend him off. I don't know what possessed me, but I shouted at him in my loudest Russian, "*Astav yeyo* [Leave her alone]!" For a moment I was frightened by my own daring. As though by magic, the drunken brute, hearing his native tongue, gave up and staggered out of the building. The astounded bystanders surrounded me, showering me with thanks and friendly smiles, the kind I hadn't seen for a long time. I'm sure it wasn't my "*Astav yeyo!*" alone that had brought about the soldier's departure. The commotion and the screaming probably would have accomplished the same result, but my part in the rescue earned me a refuge for that night.

The father embraced me while his young daughter and his statuesque wife looked at me with gratitude. They led me into a spacious, elegantly-furnished apartment, obviously the home of middle-class people. The very first thing that struck me was the blessed heat coming from a stove kindled by pieces of broken furniture and fresh-ly-cut acacia branches. Here was the first opportunity I had had all day to warm my frozen limbs. In addition, I observed that the family had probably been at dinner when Sharika, the daughter, had been attack-ed. I fervently hoped they would ask me to join them.

Before the family resumed their meal, Mr. Hajdu, my corpulent host, wanted to know a few things about the unexpected guest who had suddenly appeared out of nowhere. His first question—How was it that I spoke Russian?—was obviously prompted by fear. I explained that I came from the Carpathian part of Czechoslovakia, where Uk-rainian—very similar to Russian—was spoken. My answer was suffi-ciently reassuring that what followed was no longer an interrogation, but a narration of my story to the sympathetic family and neighbors who surrounded the huge iron stove. I noticed that Sharika also ap-peared sad when I revealed my Jewish identity. Throughout this short getting-acquainted period, I was overwhelmed by feelings of relief and pleasure at being able to unburden myself to these willing listeners.

Mr. Hajdu did ask me to eat with the family. Politely, I refused; they insisted, and Sharika quickly put an extra setting on the table. The meal was meager; food was scarce in Budapest during this time. Other than the frozen flesh of the dead horses lying on the street, which some people would rather starve than touch, meat was virtually unob-tainable. Though I doubt that the evening's meal contained any horse-meat, I would, in any case, have observed the advice in the proverb, "Don't look a gift horse in the mouth," adding, "particularly if you've had very little to eat all day!"

From time to time as we ate, Mr. Hajdu referred to the atrocities that Nazis and Hungarians had committed against the Jews, apologizing with heartfelt sincerity for some of his nation's crimes and pointing out that there were decent Hungarians who had protected some Jews.

In the course of the conversation I made sure my hosts understood that this was my first day out of hiding, and stressed the fact that I hadn't been able to find a place to stay. To my delight, Mrs. Hajdu stated emphatically that I was to remain with the family overnight, and longer if I wished. My supposedly heroic defense of Sharika assured me a welcome in their home. In fact, the family apparently felt safer with me there. There was some light-hearted joking at the table about my bravery, and it was unanimously agreed that I should become the house guard and interpreter to protect the building from the Russian intruders.

Late in the evening, my hosts, realizing that I was exhausted, asked whether I wanted to retire—a suggestion for which I had been devoutly wishing. Mrs. Hajdu led me to a little room with separate toilet facilities and a very comfortable bed. Despite my fatigue, I found it difficult to fall asleep, as I reviewed the incredible events of that day. It was unbelievable to think that so much could happen to a person in such a short period of time. In that one day, I had been liberated, almost run through with a bayonet by my liberators, missed, by very little, being shot by a young storm trooper, seen brutal hangings on a Budapest square, learned about additional atrocities committed by the fascists against my people, helped save a pretty young woman from being raped by a drunken Russian soldier and, miraculously, found shelter from the harsh January cold.

Foremost on my mind was the tenuousness of my liberation. I was still tormented by many fears. The Germans were still putting up a fierce fight just across the Danube, and there remained the possibility of their return. With the Russians, who harbored a long-standing hatred for Jews, my prospects did not look good either. I knew how vulnerable Jews could be under Soviet rule. The long history of pogroms dating back to the seventeenth century and the anti-Semitism known to be prevalent during the Soviet regime did not bode well for those few who might survive Hitler's scourge. The more I thought about my fellow Jews in their captivity, the less meaning did my supposed freedom have. My thoughts turned to Harry and Samuel, to my many relatives, to the men in Csepel, and to Jewish boys and girls I knew. Was it possible that they would not be delivered from Hitler's hands? All this turned over and over in my mind before I finally fell asleep.

At three o'clock in the morning, two Russian soldiers furiously banging on the door woke the household. Mr. Hajdu hurriedly asked me to pose as Sharika's husband if they came into the apartment to discourage them from making advances to her. We were all scared out of our wits. The Russians persisted with their pounding. Fearing that they would break the door down, Mr. Hajdu opened it. Following his instructions, I held Sharika's trembling hand, looking at her as a devoted husband might. It worked. The combination of Mr. Hajdu's offer of a bribe, Mrs. Hajdu's crying, and my protectiveness toward Sharika must have persuaded the Russians to leave us without doing any more harm than helping themselves to my host's fine Doxa watch.

I reluctantly let go of Sharika's hand and returned to my room. Before I fell asleep, I thought for a while about her loveliness and her gentle ivory hands. I even fantasized about the possibility that, since Sharika and I were about the same age, she well might some day become my real wife. It was with this pleasant thought that I drifted off to sleep once more. When I awoke in the morning, it took a while for me to realize that I was no longer in hiding, a virtual prisoner of the agricultural school. Although the bed felt soft and the room safe and warm, my first thought was that I was still running from the Nazis.

After our scanty breakfast, I spent a very pleasant morning with the family. When the conversation touched on the visit of the Russians, Sharika joked affectionately about my acting ability, and congratulated me on how well I played the part of a loving husband. After lunch I told my hosts that I was very anxious to see what was happening outside, particularly in the center of town. Having heard some shooting throughout the morning, I was afraid that the Germans might have retaken some parts of the city. Mr. and Mrs. Hajdu were concerned about my safety and tried to persuade me not to go, assuring me that a German return was out of the question. Once they realized how determined I was, they made me promise to come back, repeating that I was welcome to stay with them as long as I wished. Given my circumstances and the family's kindness, I was happy to accept their invitation.

Before I started out, Mr. Hajdu tactfully persuaded me to throw away some of my tattered attire and accept a pair of shoes and other clothing more appropriate for that penetratingly cold winter day. It was the coldest Budapest winter on record—the Danube had completely frozen for the first time since the days of King Matthias Corvinus, in the fifteenth century. As I was changing into a warm pair of trousers, I reached into the pocket of my own badly worn pants and discovered the bundle of money that Captain Weinstein had given me the day before. Mr. Hajdu helped me count the Hungarian pengos and German marks. The sum was impressive for someone who didn't own a pair of decent shoes. Mr. Hajdu calculated that once life became normal in Budapest I would be able to buy presentable clothing and have enough left to live on for at least a month.

I got to the center of town about one o'clock. It was remarkable to see the changes that had taken place practically overnight. The streets were populated now with civilians as well as Russian soldiers. Men with hand saws were cutting up branches broken by the heavy ice and loading them into old baby carriages. Many more daring souls than the day before were cutting strips of meat from the frozen horses on the streets, chasing the equally hungry birds who tried to claim their share. Some families were pulling carts laden with furniture and other belongings, probably returning home from the shelters where they had hidden during the fighting. On several corners, I saw Russian soldiers exchanging food for watches and other jewelry. The looting had apparently stopped, and so had the executions. The bodies which had been hanging in the square when I arrived in Budapest were no longer there, and the corpses of the German soldiers were gone as well. A fresh, thin layer of snow that had fallen overnight concealed the blood of the day before. It was as though nature was ashamed of what man had done, and had covered up the evidence of his hideous deeds. With all the new life that appeared on the street, the sad faces of the passersby still reflected the tragedy of war rather than jubilation at having been liberated. The city still smelled of death and destruction. It was clear that it would be a long time before Budapest would again see its boulevards teeming with happy people.

In Buda, across the Danube river, the fighting was still going on. A band of German soldiers had dug in at the King's Castle from which they wouldn't budge. Russian artillery and bombers were pounding the area. From this area, only three miles from Buda, I could actually see the bombs dropping from the airplanes. There was intermittent return of artillery fire by the Germans though the Nazis must have known that the end was near. It took a few more weeks after the liberation of Pest before Buda too was finally free.

I stayed on with the Hajdu family while I made several more visits to the center of town. In the course of my wanderings, I went to Imre's apartment, hoping that by now the family might have returned from the professor's house. The Neimanns were not there. Living in the apartment, instead, was a Gentile family who clearly resented my visit. They claimed that they had no idea who the Neimanns were nor what had happened to them, that this was their own apartment, and that the furniture I recognized as the Neimanns' belonged to them as well. This assertion didn't surprise me. During the Hitler regime, giving Jewish-owned property to Nazi faithfuls was common practice.

With the city and its environs still in a state of chaos, there seemed no possibility yet of my traveling to Mukachevo to find out about the fate of my family. In the meantime, my life was to take an unexpected turn.

Chapter 8

Call Me Nikolay

On another trip to the center of town, a Russian officer stopped me to ask for directions. As he struggled with the Hungarian words on a piece of paper, he punctuated each one with a Russian curse. I interrupted to tell him that I could understand and even speak some Russian. I took the opportunity to reveal my Jewish identity and tell him about some of my experiences with the Nazis. This was followed by an official introduction, and a very strong, almost painful Russian handshake.

Thus I made the acquaintance of Lieutenant Victor Ivanovich Smirnov, a handsome man in his early forties, who had innumerable decorations. His orderly was introduced simply as "Soldier Vanya." When I told Lieutenant Smirnov my name, he made a face. "Micky!" he said, almost with disgust. "What kind of a name is Micky? You should have a decent Russian name." Whereupon I was immediately dubbed "Nikolay Moyseyevich," possessing not only a new name but a patronymic as well.

The lieutenant asked many more questions, and I was pleasantly surprised by how well I was able to understand him and express my thoughts in Russian. As I responded to his queries, I sensed that Lieutenant Smirnov had a particular interest in me beyond asking for directions.

"So you suffered at the hands of the fascists," said Lieutenant Smirnov. "Would you like to know what I do? I belong to the Special Services, a division of the army that arrests Nazis and their collaborators. Have you ever heard of the NKVD? Anyhow, I am in charge of an investigative sub-unit that helps bring to justice those sons of bitches who wrought so much tragedy on the Russian people and on you Jews. Vanya and I are on our way to get some information about these fascists. Since we don't speak Hungarian, you could be of great help to us. Why don't you accompany me? When we return to our headquarters, I'll take you to the officers' dining room and you will have the best meal of your life. Besides, what else can you do in this dead Budapest?"

I decided to join the lieutenant on his mission, principally because I was afraid to refuse him. From the moment I met Smirnov, I had the impression that he was a moody person; in the first five minutes of our conversation I observed that his facial expression fluctuated between anger and forced pleasantness. As though possessed by a dual personality, he seemed capable of being kind one moment and severe the next. This was particularly evident when I appeared reluctant to accept his offer. His volatile nature also showed itself in his treatment of Vanya. At Smirnov's slightest dissatisfaction, the orderly was severely rebuked, but moments later Smirnov behaved as though his cruel words had never been uttered.

Smirnov pulled a German Browning out of his pocket and asked me jokingly, "Can you handle one of these? Where we are going, we never know when we will have to use a weapon." My hesitant "*Nyet*" surprised Smirnov and made me feel inadequate. I wished that I could have given him an unqualified "*Da*." Though I had had pistols and other guns pointed at me and my life threatened by them several times, I had never held one in my hands. Smirnov put the pistol back in his pocket. "Vanya," he said forcefully to his orderly, "you must teach Nikolay how to handle the Browning as well as the automatic rifle, provided of course he becomes our permanent comrade."

The lieutenant showed me the paper on which our destination was written. Since I knew Budapest well, I had no difficulty finding the place. The person the lieutenant was tracking down lived not far from the center in a modest apartment house. Apparently, our visit was a friendly one; we had come to see a Russian shoemaker who had gone to Hungary just before the 1917 Revolution and who was sympathetic to the Communist cause. He was probably involved in lower-level spying activity on behalf of the Soviets. From what Vanya told me, he was one of the sources used by the NKVD to identify military personnel and other Hungarian fascists who were involved in atrocities against Russian civilians.

Neither Vanya nor I was permitted to be present at the conversation between the shoemaker and the lieutenant, but once the official business was concluded, we were asked to join them for a bite. When we left the house, Smirnov warned me sternly not to tell anyone about our visit nor even to say anything about him and Vanya.

Around six o'clock in the evening, Lieutenant Smirnov took me to the palatial Hungarian government building where the Russian command office was located. The entrance was guarded by three armed soldiers to whom Smirnov spoke before I was allowed in. The place was teeming with officers and soldiers running from office to office. I was left in the care of Vanya, feeling rather ill-at-ease in the midst of uniformed men. I waited for the lieutenant for over an hour, worrying about the outcome of my invitation. Was it really going to be dinner? Or would it be an unexpected new calamity?

Lieutenant Smirnov arrived at last, apologizing for having kept me waiting so long. He escorted me to an elegant dining room filled with officers who were being served by chubby red-cheeked women dressed in army uniforms covered by white aprons. I was introduced to several of Smirnov's fellow officers as a probable *dobrovolyets* (volunteer) who would work with the investigative unit. The tables were loaded with deliciously prepared fowl and pork. To wash down all those culinary delights, Hungarian Tokay was served, thanks no doubt to the most recent looting of the best wine cellars of Budapest.

When the meal was over, Smirnov took me to his office, where he advised me, mildly at first, then forcefully, to become a *dobrovolyets* in the Russian army. He pointed out that the war was far from over, and that I could help to defeat, as he put it, the German *sukin sins* (sons of bitches), by working with him and other personnel as an interpreter. My knowledge of Hungarian, and even my limited knowledge of German, would be of great help to the Russian army and to him, for there was an acute shortage of interpreters. Smirnov made sure to enumerate in a very compelling manner the personal rewards that would result from my services. "Nikolay," he said, "when the war is over we will take you to Moscow, where you will be able to attend the Institute of Foreign Languages and become a linguist. And who knows, it is quite possible that for your good services you may even receive the Order of Lenin." This last incentive didn't impress me as being likely, and even Smirnov laughed at his absurd suggestion. As one might expect, I was most influenced by his reference to helping the Russians defeat the German *sukin sins.*

The evening came to an end with Lieutenant Smirnov exacting from me a solemn promise that I would return the following day. He wanted to treat me to lunch and talk to me further about becoming a *dobrovolyets.* Also, I would meet Zweiker, the Jewish volunteer who had joined the Russian army in Romania, and his staff sergeant Dinsky, a native Russian Jew. As we were saying good-bye, Smirnov repeated his proposition. "Nikolay, I want to assure you that if you do join us, you won't regret it. If you don't, you might."

On the way to the Hajdu apartment I agonized over this unexpected development. Eager as I was to stand up against the German murderers, there were several concerns pressing on my mind. Would I in my capacity as an interpreter have to be involved in actual battles and in killing? If so, would I be capable of doing it? And then, of course, the possibility that I myself might be killed made Smirnov's proposal even less attractive.

I told the Hajdus about my adventures of the day and about Smirnov's offer. Sharika appeared upset and Mrs. Hajdu reacted with great alarm. It was as though her own son were being drafted into the army. Mr. Hajdu, on the other hand, was less disturbed. After listening to the entire story, he assured me that as an interpreter I was not likely to see combat, for which I obviously had no training. As to whether I wished to join the Russians, that decision could be made only by me. He did suggest, however, that if I decided not to see Smirnov again, I would have to hide out. He suspected that the lieutenant would probably try to find me, and that Smirnov's so-called volunteer system was closer to a draft, which was a prerogative the Russians didn't legally possess. Mr. Hajdu generously promised to find a hiding place for me. The fact that the lieutenant didn't know my address was very much to my advantage if I were to follow his plan.

Again I spent a sleepless night, during which decisions were made and reversed innumerable times. The idea of becoming a fighting soldier was still distressing to me. On the other hand, it was the Russians who had in fact liberated me, and I couldn't ignore what Smirnov had said about helping them defeat the Nazis and saving the few remaining Jewish survivors, even if he greatly exaggerated my possible contribution.

My inclination to join the Russian army was based on several other reasons as well. Although Smirnov's attitude toward me up to that point had been affable, I was apprehensive and never sure about his possible actions. I was afraid that if I refused to accept his offer, he would track me down and force me to serve, this time with no pretense of friendliness to me, and God knows what else—a trip to Siberia, perhaps. The thought of having to go into hiding again, this time from the Russians, was repugnant and nerve-wracking. Then there was the matter of food and lodging that served as an incentive to consider Smirnov's offer seriously. Though I suspected that meals like the one at headquarters were not going to be my steady diet, I would still prefer eating army food to living off the Hajdus. As generous as this family was, I didn't want to continue accepting free meals from them, particularly in light of the food shortage in Budapest. And so, swayed and constrained by all these factors, I decided to keep my appointment with Smirnov.

Apparently sure I was going to return, Smirnov had prepared well for the finishing touches in his recruitment campaign. Waiting for me on my arrival were Zweiker, his Romanian Jewish volunteer, and Dinsky, his staff sergeant. Both men greeted me warmly and led me to the officers' dining room, where we were seated at our own table. When they learned I spoke Yiddish, their faces lit up. Obviously, this was a pleasurable outlet they sorely missed when they were in Russian company. Throughout the meal not a word was uttered in Russian, other than *chorosho* (O.K.), which Dinsky incorporated into Yiddish as he spoke. I was, naturally, moved and comforted at hearing my mother tongue again after so many months of living in isolation from it. Other than in the stable at the agricultural farm where I spoke Yiddish to my horse Taltosh, I hadn't used the language since my escape from Csepel.

Zweiker was a small, gaunt man with little eyes that squinted as though he didn't want to have a full view of the world around him. He was about thirty years old, came from a very religious Jewish background, and had attended a yeshiva for many years before entering a Romanian university. Notwithstanding the secular influence of the university, he was at once a religious Jew and a cultivated, worldly man. In addition to Yiddish, his mother tongue, and his native

Romanian, he was fluent in German, Hungarian, and Russian, which made him valuable to the Russians. Like me, he had escaped from a labor camp. When he was liberated by the Russian army, he had joined it under circumstances similar to mine.

Dinsky, in sharp contrast to Zweiker, was a huge, formidable-looking man with a resonating basso voice. He resembled Peter the Great, not only in stature but in his facial features, down to the mustache of the powerful tsar. His erect carriage and long stride were well suited to his gruff personality. The epitome of a staff sergeant, he took his job seriously, rarely stepping out of character. He seldom spoke quietly,— almost everything he said sounded like a command. He was a soldier in every sense of the word, extremely proud of the display of decorations on his uniform that jingled with every step he took. There was nothing meek about this fifty-year-old Russian Jew from Odessa, nor did it seem that with his personality he would allow the anti-Semites in the army to intimidate him. On the contrary, as I later observed, the soldiers were scared stiff in his presence, and most of the officers treated him with deference.

During lunch, Zweiker and Dinsky spoke about matters of particular interest to us Jews: the ongoing war against the Jewish people, the courage of the men and women in the Warsaw Ghetto uprising who died fighting the Nazis, the Jewish partisans who from their hiding places in the forests of Poland and Russia helped the Russian army by destroying German military supplies. I did not know about most of these events, nor about the enormity of the Holocaust tragedy that was unfolding.

When the conversation turned to my personal predicament, I was eager to learn Dinsky and Zweiker's opinions. Zweiker felt that despite all the hardships of being a soldier, and the anti-Semitism in the Russian army, for the time being a Jew had no choice but to become part of this force fighting against the Germans. He felt it was an obligation I couldn't ignore. All this from a pious, unsoldierlike, fragile Jew who put on phylacteries every morning in the face of derision from ignorant Russian soldiers.

Dinsky, too, limited himself to a few brief sentences. "Listen, Nikolay. If you have the courage to fight the fascists, join us. By now you must realize how vital it is that we defeat the maniac Hitler. Besides, you really don't have too much choice." He then added in an uncharacteristic whisper, "You probably don't understand what I'm trying to say, but I'll explain it to you later when we're really alone. As for your concern that some of our *mamzerem* [bastards] will give you a hard time or that you will go hungry, let me assure you that while I am here everything will be *chorosho*." Dinsky's forceful words, and the demonstration of immediate friendship from both men, persuaded me to follow their advice and make a final affirmative decision despite my misgivings.

When we finished our meal Zweiker, Dinsky, and I were invited to join Smirnov. "Well, Nikolay Moyseyevitch, how did you like those fellows? Aren't they fine soldiers? Have you decided to become a soldier or do you need some more prodding?" Not knowing what Smirnov meant by "prodding," I told him falteringly that I would most probably become his interpreter but. . . Smirnov interrupted by extending his huge hand to congratulate me on my wise decision. In my unfinished sentence I had meant to tell the lieutenant that I wanted one more evening to think it over and discuss it with the Hajdu family.

Smirnov must have sensed my inner disquiet and decided that some sort of distraction would be in order. Since, for most Russians and for Smirnov in particular, drinking was a good way to celebrate anything, he decided that the occasion of my joining the Russian army merited a toast, a real Russian toast. That meant finishing a glass of vodka to the last drop. Several of Smirnov's fellow officers were invited to our table, and their glasses were filled. Smirnov lifted his and yelled out, "*K dobrovolytzoo* [To the volunteer]!" The vodka was sent down each throat in one gulp. I made a valiant attempt to imitate them but with embarrassing results. The taste of the vodka was so revolting to me that it brought on a violent cough and filled my eyes with tears. "*Nitchevo, nitchevo* [It's O.K., it's O.K.], Nikolay," cried Smirnov with a burst of laughter. "We will soon teach you how to drink vodka, Russian style!"

Once the amusement died down, Smirnov led me to his office, where he explained the procedure for my becoming an official member of the army and of this particular division. Since the papers had to be sent to a special headquarters elsewhere, it was going to take about two weeks for the approval to come. I was delighted to learn that we would remain in Budapest during that period, making it possible for me to maintain my contact with the Hajdus.

It was during this conversation that I was given a clearer picture of how the investigative unit actually functioned. Smirnov's group was part of the second Ukrainian Front headed by Marshal Malinovsky, who was part of the team that had liberated Budapest. As the Front conquered new territory, the special investigative forces moved in and arrested people who had collaborated with the Nazis. They might be city functionaries, former military men, prisoners of war, or civilian German sympathizers. In order to go after these culprits, it was necessary to stay close to the fighting forces. Smirnov explained that we might sometimes find ourselves in the thick of the action. We had to be prepared to do battle with the Germans or the Hungarians should the occasion arise. Smirnov made no secret of the fact that just a few months earlier several of his people were killed by the Germans.

This little briefing ended with the assurance that death for our unit's soldiers, although possible, was very rare. "Don't worry, Nikolay, it won't happen to us. In the meantime, Nikolay, let's have some fun while we live. Tomorrow, I want you to come back and visit a few places with me. I would also like to introduce you to my Hungarian beauty, whom I met just a few days ago. It's a shame that she doesn't speak Russian, but I know you will help us understand each other. I think she really likes me. This, you realize, is a private matter between you and me. Should you tell anyone a word about her, I will kill you like a dog." Smirnov's last words were accompanied by loud, sinister laughter which left me with the suspicion that this was more than a friendly warning.

Until my orders came through, I could continue to live with the Hajdus if I wished, but would have eating privileges at the post, albeit rarely in the officers' dining room which would be open to me only on special occasions. Smirnov handed me a typewritten paper with several official red stamps imprinted on it that were covered with illegible signatures. "Guard this with your life, Nikolay," he said solemnly. "With this document you can walk freely without being bothered by anyone."

Smirnov took me to Dinsky's supply room. "Sasha," he ordered, "show Nikolay his handsome uniform and the boots he will wear once he officially becomes a volunteer." Dinsky lazily obeyed his command, giving Smirnov an inquiring look, as if to say, "Aren't you overdoing this a bit?" Dinsky picked a uniform that he estimated would be my size. The jacket fit as though it were made especially for me. Dinsky looked at me with solicitude, as though trying to read my destiny and wish me good fortune. Before I left, he handed me a sizable paper bag of canned foods on top of which I could see two tins of red caviar and four loaves of black Russian army bread. "Here," he said, "share this with your Hungarian family."

It was already nine o'clock, long past the hour when civilians were to be found on the streets of Budapest. Dinsky informed Smirnov that he was going to accompany me home for protection. Smirnov presumably never suspected that Dinsky had an ulterior motive for doing so. During this forty-five minute walk to the Hajdus' apartment, Dinsky gave me the kind of information and advice that would help me survive in an environment about which I knew nothing. As soon as we stepped out on the street, the lesson began—in Yiddish, naturally, for even on a deserted street Dinsky wouldn't risk speaking in Russian of the matters he was about to convey. Being careful was by now a natural reflex, a way of life that he must have learned the hard way.

"First let me tell you, Nikolay, that you almost made a fatal mistake with Smirnov by vacillating when he asked you whether you had made up your mind. You must understand that when I told you that you had no choice, I meant just that. Once the Russian army decides it wants your services, or even your life, it can get both. Just in case you didn't suspect it, I'm sure that from the time you accompanied Smirnov to the Russian shoemaker you were probably under surveillance. I bet Smirnov knows your address and the name of the people you live with. Speaking of Smirnov," he went on, "be very careful what you say to him and how you say it. He can be very charming, but he is basically indifferent to people's feelings and can be vindictive." Dinsky warned me not to complain about any hardships I might experience. "The best thing you can do, Nikolay, is hold your tongue behind your teeth as much as possible and you will be all right."

In addition, Dinsky was eager to convey to me his feelings toward his country and his loyalty to the Russian army. He did this with great solemnity, in a declamatory fashion, as though addressing a large audience. He stopped periodically to emphasize his thoughts with gestures or in a stronger tone of voice. "Right now, Nikolay, the Soviet Union is a dark place, not only because of the war but because of Stalin's atrocities. I will tell you more about that some other time. I hate this Communist regime, but I still think that socialism is the best way of life. I believe that soon our country will rid itself of its oppressors as well as of anti-Semitism. As for my allegiance to the army, I am a proud Jew and cherish my tradition, but I am also a Russian. I love my country and am willing to fight for it, particularly since we are dealing with Nazis who are out to destroy us all. Don't forget, Nikolay, that those Jewish partisans who were fighting from the forests on the side of the Russians didn't do it because they liked war. I want you to be a good soldier and help us in every way you can." With this, he ended his Yiddish speech and added in Russian, in a tone of sergeant-like command, *"Pomny, moy molodoy tovarich, yazik za zubamy* [Remember, my young comrade, to keep your tongue behind your teeth]." He shook my hand affectionately and uttered a loud *"Do svidanya."*

Dinsky made a profound impression on me. I was moved by his immediate friendship toward me, by his trust, and by his concern for my safety. I was overjoyed to have as my friend a big, brave Russian Jew, who was proud of his heritage. Having recently emerged from concealing my Jewish identity, meeting Dinsky restored in me the self-esteem that had been so harshly trampled on.

When I knocked on the Hajdus' door, it was opened immediately. Mrs. Hajdu, very agitated about my late return, must have been waiting there. She embraced me before I could even cross the threshold and told me how worried she was that the Russkies wouldn't let me go once they laid their hands on me. Mr. Hajdu more calmly than his disturbed wife also expressed his anxiety. I assured them that I was all right, and told them I had decided to join the Russians because I really had no alternative. The looks they exchanged were pretty gloomy. But when I told them I would be around for at least ten days and could stay with them if they wanted me to, their faces brightened. Mr. Hajdu inquired in great detail about what had actually made me decide to join the Russians and he concluded in the end that I was probably right.

Despite the excitement and concern over my becoming a soldier, Dinsky's package did not go unnoticed. We were all curious to see what was hidden under the caviar and the bread in that heavy bundle. As we pulled out cans of sardines and a variety of soups, cheers went up with every find. With my assurance that Dinsky had given me the package for all of us, Mrs. Hajdu, whose own supply of food was meager, started preparing dinner. With her culinary dexterity, it turned out to be one of the best meals I had eaten in a long time.

Just before going to bed, I suddenly remembered the document that was supposed to ensure my safety in Budapest. I was curious to find out what it said. With some difficulty, I was able to decipher the few bureaucratically-phrased paragraphs. It read in essence: "The Russian Armed Forces are pleased to announce that the bearer of this document, Nikolay Moyseyevich Sommer, has of his own free will decided to join the Red army as a volunteer. His papers will soon be processed. In the meantime his freedom of movement should not be impeded in any way." It was signed by Major Vladimir Zhdanov, Commander of Special Units.

This piece of paper, with its one gross lie about my voluntarily having joined the Russian army was invaluable to me. It gave me, at least for the time being, a place where I belonged and an identity. I no longer had to hide from anyone. I felt a sense of relief that for the moment there were no major decisions I had to make. They had been made for me by destiny as reflected in that piece of paper. I tried to disregard thoughts of the danger that I faced as a soldier in time of war.

Smirnov's prediction about my remaining in Budapest for about two weeks proved to be accurate. Mrs. Hajdu insisted that I stay with the family, the most pleasant time I can remember having during the war years. Dinsky's largesse continued too. Though the subsequent packages weren't as grand as the first one, I was regularly sent home with groceries that the Hajdus accepted, after some polite protestation, with gratitude.

The accidental encounter with the Hadjus turned out to be a blessing for me. These good people extended their affection and hospitality and gave me a sense of belonging. Sharika, too, was a warm friend. When, at her suggestion, we took walks on the Erzsébet Boulevard, she flirted with me, giving me the impression that she was attracted to me. For my part, once I learned to overcome my timidity in her presence, I was delighted with every moment we spent together. Indeed, I was convinced that I had actually fallen in love with her.

My work with Smirnov during our stay in Budapest wasn't at all taxing, physically at least. From time to time I would accompany him on official business, but he also took me to the house of his Hungarian girlfriend. Ilona was a very pretty actress who, because of the war, was unemployed and, consequently, broke. Smirnov must have been a real find, for he adored her and showered her with gifts that came, not from Russia, but from recent looting in the area. Although Ilona was pleasant to me, I hated my role as the lovers' interpreter. I found it difficult and embarrassing to translate the passionate declarations that floated between them. It was a great relief when they learned the necessary vocabulary in each other's language and no longer needed my services.

Two days before our departure from Budapest, Smirnov took me to the major's office to receive my army book. With great solemnity, Major Zhdanov told me how vital my joining the Russian army was. He, too, reminded me that the Germans had inflicted great suffering on both the Russian people and the Jews. "Nikolay Moyseyevich," he added, "we must make those sons of bitches pay for their crimes. You understand, don't you? Now God be with you and good luck." I was touched by the words of this kindly-looking old man who seemed more like a grandfather than a soldier. I was particularly surprised by his evocation of the Lord's name. This was the first time I heard a Russian soldier mention God in any context.

On the day I became officially a volunteer, I was given a Browning pistol that I was to wear on my person at all times, and a machine gun to be carried only when on official duty. I also received an hour of instruction from Vanya on how to use these weapons. I was repelled by handling them and by the thought that I might have to point them at a living human being. It struck me however, that if every Jew had a weapon perhaps more would have been able to save themselves.

My official inauguration culminated in my getting a new army outfit—a handsome pair of Russian boots, khaki riding trousers, and a jacket with a high mandarin collar and epaulets like those worn by officers. The insignia designated my status as someone doing specialized official work. Unlike my feeling about guns, wearing my new uniform evoked only pleasure. In fact, the very uniform that appeared menacing to me on someone else looked attractive once I had it on. I liked my appearance as a soldier; the uniform made me look taller. I postured before the mirror, admiring my looks and hoping that Sharika would be able to see me this way. When Vanya helped me into a well-lined army top coat, and I realized how warm this garment would keep me, my situation seemed even brighter.

The last evening of my stay with the Hajdus included a good supper for which Staff Sergeant Dinsky had, as usual, supplied most of the delectable ingredients. Despite the satisfaction derived from the meal, the mood became somber when the conversation turned to the subject of my departure. The sadness was particularly obvious in the face of Mrs. Hajdu, who often appeared on the verge of crying. Just as would be expected from my own mother, she served advice and warnings along with the food. Mr. Hajdu also showed his concern for my fate, but in a way that would befit a proud Hungarian man not prone to revealing his sensitivity. Sharika, on the other hand, had no doubt that everything would be all right, warning me, however, that if I didn't come back to visit the family after the war was over, she would be unhappy and very disappointed in me.

I left the Hajdu apartment in time to meet my ten o'clock curfew at Russian headquarters. Mrs. Hajdu was sobbing as she embraced me for the final "*Isten veled* [May the Lord be with you]" that moved me to tears as well. Sharika, too, wept as I prepared to leave. Mr. Hajdu, continuing to show a manly restraint, tried to comfort his wife, lovingly reprimanding her for her excessive fear on my account. "Don't you worry about this young man;" he said in a robust and reassuring voice, "he will be O.K."

As I walked the war-torn streets of Budapest, I recalled all the events that had taken place since fate brought me together with the Hajdus. Foremost on my mind was the unhappy thought that I was leaving behind a dear, noble family who had demonstrated that there were still Christians who were not bent on the destruction of Jews, and who were moreover shocked and grieved by what the fascists had wrought.

My stay with the Hajdus helped not only to heal some of the wounds inflicted on me by the Hitler insanity, but also to gain the strength I needed to confront hardships yet to come. That night, before going to bed, I said a prayer asking the Lord to protect the Hajdus who, like me, were faced with an uncertain future in a new world under Russian occupation. I also prayed for our reunion, for I was most unhappy to be torn from them.

Chapter 9

My Russian Liberators

I was now one of our unit's official interpreters. The following morning, we departed for the front line in a truck loaded with machine guns, cooking utensils, and some produce. In addition to our unit, there were a dozen soldiers and their sergeant, trepidation written all over their faces. Smirnov, who was visibly disgruntled, probably because he had to leave his mistress behind, sat in the warm front cab with Katya, a pretty soldier in her mid-thirties who served as our typist and secretary.

The rest of us bundled up inside the canvas-covered truck, trying to keep warm on what was an extraordinarily cold February day. Vodka, which Dinsky supplied in great abundance, was touted as the most efficient protection against the freezing weather. I never found out whether it helped to repel the cold, but by the time we arrived at our destination, there wasn't a sober person in the back of the truck, except for Zweiker and me. In a way, I envied the drunken lot, for they were probably oblivious of the constant artillery barrages that made me uneasy during the entire trip.

In Komárom, about ten miles from the front line, we joined another investigative unit which had been carrying out similar work to Smirnov's. This was still a war zone. Tanks and trucks with army personnel were coming and going twenty-four hours a day, and the roads were strewn with the bodies of soldiers, most of whom were German and Hungarian. Seriously wounded soldiers were brought to the field hospitals to be treated, but many died from lack of decent medical facilities or because they were beyond help.

Our living quarters were located in a huge, shell-riddled farmhouse. Smirnov and the other officers occupied the top floor, where the rooms were more or less intact. I had to stay with the regular soldiers in crowded rooms with shattered windows, exposed to the elements and to the constant pandemonium of war. The basement, the safest place because it was least likely to be hit by the occasional artillery shells, was used for temporarily housing those waiting to be interrogated.

It was clear to me that sleeping in my new quarters was going to be difficult, if not impossible. Noisy and often drunken soldiers, going to and coming back from sentry duty at all hours of the night, cared little about those who were trying to get a few hours of sleep. On the third day of our stay in Komárom, Smirnov asked me how I was doing. Remembering Dinsky's warning, I tried to be cheerful as I replied that I was exhausted and hadn't slept more than about five hours the past two nights, but hastened to add that I was going to be fine. Smirnov reacted with derisive laughter. "Come on, Nikolay," he said, "you are a soldier now, not a labor-camp inmate. Soldiers in the Russian army don't complain. It's dangerous to complain." Dinsky's injunctions were confirmed. Smirnov's original friendliness and supposed concern for me faded. Nor were my special epaulets of any consequence here. In the two weeks we spent in the Komárom area, I was never invited to the officers' dining room, the only place one could get a decent meal. Fortunately for me, Dinsky remained faithful to his promise and occasionally supplemented the poorly prepared army food with meals from the officers' kitchen.

My work load at our new headquarters was heavy. Starting at five o'clock in the morning, I generally spent five or six hours working with Smirnov. At least four afternoons during the week I accompanied Dinsky to various towns and villages to obtain meat and produce for our unit from the Hungarian farmers. From time to time, Dinsky also used me as his interpreter in arresting suspected Hungarian fascists whom he then brought to headquarters for questioning.

My most hateful responsibility was doing sentry duty every night, sometimes for five-hour shifts. I was invariably assigned to a deserted location without a soul around and without shelter from the icy, howling wind. Despite the fact that I held in my hands a machine gun that could discharge seventy-two shells in a matter of minutes, I was filled with fear as I listened to the artillery which sounded frighteningly close. Although the German and Hungarian armies were considerably weakened by now, I never ceased to dread the possibility of their recapturing our location. Above all, the most difficult part of sentry duty was staying awake. The fear of falling asleep, which carried with it the penalty of a possible court-martial, constantly haunted me. I did in fact doze off several times but never during the time that I was due to be relieved.

As part of my training, my first assignment at our new headquarters was to sit in on Smirnov's interrogation of a German officer with Zweiker as interpreter. My good friend was by now recognized by the Russians as the most talented interpreter in our unit. This was the first time I saw Zweiker at work. Even with my limited knowledge of the two languages, it appeared to me that both his German and his Russian were impeccable. Though the questions posed to the German officer tended to be quite uniform and easily translatable, I was impressed with the precision and the rapidity with which Zweiker conveyed the answers to the lieutenant.

This particular interrogation appeared to be an important one from which the Russians might glean valuable information. Though I was by now cognizant of Smirnov's potential cruelty, it still shocked me to see my "friendly" lieutenant operating on a level of rage beyond what I had ever seen. Smirnov seemed to have undergone a total personality change into someone devoid of any human compassion. Several times during the questioning, he was so harsh and threatening toward the prisoner that the poor soul stuttered severely, and even Zweiker, with his excellent knowledge of German, couldn't make out what he was saying. Of all the training sessions I was obliged to attend with other interrogating officers, I saw no one who surpassed Smirnov's inhumanity.

In the sessions I witnessed with Zweiker as the interrogator, he was brilliant. Although I felt almost sorry for the disheveled, frightened prisoners, it was good, for a change, to see a Jew participating in the interrogation of Germans. I was amazed at how the normally mild-mannered Zweiker was able to translate the questions with the same authority and severity used by the Russian officers in posing them. I was glad I wasn't in the interpreter's seat, for I certainly couldn't match Zweiker's fluency, nor did I much like the fury with which these proceedings were carried out. I would have preferred a less strident approach. Nevertheless, I learned a great deal from watching both Zweiker and the Russian officers at work.

My first important job was to accompany Smirnov to a small town near Komárom. I was armed with pistol and machine gun, which gave me, along with a sense of power, a feeling of uneasiness about my ability to use either of the weapons. Our mission was to interview the mayor of the town. Smirnov and I mounted an old motorcycle with a sidecar that the Russians had inherited from the Germans. The roads were crowded with military traffic, and traveling was hazardous. Although it was a sunny day, it was pretty cold for motorcycling. In this instance I was much luckier than Smirnov, for I was sitting bundled up in the sidecar while the lieutenant was driving in the open air, swearing every time the wind blew snow into his freezing face. Luckily, it was a very short trip.

When the mayor came out onto a small porch in response to our knock, he grew pale at the sight of us. He led us to a very well-heated room where his daughter and his wife were setting the table for lunch. Smirnov introduced himself and, with my translation, stated the purpose of our visit—to get some information on a Hungarian fascist who lived in that town and was now in hiding. He had apparently served in the Hungarian army in 1941 and had been responsible for atrocities against several families in a Ukrainian village. I was very glad that Smirnov dealt with the mayor in a more civilized manner than he had with the German officer. We came away with the information that eventually led to the arrest of the Hungarian.

Once the inquiry was over, the mayor invited us to stay for lunch. We were happy to accept, I because I anticipated a good Hungarian meal which I hadn't had since leaving the Hajdus, and Smirnov because it gave him the opportunity to flirt with the mayor's daughter. Smirnov was in an excellent mood, something I hadn't seen for a good while. He was pleased with my work despite the fact that occasionally I had required long pauses to search for the correct Russian words or the Ukrainian equivalent.

All in all, the visit went well, with the exception of one incident that broke my heart. On the way back to headquarters, Smirnov's callousness showed its ugly face. This time I was driving the motorcycle while Smirnov sat in the sidecar. As we were passing through the town, a dog started to chase us playfully, posing no danger to us. The lieutenant pulled out his pistol and shot the animal between the eyes.

Its life ended with a plaintive moan. I was afraid to let Smirnov see my grief, but he must have realized how upset I was by his gratuitous cruelty for not a word was exchanged between us throughout the return trip. As I rode into the snow-blowing wind I thought about the fate of that harmless dog and how, given Smirnov's twisted personality, my life might end as senselessly. I thought about how little worth an individual human life has in war, and not always to the enemy.

The incident left me shaken and repelled by Smirnov. Working with him had become an obligation I dreaded. As a consequence, I was very pleased when I had a chance to work with Dinsky. Despite his crudeness, Dinsky was an interesting character. As far as I could tell, he appeared knowledgeable on a variety of subjects, including Russian history, literature, and folklore. When it came to Jewish learning, I could tell that he must have had extensive schooling and a good Jewish upbringing. He quoted from the Old Testament and other sources with facility. Above all, Dinsky was a master raconteur, fascinating to listen to. The fact that we spoke Yiddish most of the time increased my wish to be in his company. From Dinsky I learned firsthand about the suffering of the Russian people in the war. He spoke with deep emotion about the siege of Leningrad, and about other calamitous events that had befallen his country and his family at the hands of the Nazis.

On our trips to the farms to acquire additional food for our unit, Dinsky proved himself perfectly suited for the job. When speaking to the farmers, Dinsky softened his sergeant-like manner. He treated them with respect and made sure it was clear that we didn't come to pillage nor did we ask for the impossible. Despite his toned-down demeanor, Dinsky never appeared subservient. He was not a beggar. He gave the farmers to understand, by way of lengthy declamatory monologues, that in war sacrifices had to be made for the fighting soldiers who were liberating Hungary from fascism. My difficult task as the interpreter was to comprehend the essence of Dinsky's dramatic orations and convey in more simple terms the importance of our mission on behalf of the Red army. Dinsky's imposing figure, and the farmers' fear of refusing him, all worked to our advantage. We invariably returned with a load of produce and meat badly needed to augment the meager army rations.

The three-week stay in the area of Komárom came to an end. In the middle of March, our sub-unit received orders to move closer to the fighting front, which by now penetrated the Slovakian border. The same crew that had come from Budapest, plus a half dozen more fighting soldiers, were loaded onto three trucks with a few provisions. We drove in the direction of the Danube River, and crossed it with great difficulty over pontoons laid alongside the bombed-out bridge that led to Slovakia. We landed at the northern end of a town called Komarno, the twin city of Komárom. This entire region, carved out of Hungarian territory during the formation of Czechoslovakia that followed the First World War, had been restored to Hungary by Hitler in 1938 as part of the deal in which the Hungarians became his allies.

The combined Hungarian and German armies in this area were now retreating in disarray. The number of deserters was enormous, giving us hordes of prisoners. At this point, since it was impossible for Smirnov and his co-workers to conduct extensive interrogations, it was simply a matter of classifying prisoners as to whether valuable information could be gotten from them at a future date. For the most part, the ordinary soldiers weren't even questioned. After recording some basic information about them, the Russians had them transported to a special unit which handled prisoners of war. The officers were held captive and subjected to brutal questioning for days on end.

Between guard duty and serving as the interpreter for both Smirnov and Dinsky, I was obliged to work sixteen-hour shifts without any rest other than when I had my meals. I was more fortunate with our lodgings than at Komárom, however, for we had a large building all to ourselves which must have served previously as an institution of some kind. There were enough rooms to accommodate twice the number of our group. I was particularly lucky to share a room with Zweiker and Dinsky, each of whom displayed a sense of humor that sent us to sleep laughing. Zweiker's brand of humor was full of irony, with an intellectual tinge characteristic of a former university student. Dinsky, on the other hand, was funny in a popular folk way, always laughing heartily and loudly at his own jokes, and forgetting that he had told them many times before. His objects of ridicule were usually the stupid Russian peasant or the Jewish shlemiel.

The fact that we had left Komárom with virtually no provisions made it imperative that Dinsky, the driver, and I start our work of providing our unit with food. The Slovakian farmer we went to first was a huge man who spoke both Czech and Hungarian. The moment we informed him of our purpose, it was clear from his angry expression that we were dealing with a tough customer. He wasn't about to part with anything unless he was pushed really hard. Dinsky burst into fury, elevating his sergeant-like behavior to its peak. He began to curse beyond my capacity to understand his Russian. Fortunately, it wasn't necessary to translate Dinsky's profanities literally. His crimson face and loud voice made the point, and we drove away with excellent yields. The farmer would have been far better off had he given us some produce before enraging Dinsky who would have settled for considerably less.

Our next two stops went more peacefully, and produced enough for us to return to our headquarters with an abundant load that contained not only food, but drink as well. Dinsky, who was a heavy drinker, had a special talent for sniffing out the locations of the rich wine cellars no matter how well they were camouflaged. It was probably the good wines and liquors Dinsky managed to bring home that made him such a popular figure, particularly with the officers, who were the primary recipients of his harvests. No sooner did we get on the truck than both Dinsky and the driver helped themselves to a bottle. As in the past, Dinsky insisted that I join him. Not to spoil his mood, I acquiesced this time and took a big swallow. Seeing the grimace produced by the taste of the wine, Dinsky burst into laughter. With his characteristic heartiness, he exclaimed, "*Molodyets* [well-done], Nikolay."

On the way home, we ran into some bad luck. Several enemy soldiers, who had been hiding in the basement of a bombed-out building, came out and fired in our direction. The minute our driver stopped the truck, the three of us jumped out of the cab and hid behind the wheels. Dinsky and the driver began to shoot immediately, as the soldiers scrambled for cover. I pulled the trigger of my automatic rifle only after Dinsky screamed at me, "Come on, you bastard, what are you waiting for! Are you afraid that you might kill a German?" Frightened by our situation and by Dinsky's shouting, I began to shoot in the general direction of the soldiers and didn't stop till I had emptied all seventy-two shells—it was as though my finger were tied to the trigger. Within minutes a Russian patrol unit arrived and helped us capture the six soldiers, four of whom were Hungarians. Despite the fact that they offered no resistance, and that only the two Germans were armed, the Russians roughed them up badly. It was obvious from their meek behavior that their attack had been intended not to engage us in a fight, but to call attention to themselves so they could surrender. I could tell from their gaunt faces that they must have gone without eating for many days and were probably relieved to be prisoners at long last. In fact, as we learned from our brief questioning, they were all deserters.

As they were loaded onto a truck, I was relieved to see that none of them was wounded, which meant that the barrage of bullets I had discharged almost unconsciously did no harm. One of those captured was a young Hungarian soldier who looked to be no more than eighteen years old, just about my age. I felt genuine compassion for him. I would rather have been on the soccer field with him than witness his arrest. I believed that, like me, he didn't want to point guns at human beings and that in a way both of us were victims of Hitler's madness. I was hoping that he wasn't going to wind up in Siberia, a place from which he was unlikely to get out alive—a fate he would share with many soldiers who fell into Russian hands.

As we resumed our return trip, I had no idea whether I had redeemed myself in Dinsky's eyes when I finally pulled the trigger. To my astonishment, he praised me and referred to my action as a good beginning, reminding me that in the near future there would be even more dangerous encounters for which I must always be prepared. I was glad that Dinsky wasn't angry with me, but not at all pleased with my initiation as a fighting soldier. It wasn't that I felt guilty, but rather that I was concerned about having to repeat this revolting act.

It was almost noon when we returned. Zabutsky, the cook, was delighted with the quantity and quality of our acquisitions, which included, among other things, two calves and several pigs fresh out of the farmer's huge icebox. Zabutsky and the two female soldiers who assisted him immediately began to prepare an elaborate meal. In this location there was no separate mess hall—our entire unit, comprising about twenty-five people including the officers, ate together. Dinsky, the driver, and I received a special bravo for getting such good provisions, and the kitchen staff was applauded for its culinary prowess. Dinsky made sure to tell the entire table of my bravery vis-à-vis the prisoners, grossly exaggerating my role in their capture despite his awareness of my repugnance at the whole episode. Smirnov was happy to hear that in addition to my good work in interpreting for Dinsky, I presumably had the potential for becoming a good soldier.

Although sentry duty was still not my favorite chore, at our new location it was much easier and sometimes even pleasant. Here we performed our shifts in pairs in front of a well-lit building, and if the weather was bad we had access to shelter. Even more significant for me was the knowledge that there was no longer any reason for me to worry about a possible German recapture of our territory. The front was miles away and the booming artillery fire that used to upset me terribly was much sparser than at Komárom.

My two favorite partners on guard duty were Zweiker and our secretary, Katya Ivanovna. When Zweiker was my companion, he invariably began with the Mincha evening prayers, which he knew by heart, and invited me to join him. Then he would give lessons on German grammar or lecture me on Kafka about whom I had never heard before.

With Katya the subjects of discussion were less intellectual. Katya was a sensitive woman who always treated me with maternal affection. She told me lightheartedly several times that if she were not twice my age she would most certainly marry me. I relaxed in her company and was able to share with her many of the feelings I couldn't reveal to either Dinsky or Zweiker. She in turn confided to me a good deal about her personal life. In the hours we spent together, I was privileged to learn about her happy childhood, her former loves, and the painful loss of her husband on the Ukrainian front in 1941. Her blue eyes shining, she described her seven-year-old son, Alyusha, whom she loved so much and whom she had to leave with her mother because of the war. I was moved by her story, and flattered that she would share with me these details about her personal life and her private feelings.

With the end of March came the good news that the German army was falling apart and the bloody war was nearing its end. It was probably a consequence of this German disintegration that the Russian front in Slovakia was moving almost without resistance in the direction of the capital. Our investigative unit was given orders to move on to Koloravo, some hours away from Bratislava.

The trip to our new destination was long and difficult. Most of the dirt roads were by now softened by the oncoming spring, making travel almost impossible. Adding to the problems caused by the melting snow was the heavy traffic of tanks and slow-moving trucks that dug deep ruts into the mud from which it often took our entire crew to extricate ourselves. Our clothes were muddied and our faces, dirtied beyond recognition, provoked uproarious laughter. We poked fun at each other, forgetting how exhausted we all were. The trip that should have lasted three or four hours took a day and a half. Trapped in the darkness and forbidden to make a bonfire for security reasons, we were obliged to spend a chilly night on the side of the road. For some there was room on the floor of the trucks, but the rest of us, including me, made our beds on the ground, where my handsome coat, now bathed in mud, refused to keep me warm. I was glad to see that Russian chivalry wasn't totally dead; Katya and the other two women occupied the cabs of our three trucks.

When we reached Kolarovo it was clear that the battles fought in that area were won easily, because there was hardly the kind of devastation we had seen in other places the Russians conquered. Unlike the Hungarians, the Slovaks were friendly to the Russians. The Slovak alliance agreement with Germany had been signed under duress, and there were many Slovak underground resistance fighters who fought along with the Czech army on the side of the Russian forces. Thus, when the Russians came in, they were viewed as liberators. However, for the most part the Russians didn't treat them much better than they did the fascists who had collaborated with Hitler though there were some differences. The kind of flagrant looting that took place in Hungary, from which the Russians sent home trainloads of goods and artifacts, was less extensive here. This restraint didn't mean, however, that if the Russian army wanted something they didn't take it, or that looting by individual soldiers didn't continue. Another distinction made between the two territories was the treatment of the farmers to whom we went for food. Dinsky gave them gasoline or tires, both unavailable because of the war and badly needed to cultivate the land.

Apart from such minor differences, many of the practices of the Russian army remained the same. Families were expelled from their homes, often unnecessarily, to provide lodging for officers, and sexual aggression against women was as prevalent as in Hungary. Of the many brutalities the Russians visited on the people they conquered, this abuse was the most heinous. It was revolting to me, and incredible that men were capable of forcing themselves on vulnerable women.

At Kolarovo we were housed in a municipal building that looked like a courthouse, where a sub-branch of our division headquarters was located. It was similar to what we had in Budapest. Here, too, officers and common soldiers were coming and going all day and all night. One could see large caravans of trucks bringing in some captives and transporting others to railroad stations to be taken God knew where. Immediately after our arrival, we were told we would be staying only four or five days because we were expected in Bratislava, which was to be totally liberated within a week. Again the work was hectic. We were overwhelmed by the number of captives we were ordered to interrogate in a short period of time. The basement was teeming with prisoners, mostly high-ranking German officers but also a few Hungarians.

Zweiker was teamed with one of the captains from our unit, working exclusively with the German prisoners. I interpreted for Smirnov, interrogating Slovakian Nazi collaborators, most of whom were released at the end of the day. My knowledge of Czech and Carpatho-Ukrainian was very useful, for both of these languages, particularly Czech, were extremely close to Slovakian. I rarely experienced any difficulty in conveying Smirnov's questions and the captives' replies.

Although we spent only four days in Kolarovo, the memory of that place remains vivid and painful. It was there that the Russian brand of anti-Semitism showed itself. In the past two and a half months, my experiences had been limited to the kind of anti-Semites I was accustomed to. Smirnov himself had told a few jokes virulently poking fun at Jews, particularly Jewish women. Vanya and Zabutsky, our cook, often called me a cowardly *Zhid* (the most frequently used Russian anti-Semitic term). Vanya was just about my size. When I got good and tired of his name-calling, I put an end to it with a left hook that I had acquired around the age of thirteen while learning to box in a youth club. Both Smirnov and Dinsky were there when I displayed my pugilistic ability and were amused. I was not. In fact I felt sorry for Vanya.

The incident of anti-Semitism that took place the evening before our departure was of a different order. Two officers, one a captain, came into the dining room and sat down at the table where Dinsky, Zweiker, Katya, and I were eating. It was immediately apparent from the captain's bloodshot eyes that he had been drinking. His companion appeared sober. The captain turned to Dinsky and asked him in a loud voice that could be heard at the surrounding tables, "Are these the two Zhid interpreters that I've heard so much about?"

Dinsky responded angrily, "No, Comrade Captain, these are two Jewish volunteers in the Russian army."

The captain turned to Zweiker and said, "You must be Zveker or Zwiker, the Romanian. Are you sure that you are just a stinking Zhid and not a Nazi? Your name is really German, isn't it? You know what we do with Nazis." Jeers and loud laughter at Zweiker's expense came from the other tables. The captain's fellow officer tried to stop him from going on with his tirade. He begged, "Please, Gregory Vasilich, stop. It's not right." Gregory Vasilich paid no attention, and pushed him out of the way. Then he came to my side of the table, pushed his index finger forcefully into my chest, and screamed, "And you, you son of a bitch, you speak too many languages. You must be a spy, you bastard, working for the Germans. I think we should put you in the basement with the rest of them!" More shocking than his words were his hate-filled eyes, the sight of which filled me with terror.

Dinsky, enraged by this disgusting spectacle, grabbed hold of the captain and flung him from our table. The captain started to reach for his pistol, but he was restrained by his own companion as well as by another officer, both of whom led him out of the dining room.

Katya, Dinsky, and Zweiker realizing how upset I was, tried to make me feel better. Apparently neither Zweiker nor Dinsky were in need of sympathy since they had witnessed numerous anti-Semitic outbursts in the Russian army. Katya was particularly ashamed of her fellow Russians. Reminiscent of what my mother used to do when I was distressed, Katya embraced me, pressed me to her breast, caressing my head gently and assuring me that nothing like this would ever happen again.

The solicitude of my friends, though it diminished my wretchedness for that evening, couldn't make it go away. I felt utterly humiliated by the brutality of the drunken captain. This wasn't the first time I had met with similar kinds of anti-Semitism, and even worse. The stone-throwing in Kustanovice by the village bullies, the beatings in Jolsva by the Hungarian soldiers, and the whippings by the major in Csepel—all these were just as humiliating and painful. There was, nevertheless, a difference in circumstances.

In the other situations, anti-Semitism was sanctioned, justified by slander and nurtured by stupidity. In my village, I was an enemy because Jews had supposedly killed Christ. In the forced-labor camps, the beatings were approved by the fascists who had as their goal the total annihilation of the Jewish people. In the Russian army, I was a volunteer who had joined to help defeat the Nazis. In fact, with the passage of time I had begun to feel that I was a real soldier, making a commendable contribution. My work as an interpreter and my trips with Dinsky to obtain food supplies were certainly of use to our cause.

Before I went to bed that evening, Dinsky paid me a visit. He walked in on me in my misery and chided me. "Are you going to let a few damned anti-Semites bring your spirits down? Try to forget them for a while. Remember the decent people, the officers who stopped that *grobyan* [boor] from hurting you, and Katya who is like a mother to you. Right now we have a much larger enemy to get rid of than Captain Gregory Vasilich. Let's defeat him first, and then we will take on the anti-Semites." Dinsky concluded his little pep talk with an often-used Jewish malediction, "*Zol zeh Got stroofen* [May the Lord punish them]." This invocation, as well as his heartening words, helped me to fall asleep that night.

The following morning, as our unit was preparing for our departure from Kolarovo, a messenger from the commanding officer of the local headquarters came with a note summoning Dinsky, Zweiker, and me to his office. Zweiker and I were apprehensive, but Dinsky was totally at ease. "Don't worry, you frightened shlemiels. If we were in trouble, the commander wouldn't send a note. He would send two armed soldiers."

When we got to the office, the major received us with a forced smile. He was a sullen-looking fat man, nearing his fifties. His face was red and puffy like that of an alcoholic. His speech was listless. One had the impression that he had to force himself to speak. After we finished a lengthy salute, we were asked to sit down. He first addressed Zweiker and me. His voice was barely audible, as though it emanated from a closed box. "I understand that both of you are volunteers. Make no mistake about it, the Soviet Union is very proud of you. We need you because we are fighting a formidable foe." There was a long pause, as though he didn't know what to say next. Then, "Please don't pay attention to a few pranks that you will meet up with from time to time. Don't forget Captain Gregory Vasilich has gone through a lot." Here he raised his voice, as though the lid of the box were now open. "It may interest you to know that he fought in the battle of Stalingrad and distinguished himself as one of our best officers. I personally thank you for your service on behalf of this patriotic war and wish you luck." He then turned to Dinsky and lazily said to him in a tone half complimentary and half admonishing, "You, Comrade Dinsky, are a brave man. I know that from your files, which are right here on my desk. I am glad that you had the courage to defend these two young men, and I commend you for it." He then added sternly, but with a smile, "I would however, suggest to you, that when you challenge someone well above your rank, you deal with him more carefully. I have spoken with Captain Gregory Vasilich, and he tells me he is prepared to apologize to them and shake hands with you as well. I understand that you are leaving today. I wish you well. You are dismissed."

When we left the office, Dinsky was furious. He started using a new set of profanities I had never heard before. He was particularly offended by the idea that the major had not treated him with enough respect in disapproving how he had dealt with Gregory Vasilich. Referring to the captain he murmured, "I should have put a bullet through that Jew-hater's head. As for that son of a bitch having fought in the battle of Stalingrad, so did I. Does that, or the few extra stripes on his epaulets, give him the right to abuse people?" At one point Dinsky was about to return to the major's office and give him a piece of his mind, but Zweiker managed to dissuade him. Fortunately for

Captain Gregory Vasilich, he never showed up. Having listened to Dinsky's tirade, I was certain that their meeting would have resulted in a fist-fight or worse, rather than in a friendly handshake.

Just minutes before we were to pull out of the courtyard, Gregory Vasilich's companion of the evening before came to say good-bye to us. He introduced himself as Lieutenant Gordieyev. Turning first to Dinsky, he began with an apology for, as he put it, "the rudeness of my drunken friend," and praised him for his bravery in restraining the captain. He then turned to Zweiker and me and repeated his apology to us, adding that Gregory Vasilich had obviously been quite drunk and didn't know what he was doing. He then told us his own personal history, that his mother was Jewish and his father a non-practicing Greek Orthodox Christian. During the pogroms of 1904, his father had rescued the seventeen year old girl whom he later married. He also told us about his family's occasional encounters with anti-Semitism and how offended he was by his friend's ugly behavior. Before Lieutenant Gordieyev could continue, however, Dinsky interrupted politely, indicating that it was time for us to leave. Lieutenant Gordieyev shook hands with each one of us and gave us a warm, "*Do svidanya.*"

The lieutenant's words and manner made me feel better about the whole affair. Even Zweiker, who tended to be cynical, and Dinsky, who was not prone to sentimentality, were touched by Gordieyev's sincerity and by his eagerness to soften the blow dealt us by the captain's display of anti-Semitism. Dinsky was all smiles. It was as though Lieutenant Gordieyev had restored the pride wounded by the major.

Chapter 10

Fear and Loathing

An order came from our commanding officer that our units would be split for a while and eventually would reunite in Bratislava, the capital of Slovakia. In the meantime, Vanya, Gavrilo our driver, and I were to accompany Smirnov to Dunajska Treda, midway to Bratislava, where Russian headquarters were located. I was afraid that our separation was permanent and that I was not going to see again my dear friends, Katya, Dinsky, and Zweiker, for it was their presence in the army that had made my life with the moody Smirnov more bearable. Katya, aware of my concern, allayed my fears. She told me in confidence that she knew from official correspondence that Smirnov was summoned for a hearing for his promotion and that we would indeed meet in Bratislava. I was of course praying that he would be promoted.

The trip to Dunajska Streda was very pleasant. Although one could still see an occasional patch of snow, it was a moderately cool day. The meadows were already sporting a variety of early spring flowers—forsythia, violets, lilies of the valley, a profusion of dandelions and snowdrops. Miles and miles of open fields allowed us an excellent view of the Little Carpathians, which brought back memories of Kustanovice and of my childhood. Everything surrounding us was peaceful. Were it not for the occasional muffled sound of artillery that seemed to come from a great distance, one could be lulled into believing that everything was well with the world. Taken by the impressive beauty that surrounded us, I did in fact forget that I was still a reluctant volunteer in the Russian army facing an uncertain future.

At Dunajska Streda, Smirnov was housed in the main building of the headquarters; Vanya, Gavrilo, and I were put up in a makeshift tent where fifty wounded soldiers were recovering. We were given military cots and two thin blankets that had seen better days. Since there was no more room under the tent we were obliged to stay outside. Exposed as we were to the elements, we were lucky it didn't rain during the three nights we spent there, for it was still cold for such inadequate covering.

Vanya, whom the Lord had not endowed with good judgment, got hold of a blanket that belonged to one of the soldiers whose friends caught Vanya red-handed and ganged up on him. Had Gavrilo and I not pleaded with his attackers to let him go, they would have beaten poor Vanya to a pulp. It was probably in return for my intercession on his behalf that Vanya was careful not to divulge my Jewish identity which might have caused me unpleasantness in that particular setting. I learned later from Gavrilo that these wounded soldiers were former convicts who, for volunteering to serve in the Russian army, were eventually to be pardoned for their crimes.

During the three days stay at Dunajska I had no responsibilities of any kind. Vanya was called on to clean up after Smirnov, and Gavrilo was given mess hall duty. As for me, either Smirnov had ordered that I not be given an assignment, or I was simply forgotten. On one hand, I had a chance to catch up with sleep I badly needed. On the other hand, I felt left out. I didn't see Smirnov for two days, but Vanya reported that the lieutenant was in a very bad mood.

On the third day, early in the morning, I was summoned to Smirnov's room. I could tell immediately that he was drunk. He sat on the edge of his bed holding his temples in the palms of his hands. He looked pale and disheveled. "Well, *zhidchook* [little Jew], you may continue to call me Lieutenant Smirnov. The bastards denied me my promotion. You know, don't you, that the Russian military brass are selfish sons of bitches? They send us to fight the war, and they take credit for the victory." Smirnov, realizing that he may have revealed too much of the inner thoughts about his superiors, got up from the bed and wobbled toward me. He looked angry and said, "You know that I like you, but if you should ever say anything to anyone about what I just told you, I will blow your brains out with this," pointing to his pistol.

Smirnov must have realized how alarmed I was by his threat. He softened his tone and said with a faint smile, "Don't worry, I'm not going to kill you. As a matter of fact, we're going to have some fun.

Tonight I want you to accompany me to town, where I made the acquaintance the other day of a good-looking Slovakian woman. I think she might be willing to spend some time with me. You know what I mean." This last sentence was accompanied by a sly smile. "But I need your help. First I want you to go with Vanya and Gregory to a farm where I requisitioned three horses that will be equipped with English saddles. No more riding for us on those ugly trucks. I bet you have never ridden an English saddle, have you?" I shook my head and was about to tell him I had never ridden any way but bareback, when he interrupted me. "Tell Vanya that I want our horses to be ready at six o'clock, and then you and I will go on our adventure." Smirnov handed me a stamped document to be given to the farmer for the horses and dismissed me.

We went to the farm around noon and picked up three horses all ready for mounting. They were fine-looking animals, but none was as handsome as my dear friend Táltos. Vanya, who had begun his military service in the cavalry, was a fine rider. I watched carefully as he mounted his horse and then imitated every one of his moves. A few compliments on his excellent riding ability, moved Vanya to give me riding lessons. My bareback experience also came in handy, and we spent the entire afternoon on horseback. By the time I was to meet Smirnov, I was fairly comfortable on the frisky mare, able to post with her in almost perfect rhythm.

When I reported to Smirnov at six o'clock, he was in a better mood and surprised me with an invitation to the officers' dining room for supper. After the meal we rode into town, where we left the horses in the care of a Russian guard and proceeded on foot toward the center. Although the scars of war were evident, a few stores were already open and people were going about their business trying to emerge from the wreckage. In front of the few food stores, crowds pushed each other in an attempt to get to the front of the line before word came that there was no more food to be had.

Besides the civilians, there were many rowdy Russian soldiers prowling the streets in search of *Fräuleins*—girls who were willing to flirt and go beyond flirting for valuable gifts the Russians possessed as a result of their looting. But these *Fräuleins* did not interest Smirnov. He was out for a real conquest, a challenge that would prove his wooing talents. Smirnov led me to a bakery shop, peeked through the window, and suddenly grabbed me be by the shoulder. "There she is! Come on, let's go in." We entered the store. Smirnov greeted the young woman in Slovak and followed it up with a compliment on her good looks. Part of his technique in pursuing women was to learn some flirtatious expressions in the language of his prey. Smirnov introduced me to Vera Sokolova as his official interpreter.

Vera Sokolova was a good-looking woman in her early thirties. In fact, she very much resembled Ilona, Smirnov's Budapest girlfriend. Like Ilona, Vera had fine features, as though specially carved for symmetry. Vera was about to close the store, which by now had sold out of baked goods. Through my interpretation and Vera's limited knowledge of Russian, Smirnov managed to communicate to her that an officers' party was being held at headquarters to which several girls from Dunajska Streda were invited. He, Smirnov, would like her to come as his guest. He would fetch her personally by jeep and bring her back home after the party. It was apparent from Vera's attitude that she was apprehensive about accepting the invitation, but his subtly menacing insistence made it impossible for her to refuse. A rendezvous was set for nine-thirty. Smirnov was delighted with himself.

"Well, Nikolay, how did you like this piece of work? I don't believe that Don Juan could have done better. Do you know where that party will be?"

"No, sir."

"Of course not. Have you ever screwed a girl in a jeep?" "No, sir."

Smirnov burst out into uncontrollable laughter.

When we arrived home, Smirnov told me I was no longer needed and could retire for the night. I never knew the details of what transpired that evening, but the next morning, when we rode through the town on our way to Bratislava, Vera noticed us from her shop. She ran out with a broom in her hand, swung at Smirnov, spat at him, and shouted curses. Smirnov, sitting on his horse like a coward, urged the animal to move faster in order to avoid Vera's blows and the stares of the few curious onlookers who gathered around us. My horse reared, frightened by the shouting and the commotion. I held on for dear life and barely managed to stay on the distraught animal.

Apparently Smirnov, like some of his fellow Russians, had behaved crudely the night before and may even have raped the poor woman. I felt awful. It was as though I had been a partner in his brutality by using my limited Slovak knowledge to help carry out his villainy. For a while I believed that the shying of the horse was God's reproach to me for my part in this terrible episode.

On the way to Bratislava we stopped for a few hours at a time at several military installations, where Smirnov had official business. This was a boon, because after the first day of riding I could barely sit on the horse or stand up straight when I dismounted. I kept my pain a secret because had Smirnov been aware of it, instead of sympathy I would have been reprimanded and made fun of. I was jealous of Vanya and the lieutenant for their endurance. For the rest of our two-day trip to the Slovakian capital, Smirnov was in a foul temper. Vanya took a couple of beatings from the brooding lieutenant. I was luckier; I escaped Smirnov's heavy hand, but not his angry tongue.

We arrived in Bratislava toward the end of April, some two weeks after it was liberated. The city had not suffered as much damage as Budapest, and had managed to get on its feet more quickly. By the time we arrived, it was already bustling with people. The fact that some forms of transportation remained intact made it easier to bring in food from surrounding areas. Nevertheless, the destruction of war and the suffering on the faces of the people were everywhere visible. Only the natural beauty that surrounded Bratislava was not marred by the fighting. The Little Carpathians, the fields with red and white poppies, had defied destruction and retained their former splendor.

I did not know then, nor could I have imagined, the horrendous Jewish tragedy that had taken place in that once charming city. I later learned that out of some 15,000 Jews who lived there in 1938 only a small fraction survived the Holocaust. The Jews of Slovakia had met with the same fate as the German Jews. As early as 1938, a year before Slovakia broke away from Czechoslovakia to become a puppet regime of Germany, synagogues and institutions of Jewish learning were desecrated and anti-Semitic terror was in full force. Some thousand students were expelled from the University of Bratislava. In 1939, Jewish shops were confiscated, and in 1940, Jews were obliged to surrender their homes. Deportation to concentration camps continued until just a few weeks before the collapse of the Nazi regime.

The beautiful Carpathians had been witness to untold human suffering.

When the investigative unit reunited in Bratislava I learned that Katya was soon to be discharged. She was returning home to Leningrad to be with her son Alyusha and the members of her family who survived the siege of that great city. I was happy for her sake that her military service was soon coming to an end, but I hated losing a dear friend and protector.

In the two days before Katya's departure, I had no official responsibilities and was pleased that she wanted to spend her free time with me. We took long walks through the city, and visited many of the historic sights. Our conversations covered a variety of subjects that allowed me yet another glimpse into her sensitive Russian soul.

Most unexpectedly, Katya brought Smirnov into our conversation. She wanted to know how he had been behaving lately, and how he had been treating me. She was particularly interested to learn what had taken place during our separation. I told Katya about the shameful episode with Vera Sokolova. I knew that she would under no circumstances reveal to Smirnov what I told her. Besides, I was more comfortable sharing with Katya the things that pressed on my mind than with Dinsky or Zweiker.

Swearing me to secrecy, Katya entrusted me with her own bout of harassment by Smirnov and other officers. She was particularly bitter about Smirnov who would not take no for an answer, in spite of her threat to complain to the commanding officer. She told me that other women were subjected to this kind of behavior with no recourse, particularly from officers, who acted as though women were there not to support the war effort but to satisfy their sexual needs. Often they were guilty of rape, for which they were never punished.

Like Dinsky, Katya was intensely aware of Russian corruption, and both were unhappy with many aspects of their regime. What was surprising to me was that among themselves the Russians never spoke critically about the army or about the regime. It was clear that they were afraid of each other, and were looking for someone other than a compatriot with whom they could share their dissatisfaction. I often felt as though I were a kind of repository to whom they could entrust their secrets. In our last private conversation, Katya implored me to come to Leningrad when the war was over, to see her and meet her handsome little boy. At the farewell party in her honor, Katya and I danced a swift polka played by a skilled Russian accordionist. I still remember the affection with which she looked at me while we spun around the floor. The occasion brought back memories of my mother, with whom I had danced many times.

The following morning, Dinsky, Zweiker, I, and a few other friends accompanied Katya to the railroad station. We each got our final Katya embrace—mine felt as though I were wrapped in a soft woolen blanket. She mounted a train crowded with Russian soldiers, some of whom were hanging from the doors. As she was waving her good-byes, tears rolled down her face. All of us were deeply moved by her departure. Even the tough staff-sergeant Dinsky's eyes watered. Circumstances prevented me from making the attempt to see Katya again. In 1971, however, when I did get to Leningrad, I made every effort to find her but without success. I did however visit her many times with loving thoughts and appreciation for her kindness to me.

A few days later, Smirnov got the good news that his promotion to captain had finally come through. With it came an assignment to head a small investigative unit in Trnava, a Slovakian town not far from Bratislava. Smirnov was delighted, and so was I, hoping that his new rank would put him on a more steady emotional keel which would make life more pleasant for me.

Along with Smirnov's promotion, came the bad news that Dinsky and Zweiker would not accompany the captain on his new assignment. Both of them were being sent to Budapest despite the fact that they would have preferred to remain in Bratislava. How ironic I thought, that they who would have preferred to remain in Bratislava, were sent to Budapest, while I desperately wanting to go there to begin to search for survivors in my family could not. I was of course unhappy that I was going to be permanently separated from my two friends, particularly Dinsky, without whose protection life with Smirnov was going to be difficult and even dangerous. Dinsky, aware of my uneasiness about our separation, tried to bolster my spirits. He also warned me once more not to do anything that would incur Smirnov's wrath, reminding me that Smirnov, despite his relatively low rank as an officer, wielded a great deal of power. "You know of course that Smirnov is serious about taking you to the Soviet Union. I am sure he thinks that with your knowledge of languages and with additional training you will be an asset to our country.

"Most of all, Nikolay, I must caution you not to do anything stupid. Should you contemplate a way out, be sure that you do it right. If however, you are willing to come to the Soviet Union, don't worry; you will not be the only Jew. In any case, I hope that you won't forget the old man and come to visit me in Odessa." These last words were accompanied by the loud, characteristic Dinsky guffaw.

Although Dinsky's words were reassuring, his reminder about Smirnov's potential for making life difficult made me uneasy. I was even more bothered by his warning "not to do anything stupid." Did he actually suspect that by now it had occurred to me more than once that I must find a way out of the Russian army, that I did not want to go to the Soviet Union?

Both Zweiker and Dinsky were sent off to Budapest without any expression of gratitude or a proper farewell from their superiors; Smirnov showed his utter dislike for Dinsky to the last moment. Dinsky, aware of this, didn't really care and was in a good mood, probably very glad to get away from the surly captain. The night before his departure, Dinsky dispatched a good quantity of vodka in his room with several close friends, including me. When the evening came to an end and I was about to leave, Dinsky gave me a Russian bear hug. "Don't worry Nikolay; everything will be O.K." Zweiker said goodbye in his more restrained fashion. Since both were leaving very early in the morning, these were our final adieux.

I never went to Odessa nor did I ever see Dinsky again. But the memory of this unique character has never faded. A man who appeared at first sight to be a typically gruff sergeant turned out to be a complex personality in whom goodness, duty, kindness, loyalty, and Jewish pride cohabited without conflicting. In his peculiarly Dinskyan way, he treated me as he would his own son, and I am sure that without all his helpful advice I would have made many serious blunders.

After a few more days of work in Bratislava, preparations were made for our transfer to Trnava. Vanya, Zabutsky, and a driver were to travel in a newly acquired American army jeep. I was to accompany Smirnov in the motorcycle we hadn't used since Koloravo, where

Smirnov shot the poor dog. I was always apprehensive riding with Smirnov, who loved to drive at lightning speed with very little regard for his or anybody else's life. Many times during the trip I sat petrified, holding on for dear life as he made sharp turns at fifty miles an hour, tilting the sidecar to a 45-degree angle.

Unlike the roads between the smaller towns, the highway to Trnava was easy to travel despite the heavy military traffic. At this point in the war, we were far away from what was still left of the German front. The only reminders were the high-flying bombers heading toward Berlin to inflict on Hitler the final blow. Smirnov was excited about going to a new location. He kept shouting over the motorcycle noise that as soon as we got to Trnava I must help him find a Slovakian *Fräulein*. With Smirnov's speeding, we made the trip from Bratislava to Trnava in an hour.

Our new headquarters were close to the center of town, in an impressive-looking three-story apartment building untouched by the bombing. Thirty-five people were going to work under Smirnov's supervision, among them a few lower-ranking officers, a young, good-looking secretary, and a fat cook in her forties. Within an hour of our arrival, Smirnov's new staff was assembled in what was to be our dining room. Smirnov made a short speech to a nervous staff warning them to stay in line. By the time Smirnov finished his speech, the jeep arrived with his luggage. He ordered Vanya to get a fresh suit of clothing ready for him, and informed me that we were driving into town. Like Bratislava, Trnava was filled with military personnel, but not too many young women were to be seen in the streets. The few attempts the captain made led to no conquests that evening. Obliged to go back empty-handed, he reprimanded me for not helping him get a *fräulein*. I learned the following day that after our return Smirnov had tried his luck with the pretty secretary. I hoped for her sake that whatever happened that night was of her own volition and not a consequence of Smirnov's brutality.

The rapidity with which the Germans were retreating made the Nazi defeat imminent, but it came even sooner than expected. On May 9, about a week after our arrival in Trnava, we learned that the Germans had capitulated. The thrilling news inspired celebrations by Slovakian civilians and Russian soldiers alike. Jubilant crowds danced in the streets and, with the celebrating there was a great deal of drinking which led to the usual coarse behavior toward women. Smirnov who was also drunk, actually behaved relatively well during the festivities. With my help, he organized a party at our headquarters to which a few local dignitaries and some Slovakian girls were invited.

Among the guests there was an attractive blonde young woman of about thirty who, after some crafty wooing on Smirnov's part, became his girlfriend. Marina had been a member of the Czechoslovak Communist Party before the war, had studied Russian and spoke it quite well. When Slovakia broke away from the Czechs and became "independent," Marina joined the antifascist underground. Now that Slovakia was liberated, she was eager to continue her Communist activities. Because she wanted to visit the Soviet Union, meeting a Russian officer must have been her dream. She fell in love with the handsome captain, not knowing that he was married—nor would she have cared in any case. For about a week Smirnov hardly did any of his work, passing most of his time with his new love Marina, who slept in his apartment almost every night. Their romance not only spared me the repugnant job of abetting him in his constant search for female companionship, but left me with some time to myself.

Marina and I liked each other. She inquired about my past and expressed sympathetic interest in how I had survived the labor camps. The fact that I was a volunteer in the Red army, and a Czech, led her to suppose that I too was loyal to the Communist cause. She admired me for having joined the army. Marina didn't possess the sensitivity of dear Katya; nevertheless, she became a good friend who was later instrumental in helping me gain my freedom.

Now that the war with Germany was officially over, I was hoping that Hitler's defeat would bring with it my liberation from the Russian army. I approached Smirnov very tactfully, telling him I would be most grateful for his permission to return to Budapest in order to find the few survivors of my family; I made sure he understood that I was asking only for a few weeks of furlough. In reality, this was the first step in my plan to escape, for Dinsky's parting reference to leaving the Russian army weighed heavily on my mind. But Smirnov must have been in one of his bad moods. He responded with a surprised, annoyed look, as if to say he didn't want to be bothered, and told me to speak to him some other time. I was disappointed, but at least it wasn't an un-qualified rejection.

Working in my favor was the fact that our division had captured about 500 Russian soldiers who had defected to the German side with General Andrey Vlasov in 1942. Vlasov, who later formed a 50,000-man army of deserters and fought against his countrymen, was himself captured and executed in 1946. These men, known as "Vlasov deserters," were now in our unit's hands for interrogation. Because they spoke Russian, my services were not needed for at least three weeks, giving me practically nothing to do. This, I thought, might sway Smirnov to grant me my furlough. In the meanwhile, I had no choice but to bide my time.

On Saturday morning Smirnov sent for me. Though he was ob-viously tired, he greeted me with a genuine smile and asked how it felt to do nothing all week long. "You know, Nikolay, that I have been working hard with these Russian Vlasov traitors. Can you imagine, these bastards were willing to kill their own brothers? We write too many reports on them. I think we should line them up against the wall and blow their brains out. Don't you think so? You wouldn't desert from the Red army, would you?" Considering my own plans for a per-manent furlough, Smirnov's words sent a chill through my body. "The reason I sent for you is that today is Marina's birthday. I decided to give her a small party, and I asked her to invite some of her girlfriends. A few of my fellow officers from the central investigative quarter will also be there. By the way, if we can help it, I don't want anyone from our group to know about this party, but you are invited. I bet there will be a girl among them that you'll like. You know, Nikolay, it's about time you too got yourself a girlfriend. I've spoken to Zabutsky about preparing the food. Your responsibility is to get lots of flowers and some good drinks. I'm tired of vodka. Besides, vodka is really made for peasants. I want you to get champagne, good wines, and liquors. Tell the driver to take you wherever it's necessary; be sure you don't come back empty-handed. You should also tell him that I'm advising him to keep his trap shut about all this if he wants to live to see another birthday. Take along some tanks of gasoline to pay the bastard vineyard owners for what they give you. I don't want them to complain to our commander that they were robbed."

For a moment I thought this was the time to ask Smirnov once more for my furlough. I decided my chances would be much better if I came back with the drinks—after all, there was always the possibility of failing to fulfill Smirnov's demands. The fact that we were ready to barter four twenty-gallon tanks filled with gasoline, a very precious commodity, made me feel fairly confident of success. I wished Dinsky were there to help me with this very important mission. I ran straight to the driver with Smirnov's orders and his threats. We drove to a wine cellar in the outskirts of Trnava where I had once been with Smirnov—on which occasion the captain had neglected to remunerate the proprietor for his three bottles of wine.

The corpulent Slovak vineyard owner wasn't at all happy to see us at first, but when I showed him the fuel he was not only amenable, but eager to make a deal with us—some six bottles of champagne and as many bottles of wine in exchange for one tank of gasoline. Feeling good about the fact that I wasn't involved in pillaging but in a business deal, I gave him two tanks, thus leaving the door open for a future transaction. In return for my generosity, the farmer directed me to another grower whose specialty was the production of fine liquors, and who was probably just as much in need of fuel. We were successful there as well, acquiring a good supply of a potent homemade brandy called pálinka. This was actually similar in taste to vodka, but Smirnov liked it very much and consumed a good bit of it.

The party was a huge success. Zabutsky, in addition to preparing abundant food, also served as the musician for the night. Smirnov's guests danced with admirable grace to the accompaniment of Zabutsky's accordion. To make me feel more at home at the party, Marina had brought with her a young neighbor of Czech background. Jera was a vivacious, bright girl about my age, with whom I danced a few times, but who must have been disappointed in me because I wasn't in tune with the festivities. Besides suffering from my usual clumsiness with girls, my mind wasn't on having fun but on finding a way to get out of the Russian army alive and eventually gain my freedom. Although Jera was the kind of girl I would have been delighted to have a date with, that sort of socializing would have to wait for other times and other places when I was not a virtual prisoner living with daily anxieties. At the end of the party, a young officer accompanied Jera to her house, leaving me jealous and annoyed with myself.

The next morning, Smirnov invited me to have lunch with him in the officers' dining room, for the first time since we had come to Trnava. Ever since Dinsky left our unit, I hadn't had a decent meal— to this day I remember the disgusting fish soups that were served to the ordinary soldiers while the officers were feasting on fine cuisine. I could tell immediately that Smirnov was in the best frame of mind I had seen him in for a long time. "Well, Nikolay, how did you like the party? Wasn't it something? What happened to you and Jera? Didn't you like her? I think I will have to teach you how to deal with women. Anyhow, I wanted to show you that I appreciated your good work, so I invited you to have lunch with me."

Well, I thought, this is my chance to broach the subject of a furlough. But I was filled with anxiety, anticipating the worst possible scenario, a flat rejection. As we started to eat, I quietly said, "Captain Smirnov, I don't know whether or not you recall my mentioning to you that I would very much like to go on a short furlough."

"Oh, yes," said Smirnov. "I remember that you did say something about it before. Would you tell me again why it is that you want a furlough? Don't you like the Russian army?"

I started to tell him that I wanted to find the survivors of my family, but couldn't finish my sentence. This was the first time I ever saw Smirnov moved to compassion. "Now, Nikolay, stop those damn tears. Let me see what can be done about that damned furlough of yours. I can tell you now that you must wait at least till the first week of June. In the meantime, stay out of trouble. Here is what may happen. At the end of May or the beginning of June, I am returning to the Soviet Union by way of Budapest. If I can get you the furlough, you will have about four weeks to do your business. At the end of those four weeks, you will meet me at the Budapest headquarters. You understand that my superiors and I have decided to take you to the Soviet Union. This will be the best thing that could ever happen to you. Once you are there, the army will make arrangements for you to complete your education and then send you to Moscow University to study languages." All this was said in a benevolent tone, as though a father were mapping the future for his own son.

Suddenly, Smirnov assumed a cold, intimidating posture. "Now remember this. I'm pretty sure I can get you your damned furlough. But I don't want any funny stuff. I don't expect to have to look for you in Budapest or any other place. You understand that you are officially a soldier in the Russian army, certainly a better place than a German concentration camp or Siberia."

I was shaken by Smirnov's threatening words, but I managed to muster enough composure not to betray the slightest sign of my inner fear. In fact, his threats intensified my determination that, once I had that leave in my hand, the captain would never see me again. I knew then beyond any doubt that the only way to gain my freedom was to escape from the Russians no matter how dangerous the attempt would be. I thanked the captain for giving me the opportunity to go to the Soviet Union and assured him that I had every intention of meeting him in Budapest. Smirnov appeared satisfied. Turning pleasant once more, he spoke about the success of the party and about his affection for Marina. Because he was so busy with his work, he asked me to make sure that Marina had everything she wanted while he wasn't around.

"Incidentally, Nikolay, I have good news for you. Over the weekend, I intend to take Marina with me to Vienna. She has been there many times before the war and longs to see it again. She tells me that Vienna is as beautiful as Paris. As a sign of my appreciation for your good services, I will take you with me. I know that you will like it. Don't say a word about this to anyone at our post. As for the major at the command post, we should not have any problem with him. I will take care of him as I have done in the past. You understand, don't you, that all these guys can be bribed. I intend to give him a Doxa watch and some other trinkets. You know, Nikolay, a Russian would be willing to kill his mother for a good watch."

The jeep Smirnov had obtained by bribing the commander was brought to his front door at the appointed time. Marina, who had spent the night there as she had many times before, was dressed elegantly. Except for her shoes, the clothes she wore were clearly of much better quality than any she could have bought with her own money. In fact, I recognized the red silk dress and large-brimmed white hat as having come from one of the suitcases the captain kept in his room. These suitcases contained all sorts of women's clothing, men's suits, fur coats, watches, gold bracelets, necklaces, and other valuables. Smirnov, like some of the other officers I knew, had collected or, to put it more bluntly, stolen these objects—either directly or by taking them away from ordinary soldiers whom they reprimanded for being thieves. The larger booty such as cars, trucks, and art collections plundered by the higher army brass were regularly sent by train to the Soviet Union.

Marina was in excellent humor and obviously thrilled about going to Vienna. We all got into the freshly polished jeep, I, in front with the driver, Smirnov and Marina in the back. After a few glasses of wine, Smirnov asked all of us to join him in singing. In a surprisingly fine baritone voice, he gave us his Russian repertoire with the assistance of the driver, who knew only half the lyrics of every song. Marina and I gave our own performance of whatever Czech songs were familiar to both of us. In addition, Smirnov entertained us with jokes and anecdotes, making all of us hilarious for almost the entire two hours it took us to get to Vienna. I became so caught up in the merrymaking that I completely forgot my recent preoccupations.

Once in Vienna, Smirnov gave me a bundle of Austrian money and told me to pay whatever was necessary to find lodging for all of us while he was sightseeing with Marina. He whispered to me that he didn't want to go to the Russian headquarters with a woman in our company. I was to meet them at six o'clock for dinner.

Vienna, to our surprise, turned out to be in worse condition than both Smirnov and Marina anticipated. The Red army siege of April 1945 had laid waste to large areas and the once-beautiful city was in ruins. More than a month after its liberation, it was still in a state of chaos. The food shortage was so bad that the small amount of produce available was prohibitively expensive, and only the very rich were able to afford any, while many residents were actually starving. There were no restaurants open. In order to get an evening meal, we had to go to a Russian army post, where Smirnov and the driver got some rations while Marina and I waited in the jeep.

We were more fortunate with lodging when I persuaded the owner of a small hotel that wasn't really open for business to let us stay overnight. She was a young, pregnant woman whose husband, though partially disabled, had been drafted into the German army five months earlier. She didn't know whether or not he was actually involved in fighting, or even if he was alive. We all sympathized with her and Smirnov showed his compassion by having me give the young woman the entire bundle of Austrian money.

The next morning, Smirnov gave in to Marina's urging and consented to spend a few more hours driving through Vienna. Notwithstanding their disappointment at finding the city in ruins, Smirnov and Marina were in a cheerful mood and their singing and merrymaking went on for the entire return trip to Trnava.

Chapter 11

A Permanent Furlough

True to his word, about a week later Smirnov took me to see the officer responsible for passing on my furlough. Major Sulima Achmatovich was a very short man of Uzbek extraction. His voice resembled that of a bleating sheep, and he spoke Russian with a heavy accent peculiar to the Samarkand area. The faintest of smiles exposed his pearl-white teeth and his blackened gums; it was as though Nature had not provided him with an upper lip. He greeted us not with a salute, as was customary in the Russian army, but by bowing, seeming even shorter as he stood before the towering Smirnov. He looked like a toy soldier, not a real one who had earned such a high rank.

Major Sulima led us into his office with tiny, quick steps, as if in a hurry to get to the business at hand. His small stature was particularly pronounced when he sat down behind his desk, for one could see only the part of his upper body from which innumerable medals jingled with the slightest movement. The major began our meeting by paying me several compliments. "Nikolay," he said, "Captain Smirnov has told me quite a bit about your good work with the Russian army, and something about your background. I understand that you are a Jew. It is a shame that you had to suffer in Hitler's labor camps, but the brave Russian soldiers took care of that, didn't they? As you know, Nikolay, the bastard blew his brains out and you are now a free man. I want you to know that I too paid the price in fighting the Nazis." The major exposed his left hand and showed me his scarred palm with two missing fingers. "I am, as you may already know, a cavalry man in the great tradition of Mongol horsemen. My forefathers probably fought in the army of Genghis Khan. I should also tell you that one of my sons lost his life and another was heavily wounded fighting the Germans. So you see, we have all suffered.

"Anyhow, I am glad that you became a volunteer in our army. I understand that Captain Smirnov recommends that you be granted a furlough, after which he intends to take you to the Soviet Union, where your talents as a polyglot will be further developed. You should consider your opportunity to go to our country as a special privilege. I see no reason why I shouldn't grant you a furlough. At the suggestion of Captain Smirnov, I will date your leave from June twelfth. Now I must say good-bye to you. I have some business with Captain Smirnov. You can wait for him outside." Major Sulima bowed as he dismissed me. I, too, inadvertently bowed to the major instead of saluting, eliciting a broad smile. I could once more see his entire set of white teeth and his darkened gums.

As I waited for Smirnov, the usual contradictory thoughts ran through my mind, fluctuating between hope and despair. I was at once happy that my furlough was actually being granted and worried about the outcome of my entire scheme. I hoped for the remote possibility that Smirnov was lying about wanting to take me to the Soviet Union and in reality planning to "disappoint" me, not knowing that the very idea of going there made me ill.

Smirnov emerged from the major's office a half hour later. He approached me with a wide grin on his face. "Well, Nikolay, am I or am I not good to you? Who else but Captain Smirnov would be able to swing a furlough to Budapest for you, and then take you to the Soviet Union and send you through school?" Once more I thanked him for his kindness, then followed him to a large hall where Smirnov participated in the interrogation of the "Vlasov deserters."

The hall was filled with officers of all ranks, as well as ordinary soldiers presumably invited as observers. Dispersed in several locations, there were stony-faced guards who stood at continuous attention. The place was totally silent, except for an occasional cough. The atmosphere was ominous; looking at the solemn faces of those in attendance, one had the feeling that something calamitous was about to take place. On a specially constructed stage, five officers sat at a table, Smirnov among them. At a separate, smaller table sat a menacing-looking officer in charge of the proceedings. Facing the two tables was a little stool, more appropriate for a child than for an adult, on which the prisoner was to sit, with a desk on either side occupied by the recording secretaries. At the sound of a gavel struck by the officer in charge, two guards brought in a handcuffed, pale, and bedraggled man and sat him down on the stool. He was wearing a soiled officer's uniform. The epaulets and other insignia were torn off the jacket, making it impossible to establish his rank right away. When he was asked to state his name, he also identified himself as a lieutenant. This was the only time through the entire questioning that his rank was mentioned. He was never referred to by his interrogators as lieutenant, nor was the usual term *tovarishch* (comrade) employed. He was addressed either by his last name or by his first name and patronymic. This was apparently done as a sign of contempt. As far as the Russian army was concerned he was no longer either a *tovarishch* or a lieutenant.

The questioning lasted for about an hour and a half. It was painful for me to watch a man being subjected to such abuse. The lieutenant was accused of being part of the so-called Vlasov conspiracy and for having allowed himself to be captured by the Germans without resistance. Although he hadn't joined the Vlasov contingent that eventually fought on the German side, he was still considered a traitor. According to the officer in charge, the least the lieutenant could have done was to observe Stalin's mandate that no Russian soldier, and particularly no Russian officer, should allow himself to be captured alive by the enemy. The interrogating officers were blatantly cruel and showed no compassion for the wretched man who had spent three long years of torment in German hard-labor camps. The lieutenant tried to justify his actions at the time of his capture, repeatedly assuring his interrogators that he was still a loyal Russian willing to die for his country, but to no avail. Although no sentence was pronounced during the proceedings, it was clear that his guilt was irrevocably decided. I later learned that some of those accused of participating in the Vlasov conspiracy were never sent back to the Soviet Union but were executed following the kind of kangaroo trial I had witnessed.

Though the six days before the start of my furlough seemed long, and were anxiety-ridden, everything looked good for my departure— except for one disastrous incident. Not having to interpret for Smirnov, I was needed only occasionally to help out a few of our staff members when contact was necessary with Czechs or Slovaks in Trnava. Otherwise, I was free most of the time. Marina, who was at loose ends because Smirnov was very busy, invited me to spend some time with her. She, like Smirnov, loved motorcycles and asked me to take her for rides. I had at my disposal a BMW motorcycle that Smirnov had gotten from a fellow captain, who had probably appropriated it from some Slovak. Aside from the fact that I couldn't refuse her even if I wanted to because Smirnov wanted me to accommodate her, I was glad to have her company during those lonely and suspenseful days. I would drive her all over town and to various parks where we sat and talked, or rather, where I listened to Marina's interesting stories of her past activities. She reminisced about her childhood, about her experiences in the Czech underground, and about her former loves. She also spoke about her present happiness with Smirnov and how much she looked forward to accompanying him to the Soviet Union.

Just two days before I was to leave, Marina and I took a walk in the nearby park that the two lovers used to go to after Smirnov's return from work. As we sat on a bench, I noticed Smirnov walking menacingly in our direction. When he got closer, he pulled out his pistol and pointed it at me. Obviously drunk, he raged about my having deceived him. "I know what you're trying to do, you Jew bastard! You're trying to take Marina from me. But before that happens your brains will be blown out! I want to see you later in my office!" Marina was beside herself. She cried, embraced him, and begged him to put the gun away.

Smirnov ordered me to leave. I was petrified; not only would I not get my furlough, but I might very well lose my life, for Smirnov was capable of carrying out his threat, whether personally or by order. There were only two possibilities to hope for—either Smirnov would sober up and realize he had acted foolishly, or Marina would be able to persuade him that he was mistaken in his perception. After hours of agonizing and mourning for my life, I was summoned, not to Smirnov's office, but to his apartment. As I entered, Marina walked toward me with her arms extended as though to embrace me, but I avoided coming close to her. "Come on, Nikolay," she said soothingly, "everything is all right. Victor realizes that he was mistaken about our friendship. You know that he has been working very hard lately, and he was also a bit high. Come on, darling," she said to Smirnov, "make Nikolay feel better."

At Marina's urging, Smirnov approached me and extended his hand, showing a little remorse. "I'm very glad I was mistaken," he said almost inaudibly, "because I was prepared to send you to hell and not on a furlough. You should be grateful for the rest of your life to Marina, who saved you. Anyhow, here are your furlough papers. You have three weeks before we meet in Budapest, where we may spend some time before we depart for the Soviet Union. Before you leave us, I want to give you a few gifts, as well as some spending money." Smirnov pulled out from his suitcase a gold watch and a pair of good-looking leather boots and handed them to me ceremoniously. "There, in case you can't wear them, you can give them to one of your relatives when you find them." He also took out of his large portfolio bundles of mixed paper currencies, among them some five hundred German marks that were of greater value than he may have realized. Finally, he told me I would have to catch a train from Trnava to Bratislava, where I could make a direct connection to Budapest.

The night before my departure, I had the honor of dining at Smirnov's apartment in the company of my savior, Marina, and the pretty secretary whom Smirnov had abandoned in favor of Marina after his one-night courtship. She came with a young officer who had joined our unit just a week earlier. Marina brought along Jera, with whom I had behaved so clumsily at the birthday party, assuring me that Jera herself had asked to come. I had thought about Jera many times, and was eager to see her again and make up for having been so somber at our first meeting. This time in a happy frame of mind I felt at ease with her and, thankfully, did not redden in embarrassment every time she looked at me.

When Zabutsky, our cook and accordionist, started playing dance music, I approached Jera without hesitation. I could tell that she was having a good time simply by looking at her ebullient face. The food and drinks were delicious and abundant, all the more enjoyable since, for a change, I had had nothing to do with their acquisition. Smirnov made sure to tell all of those present about how he intended to take me to the Soviet Union, and about the great opportunities that were waiting for me there. As usual, a great deal of alcohol was consumed. I, too, had a few drinks, partly because the liquor tasted good and partly because everyone urged me to drink at what was billed as my farewell party.

The drinks inspired not only singing but some good-natured teasing, mostly at my expense. We played a game of Spin the Bottle, Smirnov style, in which two kisses were due the winner instead of the customary one. According to Smirnov's dictum, each kiss was to be accompanied by an animated "*Molodyets!*" repeated three times. As fate would have it, I got to kiss Jera on two of my turns. Of course I didn't at all mind kissing her, but would have preferred to do it without so many onlookers and certainly without those prolonged cheers.

The party broke up at about one o'clock, by which time with the exception of Jera and myself there wasn't a sober soul among us. Smirnov was so drunk that Marina had to put him to bed in his clothing, boots and all. Since the driver was also too drunk to take Marina and Jera home, both of them remained in Smirnov's apartment for the night. I said goodnight to everyone. As I was leaving, Jera asked whether I wanted to take a walk before retiring. I accepted the invitation willingly. Once outside, Jera was very demonstrative with me, taking my arm and synchronizing her steps with mine as we walked. She spoke with almost childlike enthusiasm about her future plans. Now that the war was over, she expected to enter the University of Prague and become an elementary-school teacher. She wanted to know more about my family and asked me many questions. Among other things she asked if indeed I intended to go to the Soviet Union. Without waiting for my answer, she told me she didn't think it was a good idea. "Nikolay," she said in her melodious voice "you should remain here. You too should enter the University of Prague and become a linguist. Why would you want to go to the Soviet Union, so far away and where you have no one?" I wished I could tell her how determined I was not to go, or about my plan to escape that fate, but I didn't dare.

Our little promenade lasted for an hour. Encouraged by Jera's charming flirtation and by the surrounding silence of the night, our stroll ended with several kisses that were very different from the ones we exchanged during Spin the Bottle. As we were saying good night, Jera insisted that she wanted to accompany me to the train station the following day.

At noon, I was picked up by the jeep with my few possessions contained in an army knapsack, wearing the better of my two uniforms for the journey. I said good-bye to Zabutsky, who arrived with a package of food rations sufficient for two days. Vanya and a few other people also came to see me off. Smirnov couldn't be there because he was at work, but sent Marina to accompany me to the station. Just as we were about to pull out, Jera appeared. She walked toward us in brisk dancing steps. "Nikolay," she scolded, "you weren't going to leave without me, were you!" As we left the courtyard, I looked at Vanya's sad face and felt sorry for him. I was hoping that the hapless orderly would not continue to be beaten by his heartless taskmaster, Smirnov.

On the way to the station I sat between Marina and Jera who appeared downcast. From time to time she squeezed my hand and looked at me affectionately. At the station we learned that there wasn't going to be a train to Bratislava for the next three hours. Of course the driver couldn't wait all that time. I told Marina I was going to be all right and that both of them should go back with him. Marina accepted my suggestion reluctantly, embraced me, and assured me that we would see each other in Budapest very soon, implying that she was going to the Soviet Union.

Jera refused to return with Marina despite my half-hearted urging. We spent three wonderful hours waiting for the train, time for which I was grateful. However, I got more than I bargained for. At the end of the three hours, an announcement was made that there were no trains going to Bratislava that day. Angry shouts and curses were heard from the few Russian soldiers who were also waiting, and meek moans from some fifty civilians who were hoping to get to the Slovak capital. As much as I wanted to spend more time with Jera, I began to think of an alternate way to get to Bratislava. Outside the station, I saw two Russian soldiers loading sacks of flour onto a truck. When I inquired whether they were going to Bratislava, I found they were going to a military post halfway between Trnava and the capital. I showed them my furlough papers and asked if they would be good enough to give me a ride. The driver saw the **DOBROVOLYETS** that was printed in bold type. "*Dobrovolyets,*" he exclaimed "*Mo-lo-dyets,*" dividing the word of approval into prolonged syllables and told me that he would be glad to give me a ride. "You have ten minutes to say good-bye your pretty *Fräulein.*" Just before I boarded the truck, a few more kisses were added to the ones we had exchanged the night before. I promised Jera that I would write to her and actually did write a letter from Budapest but did not stay there long enough to receive the reply that I am certain came.

My two traveling companions, both in their thirties, were affable fellows. They offered me food, and insisted I take several gulps from the bottle of vodka they shared. I was glad that they didn't use glasses since I could pretend to be drinking more than I actually did. Both of them spoke with great pride about knocking the hell out of the Germans. "We really gave it to them," said the driver. "My toes were blown off my left foot but I don't mind." I am sure that if he had not been in the driver's seat he would have shown me his foot. "We must pay them back for what they did to us," added his companion. "Defeating those Nazi murderers isn't enough punishment for their crimes. We should hang all of them by their balls."

At the small Slovak town where they dropped me off, it took only a few minutes to hitch a ride on a truck that was going to Bratislava. Since there was no room in the cab, I got into the back with three soldiers sitting around a huge barrel of wine. The two younger fellows were drunk. The third, about forty-five years old, appeared sober though he too was holding a canteen. One of the drunken soldiers offered me wine. When I declined, he became angry and started shouting obscenities. "What are you, some kind of stuck-up officer who refuses to drink with ordinary soldiers? You have strange epaulets with nothing on them. Were you debarred or something?"

I pulled out my furlough papers and tried to tell them I was a volunteer and an interpreter for the NKVD. The document was knocked out of my hand and almost flew off the truck. The older soldier tried to intercede on my behalf but the two brutes wouldn't listen. "You bastard," said one of them, pointing his gun at me, "you have a foreign accent. You are probably a spy, and I think we should shoot you like a dog." The threats and the foul cursing went on intermittently for a long time.

Frightened out of my wits, I contemplated jumping off the truck, even though it was going about thirty miles an hour. Fortunately, a soldier in the cab overheard the shouting of the two drunkards and alerted the driver. He pulled over to the side and came to the back to find out what was going on. The sober soldier gave him a brief report. The driver asked to see my papers, which he hadn't bothered to look at when he picked me up. After examining them, he yelled at his drunken comrades, but suggested that I get off anyway because he couldn't be responsible for what they might do to me. "As it is," he said, "you're lucky these idiots didn't pull the trigger on you."

There I was just about half an hour by car from Bratislava with night quickly falling. Since there was no transportation in sight I started walking at a fast pace. Although shaken at first by what had taken place on the truck, I quickly recovered. The fact that I had survived one more threat to my life, and that I was actually on my way to freedom, gave me hope that I would be able to overcome even larger perils. I hadn't walked far before a chauffeur-driven jeep stopped beside me. The major seated inside waved me over and asked me where I was going. He immediately asked to see my papers. After looking them over carefully, he pointed to a spot near him in the back of the jeep with a brusque *"Davay, davay* [Get in, get in]." On the way to Bratislava, I explained my situation to him.

By the time we got to the city, it was completely dark. Since the major thought that it might be too late for me to try to make a train to Budapest, he invited me to spend the night at his headquarters from which I would be driven to the train station the following morning.

On our arrival at the post, the driver was told to take me to the mess hall where I had a good meal, and later to a room where I spent the night with four other soldiers. Before I fell asleep, I thought about the people I left behind in Trnava, about Jera and about the drunken soldiers on the truck who were ready to blow my brains out. I wondered whether other people were as danger-prone as I was.

The next morning I was driven to the train. What was supposed to be a six o'clock train came at eight. The cars were packed with Russian soldiers and even the steps were fully occupied. The only place that still had room was the roof of the train. Since we had no other choice, some of us who had been waiting found places on the top. The engine was pulling such a large number of wagons that the train moved very slowly, posing no danger to the passengers "riding high."

The only constraint on us was that we could not stand up straight when the train was passing through tunnels.

Most of my fellow-passengers were emaciated Jewish men and women, survivors returning from various concentration camps. They sat in little circles and talked about their respective nightmares. I wanted to join those wounded beings who had endured far more than I. Listening to their harrowing stories introduced me to yet another dimension of the Nazis' atrocities. I realized that what I had learned about the Nazi abomination paled in comparison to what these survivors had seen and undergone. It was from the lips of these people that I heard for the first time the vile word "crematorium" and the horrors associated with it.

Those few survivors who still had some strength to move about after many days of this kind of travel, dragged themselves from car top to car top in search of relatives or fellow townsmen. The question, "Where are you coming from, have you come across. . . ?" must have been repeated a hundred times only to be answered by a negative shake of the head. I too made a few inquiries about my family and friends, but with no success.

Chapter 12

The Joy and Grief of Reunion

Normally the trip between Bratislava and Budapest should have taken about three hours. This one took almost seven. When we arrived, it was immediately apparent that much had changed in the five months of my absence. Although a good deal of the rubble in the streets was still there, the city was already bustling with activity. People were getting on and off the streetcars, most of which were restored by now.

I made my way first to the Hajdu apartment, assuming that I could stay with them temporarily. I could have gone to a Russian army post for a few days, but considering that I was determined not to return to my NKVD unit that would have been a foolhardy choice. In fact, my plan was to get out of uniform as soon as possible, start behaving like a civilian, and have no contact with anything or anyone Russian. The only thing I intended to keep until I was sure of my freedom were my furlough papers.

When I got to the apartment, I learned from the new occupants that the Hajdus had moved from Budapest. They couldn't tell me exactly where, but they thought it was to Debrecen, where Mr. Hajdu had gotten a job. I was disappointed, but glad to know they were all right.

My next hope lay with finding my dear friend Imre and his family. I got on a streetcar, praying that the Neimanns had returned and had been able to get their apartment back from the unfriendly occupants who were living there in January. When I rang the doorbell, Imre's mother appeared. She looked at me for a while, scared at first of the Russian uniform. A few seconds passed before she recognized me. "My God," she said in a weak voice. "Micky, Micky, it's you! You're alive!" She embraced me and wept. "I know why you are here. You are here because we prayed for your return every day. You can't imagine how unhappy we were that we had to leave you out in the street. Come sit down and tell me, how did you make it? How did you survive the murderers, and how did you get into this Russky uniform? Oh my God, you must be hungry. Let me give you some food. I expect Imre home any moment now."

I could tell from Mrs. Neimann's face and debilitated voice that hiding from the SS had taken its toll. She had aged dramatically since my escape from Csepel. She was now totally gray, her eyes swollen, and her walk considerably slowed down. I had the impression that she had been crying just before I came. After I told her briefly about my adventures and how I came to join the Russian army, Mrs. Neimann opened her heart to me. I learned that her youngest daughter, a lively dark-haired young woman, had not been able to get out of the ghetto and join the family in hiding. She was most likely taken to Auschwitz, where she must have perished. Mrs. Neimann's recounting of the last time she saw her daughter was interrupted by the arrival of Imre. She wiped her tears and said, "Please, Micky, don't tell Imre that I cried again. He becomes very annoyed with me."

When Imre saw me, he couldn't believe his eyes. We ran toward each other and embraced. Neither of us could say anything for a good while. "Micky, *picy haverom* [my little friend]," he said in a cracked voice. "You see, Mother, I told you he would make it." Imre too wanted to know how I had survived and what I was doing in that "damned Russian uniform with a pistol strapped to your waist." He was abjectly apologetic about not having been able to take me to their hiding place with his family. I assured him once more that I understood there was nothing he could have done about it, and that I was very grateful to him for having engineered our escape.

At dinner, I explained that one of my reasons for coming to Budapest was to start looking for surviving members of my family, and that I hoped there was some way they could help. Mrs. Neimann was able to give me the name and address of a Jewish organization that was involved in such searches, and Imre volunteered to take me there the following morning. As we reminisced about our experiences in Csepel, I asked Imre whether he had any idea about the fate of some of our friends. It was then that he gave me the horrendous news about our unit. He had recently learned that out of some three hundred of our boys only a dozen or so survived after they were taken from Csepel. In fact, just a few days earlier they had a reunion, to which they invited the old Hungarian officer who had tried to protect us from the camp commander. This upsetting news triggered my anxiety about what might have happened to my family, and I was impatient to start my search.

Among many other things, I told Imre of my experiences on the farm, and with the Russians. I also told him about my present predicament and the fact that Smirnov seemed determined to take me to the Soviet Union. Before I had a chance to tell him about my "permanent furlough plan," Imre looked at me in amazement and interrupted. "Dear *picy haverom,* don't tell me you're crazy enough to do such a stupid thing as to actually go to Russia! Are you out of you mind? From what you've told me about your work with the Russians, it appears that you know too much about their operations. I wouldn't be surprised if, once you got to the Soviet Union, they sent you to Siberia. Or even worse, they might simply dispose of you, if you know what I mean. We must do something about this, and soon. You escaped from the Nazis. I think you can get away from the Russians as well. You know you can count on me. We will figure out something."

Imre was ready to disregard the fact that the slightest participation in my escape posed considerable danger to him, should anything go wrong. He led me to one of the closets and pulled out a pair of trousers. "Here," he said, "try these on." Imre was a good bit taller and heavier than I, so when I put on the trousers I looked like someone who had lost a lot of weight. Mrs. Neimann smiled benevolently.

"Micky, my dear," she said, "we will have to fatten you up." "The next thing we must do," Imre said, "is to get you some false papers. You must also get out of Budapest before Smirnov's arrival, if indeed he is going to come. But in any case, if you don't report to the command post at the end of your furlough, you, my dear friend, are a deserter."

It was getting late, and I was totally drained, physically and emotionally. Just as a formality, I asked Mrs. Neimann whether it was all right for me to stay overnight, knowing full well what her answer would be. My question precipitated a feigned angry expression on her face, accompanied by a good whack on my neck with her dish towel, and followed by hearty laughter for the first time during the evening. Mrs. Neimann assured me that I could stay as long as I wished.

To be sure the Neimanns understood that I didn't intend to be a freeloader, I showed Imre my bundle of money. This is when I learned to my pleasant surprise that the German marks were especially valuable. Imre informed me that on the black market my marks were the equivalent of some two hundred American dollars, the American dollar being even then the most prized currency in Europe. I possessed a veritable fortune. Had Smirnov known, he surely would never have given it to me. "Well," said Imre jokingly, "now you can really stay with us as long as you want to."

It was reassuring not to sleep in a place surrounded by Russian soldiers for a change. This was the first time in six months that I didn't experience perpetual fear of Smirnov and everything that went with being in the Russian army. Though I was still worried about the outcome of my desertion and about finding my family, I slept well, comforted by the realization that I was at last on the way to becoming a free person.

After breakfast the next morning, Imre accompanied me to the Erzsébet School where the Jewish organization was quartered. The steps were almost impassable, jammed with men and women circulating in hopes of finding surviving family members. Even for the few who were lucky enough to find a member of the family there was always the awful news of countless losses.

Inside the school, there was a desk where new arrivals registered and were told to wait in case a matching survivor might either arrive or already be somewhere on the steps. We were told to check every hour or so the lists that were posted on a bulletin board. I went to the desk and registered. As far as I could tell from the virtually inaccessible bulletin board, surrounded as it was by crowds of people, neither Harry nor Samuel's nor the names of some forty relatives were listed. I asked Imre to leave me there, saying that I would get back by myself. I gave him the German marks to exchange for dollars as well as for Hungarian currency so we could go shopping for some decent clothing for me.

I returned to the steps and circulated among the people. Finally, I recognized a young man I knew from Mukachevo—Chaim, a cart driver, who when I last saw him about three years earlier was a strong young man with a robust voice. Samuel and I used to transport lumber with him and listen all day long to his jokes. He now looked half his former size and spoke in a thin voice that was barely audible. "Chaim," I said, "how glad I am to see you. How are you?" "Not so well. You know. . ." Just as he was about to continue his sentence, he broke out in a sob. I embraced Chaim's bony frame and held him in my arms till he could talk again. As was almost a given among the few survivors, the list of family casualties was a long one. When Chaim finished his enumeration, I asked him if he knew anything about Samuel. He told me that the last time he saw him was in May of 1944, in the Mukachevo ghetto. But Chaim couldn't tell me anything about other members of my family. Like many of those of whom I inquired, he shook his head sadly to indicate that he had no news for me.

I came home disappointed. Imre and his mother tried to cheer me up—she with a warm motherly embrace and a good meal, and Imre with the bundle of dollars and pengös he had gotten for the German marks. "Micky," he said, "tomorrow we are buying you new clothing. You are going to be so elegant that Smirnov wouldn't recognize you even if you stood in front of him."

I insisted that Mrs. Neimann accept some of the money because I knew the family was in a bad financial state. Though Imre had a job working for a friend of his, he was still not earning enough, given the exorbitantly high food prices in Budapest. Mrs. Neimann protested for a while but acquiesced when I insisted.

The next morning, Imre and I went to the center of town. Although a few clothing stores were already open for business, it was far better to buy at the open market where prices were considerably lower. The market was loaded with men's and women's apparel, new and secondhand, and one could buy directly from individuals who were pressed for money. Selling one's belongings or bartering them for food was one of the ways people survived the deprivations of the war. Among the traders there were also Russian soldiers who, with impunity, were exchanging a variety of stolen items for watches, jewelry, or alcohol. I bought a pair of shoes, some shirts, and an elegant light gray suit of excellent quality that must have been worn only once, the kind that in the past I could only dream about. I could hardly wait to return home and try on my new wardrobe. When I came out of the bedroom, Imre and his mother complimented me profusely. "I was right," said Imre, "you don't have to leave Budapest to avoid Smirnov. He would certainly not recognize you." I too was satisfied with the way I looked. But there was more to my new appearance. Being totally dressed in civilian clothing gave me a sense of freedom, as though I were now ready to resume the life I had lived before the Nazi nightmare.

When I returned to the Erzsébet School to continue my search, I saw many of the same people on the steps. I wondered why they had come back. After all, by now enough time had elapsed since the liberation of Auschwitz and other camps for them to realize that the chances of finding surviving relatives were next to nil. After a few more encounters I understood that they had come there to be among those who could understand what they had been through.

I visited the registration desk once more. This time there were fewer people than the day before. The bulletin board, too, was less crowded, but I still couldn't find any of my family's names on it. Going back to the steps, I saw poor Chaim sitting alone in a corner with his head in his hands, totally forlorn and depressed. "How are you, Chaim?" I said.

"Do you have to ask?" he answered with a faint ironic smile, "What do you think, that between yesterday and today I have forgotten that my family was massacred?" I tried to distract him from his misery. "Melach, my dear friend," he said. "I know that you are trying to make me feel better, but you understand. . ." He couldn't say any more. I wept with him and then sat with him in silence. Finally, he said to me, "Let's meet tomorrow. Perhaps I will be in a better frame of mind." I left him as I had found him, his head buried in his hands.

As I was leaving, a middle-aged woman called my name. It was Dvoyra a friend of my mother who spoke of her affectionately, and remembered her cleverness and humor. Just meeting someone who knew and liked my mother, hearing her memory evoked by someone, reinforced my feeling that she was still with me and a part of my life. Dvoyra brought me the first good news of a family survivor; my aunt Irene, Mother's youngest sister, was alive. Dvoyra had seen her a few days earlier here at the Erzsébet School, and she told me that Irene was in fairly good physical condition by now and intended to return to Mukachevo. Unfortunately, she didn't know where Irene was staying.

Dvoyra herself, like the rest of those congregating on the steps, had her own heart-rending story to tell. She knew for certain that her two sons, as well as many relatives, had died, but she was still hoping that by some miracle her husband was alive. She too was about to return to Mukachevo where they had a small house before the family was deported.

Though I was heartened to learn that at least one member of my family was still living, I was becoming despondent about my lack of success in finding my brothers, or at least somebody who had seen them. I decided to give it one more day at the school before going to Mukachevo to continue my search. As I entered the building, someone tapped me on the shoulder. It was Mottel, a fellow mechanic, whom I knew from trade school. "Is it really you, Jehudah Melach?" he cried. "What are you doing here? Don't you know that your brother Harry is looking for you?" He dragged me toward the steps. "Hurry up!" he shouted. "Let's run, let's run, I just spoke with him." I saw Harry at the base of the steps with a girl I recognized as Lilly, his girlfriend back in Mukachevo, on their way home. I wanted to call after him, but no sound came out of my throat. It was Mottel who managed to get his attention.

Harry stopped to see who was calling, stood frozen for a moment, then broke into a sprint toward us. I ran in his direction, and within seconds we were locked in an embrace. Harry cried out, almost in a tone of reprimand, "Where were you? I have been looking for you for months!" In our exultation at finding each other we sobbed, we laughed, we were silent. Lilly joined us in our embrace and for a long moment we stood together, mute.

Harry burst out with a torrent of questions, hardly giving me the opportunity to answer even one of them. "Where were you? How did you survive? Where are you staying? Why do you look so pale?" We returned to the steps—we seemed to feel intuitively that the steps were the right place to exchange sad stories. There I gave Harry an abbreviated account of my experiences and of my present condition. It was more pressing for me to learn what he knew of the fate of our family.

Foremost on my mind was to find out what had happened to Samuel. "Did he make it?" I asked impatiently. Harry, barely able to contain his composure, after a long pause, told me haltingly that it was pretty certain Samuel had not survived. As he began to give the account of Samuel's murder, I could not cry or speak. I bit my lips and uttered an anguished moan, sounding more like a wounded animal than a human being.

The source of Harry's information was our niece Zlate Raizel, the daughter of our half-sister Sarel. About the time of Mother's death, Samuel and Zlate Raizel had started a boy-girl relationship. Jewish law frowned upon such a relationship, but there were instances of marriage between uncle and niece. Their tender ages, however, made marriage a remote prospect.

In April 1944, immediately after the Passover holidays, all the Jews of Mukachevo were herded into two large ghettos. Because Samuel and Zlate Raizel were living in the same general area, they were taken to the same one. In early May, the Jews of both ghettos were crowded into a brick factory located on the outskirts of Mukachevo and in that same month the transports to concentration camps got underway. The two managed to get on the same car in a cattle train. Throughout the trip Samuel spoke about escaping by some means, of perhaps making his way to the Russian side in order to fight the Nazis and help in the liberation of his fellow Jews. He did not want to go like a lamb to the slaughter. When they were just a few hours away from Auschwitz, he made a final decision to escape. Ignoring the pleas of Zlate Raizel and others in the car, he began to remove the barbed wire from the window with the intention of jumping out at some juncture. He urged his sweetheart to come with him, but she was too afraid. After many apologies for leaving her, his last words were that he would rather die than be a slave to the Germans.

Samuel jumped as they were crossing a river. He succeeded in swimming to shore, but a guard spotted him. It was apparently so important to the Germans to kill one more Jew that the train was stopped and backed up for some distance. A band of soldiers got off and pursued Samuel. Zlate Raizel and a few other witnesses heard shots. Samuel must have been killed on the spot. He never reached his eighteenth birthday.

I have gone over in my mind a thousand times the circumstances of Samuel's death. I have grieved over the fact that he might have survived if he had waited. Strong, resourceful and bold-spirited, he had a chance of withstanding the torments ahead of him. And yet, it was entirely in character that he made the attempt.

Despite the certainty of Samuel's death, Harry and I still hoped that our dear brother had escaped and would somehow appear. However, in time we realized that we hoped in vain. The only thing left for those of us who loved this valiant boy was to continue to mourn him and observe the customary memorial services held each year for the six million who died at the hands of the Nazis.

In answer to my questions, Harry told me of his experiences. I learned that he had spent almost two years of Nazi captivity in the Ukraine. He was primarily engaged in retrieving dead German soldiers for burial, digging trenches for the German and Hungarian armies, and building huge traps equipped with explosives in case of retreat. Harry was luckier than those Jewish boys who were used, at the cost of their lives, to clear mines that had been laid by the Red army.

Digging ditches and carrying huge cement blocks from dawn to dusk without rest and on a starvation diet had debilitated him. In desperation, to get some relief, he jumped from a tree hoping that he would break an arm or a leg. Instead, he got stuck on the lowest branch with no more than a scratch. "Can you imagine such bad luck?" he asked. As a kind of emotional release, we all burst out laughing at this comic episode in an otherwise melancholy story.

In the early fall of 1944, the Nazis were retreating from the Russian front, or rather, running for dear life. But the Germans still found time to carry out their atrocities on innocent Russian and Ukrainian people and burn their homes. Even more important to them was to leave no living Jews in their wake. Harry and a few of his fellow inmates were lucky. In the confusion of the retreat, his detail was left behind with a Hungarian sergeant who was not eager to catch up with his unit. The Jewish men, feeling that they had the upper hand, made a deal with the sergeant. If the Germans returned, their alibi was that they couldn't find their way back.

The Germans did not return. It was at this time that Harry, the sergeant, and the other men deserted from the Germans. The sergeant was smart enough to get civilian clothing and disappear. Harry and the other young men were found by Russian soldiers in a hayloft in a small village in the Carpathian mountains. Frightened by their liberators, they hastened to inform the soldiers that they were Jews from forced-labor camps. Harry kept saying to one of the soldiers, "*Me Yevrey* [We are Jews]."

One of them approached him and said in Yiddish, "Take off those Hungarian army caps before the Russians take you as prisoners of war by mistake." The men were given some food and their freedom.

Harry made his way to Mukachevo to begin his search for family members, and for his sweetheart, Lilly. What he found there were some other young men who, like himself, had been in one of the labor battalions that were now liberated. In November a few more survivors drifted to Mukachevo, each one bringing tales of suffering at the hands of the Germans. Still not aware of the enormous loss of Jewish lives, they were confident that many of their relatives were going to return. Their suffering notwithstanding, they intended to rise out of the ashes and start life anew.

It was not until the first few months of 1945, after the liberation of Auschwitz and other camps, that the colossal extent of the Nazi slaughter began to unfold. Much of that terrible news was brought by the few survivors who continued to straggle back to Mukachevo. The hope that great numbers were going to return was shattered. It was then that Harry learned about Samuel's tragic end and more. On my mother's side, in a family that consisted of at least sixty people, six survived concentration camps. Among the many who perished was my dear Uncle Joseph, who died in the arms of his son Martin on the day of liberation. Martin came home, but died a few years later of tuberculosis.

On my father's side, the massacre was even more thorough. Of my four half-sisters, three half-brothers, and their spouses only one, Jacob Hersh survived. Of the many children that they had among them, two survived—Zlate Raizel, who brought to us the sorrowful news about Samuel, and her brother Moomoo.

Among the dead there was another Zlate Raizel, the daughter of my half-sister Rachel. I had been particularly fond of her. She was about my age and, like her mother, a captivating beauty. When we were still children, Zlate Raizel and her mother often came to our house on Saturdays. Zlate Raizel too loved to dance and was always there when

Brindel gave his dancing lessons. Whenever I didn't dance with my mother, I would run to Zlate Raizel and ask her to dance with me. When Rachel came to visit us during the summer, Zlate Raizel and I used to stroll hand in hand along the banks of the river. We were often teased and told to remember that we were cousins and could not get married. Indeed, such thoughts had crossed my mind because our friendship was not that of an uncle and niece. Zlate Raizel had often, in very shy ways, displayed her affection for me. She was a very bright girl. Had it not been for the Holocaust she would most likely have attended the gymnasium despite the poverty of the family. I was deeply moved by this particular loss and have never stopped thinking of her.

Almost two hours went by and we were still sitting on the steps of the Erzsébet School. The exchange of woes had been mostly between Harry and me. Lilly was sitting between us with an anguished expression waiting for her turn to speak. Once in a while she would nod her head to indicate that she was listening to our accounts, but I had the impression that her thoughts were elsewhere. She was silently counting her own losses which were of staggering proportions.

Lilly told me she had learned from other survivors about the extermination of virtually her entire family. Among those who had perished were her parents, four brothers, aunts, uncles, and a host of others at Auschwitz. The selection process devised by the Nazis as to who was to live and who was to die was simple. Thumbs to the right were given to the young who appeared strong enough to work. The elderly and the children were pointed to the left which meant extermination in the gas chambers. Lilly's parents were sent to the Auschwitz gas chambers almost immediately after their arrival. Lilly did not know how her four brothers met their end.

Besides herself, those of her family who miraculously survived were her older sister, Regina, and her two younger sisters, Helen and Miriam. The four young women were sent to the right and remained in Auschwitz for a few months before being transferred to a labor camp in Wustergiersdorf, not far from Auschwitz, where they worked in factories that produced war materials for the Germans. The sisters were liberated in May of 1945. It took them some three weeks to get to Mukachevo which seemed like a graveyard whose dead were buried or incinerated somewhere else. It was in a way thanks to Lilly that I met Harry in Budapest. At her prompting he left Mukachevo, where he had been prepared to remain. Lilly had visions of a better place to live than our home town which would be a continuous reminder of the Nazi massacre.

As soon as Lilly finished her abbreviated account, the three of us stood up, almost in unison. It was as though we understood that at least for the time being there would be no more talk about Auschwitz or any other place connected with the recent past. We had to leave behind us the steps of the Erzsébet School, where we could dwell only on our tragedies. It was now time to find our way out of the past, to resume life and look to the future.

As we walked out of the schoolyard, Harry announced with great joy that the two had decided to get married. "You came just in time," said Lilly with the smile characteristic only of a bride-to-be. "The wedding will be next week."

"The plan is," broke in Harry, "after we get married, to make our way to Israel or to America, the *goldene medina* [the golden land]." He added jokingly, "You know that in America the streets are paved with gold."

Harry told me that they were staying in a kibbutz on Aréna Street that was supported by the Jewish Committee for Relief Abroad. In a few weeks they would be smuggled to the West by the Berihah. This was an organization consisting mostly of former Israeli soldiers whose underground mission was to get Jewish survivors out of Eastern Europe by illegal border crossings. Their first destination was Austria where displaced persons camps were set up to receive them. Once there, they would decide their next step. Harry urged me to move into the kibbutz with them. Although the kibbutz and the Berihah people would encourage us to go to Palestine, they were willing to accommodate anyone who wanted to get away from the scene of Nazi terror.

Finding Harry and Lilly, and learning about their coming marriage was uplifting. Their union would begin the rebuilding of two families that were nearly wiped out. We could turn away from death and take up the threads of life once more. Also, joining them in their exodus from Eastern Europe was a solution to my agonizing concern as a deserter. Before I found Harry, I did not have a clear idea of what I was going to do once my furlough was officially over—I only knew that remaining in Budapest or living any place in Eastern Europe under Russian occupation was risky. Getting to Israel or to the *goldene medina* was more than a means of escaping from the Russians. It also meant that there was a new beginning, a new life for me on the horizon.

The preparations for the wedding were filled with joyous anticipation. There was, nevertheless, an underlying melancholy; we all knew that had it not been for Hitler's devastation this would have been a very different celebration. At least during the wedding everyone refrained from making reference to the recent past. It was as though we had all agreed that looking back was not permitted. Even the rabbi, in his speech, observed this temporary covenant.

The list of invited guests was very short—a few of Harry's and Lilly's friends, Lilly's three sisters, and the members of the kibbutz living in the same building with the future couple. Lilly looked radiant in her borrowed white wedding dress. Harry, on the other hand, appeared pale and nervous. When the rabbi pronounced them man and wife, it took Harry three attempts to break the glass that according to Jewish superstition is supposed to turn evil spirits away from the happy event.

Once the solemn ceremony ended, the large dining room of the kibbutz was suddenly filled with shouts of "*mazel tov* [good luck]" and "*siman tov* [good omen]." The meal consisted of a few hors d'oeuvres. Afterwards, we sang, standing around an old upright, to the accompaniment of a gifted concert pianist, another Holocaust survivor whose professional career had been interrupted by the Nazis. When the meal was over, we danced to the music of the kibbutz band. The floor of the dining room must have been really strong to support the strain of the stamping feet moving with rapid steps. We danced the horah, the Russian two-step, the kozachok, and the Hungarian czardas. During the five hours of merrymaking there were no despondent faces to be seen. The joyous occasion allowed us a rare opportunity to lapse into a brief period of forgetfulness.

We had about two weeks before being taken across the Austrian border. I was now more confident that my escape from the Russian army was not going to pose any serious problems. Moving into the kibbutz, even if it was only for a short time, gave me a feeling of safety as well as a sense of belonging. The fact that the kibbutz consisted almost exclusively of young people as well as a few children who had been in hiding gave the place an atmosphere of hope. The cultural life, too, played an important part in having the feeling that one was indeed embarking on a new life. There were nightly programs which included lectures on life in Israel, Hebrew lessons, music lessons for a variety of instruments, and group singing every night before retiring.

During our stay, preparations were made for our eventual departure for Austria. We had to secure false papers that would give each one of us identities as Austrian Jews who were returning to their homeland. At the border crossing, these documents would be shown to the Russians, who often had to be bribed whether or not the papers presented to them were legitimate. Although there was always some danger involved in these operations, the procedure had apparently been well tested with earlier groups.

The day before we were to leave Budapest, I went to say good-bye to my dear Neimann family, whom I had visited regularly during my stay in the kibbutz. They had mixed feelings about my leaving them for good. Mrs. Neimann was particularly concerned about my safety with respect to the Russians. She embraced me for the last time, and kept repeating, "Micky, my dear, I'm so happy for you. I'm sure now that the Russkies will not get you." She added, "If only I were younger, I, too, would try to get out of this place which will always remind me of the loss of my dear child and my family. " Imre too embraced me and expressed optimism about my future. I was deeply moved by the separation from these two people who had been so good to me and who had played a part in my survival.

My group consisted of some thirty-five people, among them Harry, Lilly, her sisters, the concert pianist, and a couple who had two children. Our first stop was going to be a Hungarian town called Szombathely, located on the Austro-Hungarian border. The night before our departure, the director of the kibbutz made an inspiring farewell speech that was filled with optimism concerning our fate. As we were given our forged papers, we were told to either hide or destroy any documents that could give away our real identity should problems develop. I burned a few of my papers, including the furlough

Rehearsal of a dance choreographed by Jay Sommer for the Purim festival play at the DP camp in Cremona.

document. Harry tore up his marriage license, among other items, leaving himself with just the minimum identification that might be necessary for future occasions. The last evening, like all the previous ones, ended in singing the *"Hatikva,"* the Zionist anthem of hope. Inspired as I was by the director's speech and by the anthem we sang, I nevertheless felt tense. From time to time, it struck me that crossing a border guarded by Russian soldiers was like walking into a trap.

The next morning, two Berihah guides took us to the Keleti train station and we left for Szombathely. We had to spend a week there before the time was right for making the crossing to Austria. While we waited, we rehearsed how to behave at the checkpoint. Because the Berihah people knew about my deserter status, I was warned that under no circumstances should I open my mouth. Every one of us was told to memorize our new identities and know every detail of our documents. It was obvious from this thorough preparation that these Berihah fellows were experienced and well prepared. They knew exactly on what day, at what time, and at which checkpoint the crossing was safest.

The appointed time was Sunday at noon. This, we were told, was the best day and the best hour because at most checkpoints single guards were posted, making bribery easier should it become necessary. As we approached the crossing gate, the guard raised a little red flag and yelled out *"Stoy* [Stop]!"* As much as we were assured by our guides that everything was going to be all right, that loud *"Stoy"* produced many pale faces and eyes that revealed fear. I felt my heart beating at a faster pace as well.

Our guide, who spoke Russian fluently, produced an envelope in which our documents were stored and said to the guard in a confident voice, *"Eto grupa austritzkich Yevreyev vozvrachayuchiyesa domoy iz concentracionovo lagera* [This is a group of Austrian Jews returning home from concentration camp]." The guard led our guide to a small hut a few meters from the barrier at which we were all lined up. Within minutes, the Russian soldier and the Israeli returned. The guard raised the pole and waved us on with a loud *"Davai Yevreyi* [Let's go, Jews]."

As we walked quietly toward the Austrian side, I saw the expressions of apprehension on the faces of my companions turning into silent elation. Once we were well into Austrian territory, we were met by two members of the Berihah driving trucks that were to take us to a displaced persons camp in Judenburg. Only when all of us were already on the trucks, was there an outburst of *"Mazel tovs."* I felt as though a nightmare of many months had finally ended. Harry told me in a whisper how much he had worried and prayed for my safe crossing, and then joked, "You know these Russkies might have been pretty annoyed with a Jew who is taking a permanent furlough from their army." As the guide who had negotiated our crossing was taking his leave to return to Szombathely, he said with a smile to all of us, "You see what miracles can be produced with the help of a gold watch."

Jay Sommer with his pupils in front of the schoolhouse that he helped to renovate.

Chapter 13

Refugee Life

Judenburg, meaning "Jewish town," is situated in South Central Austria, a very short distance from Graz. The small Jewish population, dating back to the eleventh century, had been subjected to repeated anti-Semitic attacks, culminating in complete expulsion in 1496. It was not until the second half of the nineteenth century that any Jews returned to Judenburg, and only about sixteen Jewish families were living there when Hitler occupied Austria in 1938. Most of these left for Vienna, hoping to become part of a larger Jewish community that would protect them from the Nazi onslaught. But, as we learned at the end of the war, the move did not help. They, with the rest of the Austrian Jews, were rounded up and sent to concentration camps from which only a few returned.

The displaced persons camp established by the Allies in Judenburg in 1945 for Jewish refugees, mostly from Eastern Europe, represented yet another return of Jews to Judenburg, not as permanent settlers but as transients who were hoping for a quick departure.

On our arrival, we were received by a camp committee consisting of several different Zionist groups and kibbutzim. Each of us was given a mess kit, a wood-framed canvas army cot which we had to assemble, bedding, and a blanket. Our sleeping quarters were crowded, a far cry from what we had in Budapest. Some seventy people were placed in one large room with a passageway in the middle and only a little space between cots. All of us had to stay within the same four dreary walls, and there were no separate quarters for married couples, or for the few families with children. One distinction was made; single men and women had to be located on opposite sides of the aisle. This one-room arrangement was particularly difficult for the women, since they had no privacy. The only thing that might provide some cover or separation between cots was rigging curtains made out of blankets, if one could afford to buy them.

Despite the hardships we had to face in Judenburg, being there represented the first step on the road to our desired destinations. The thought that we had managed to free ourselves from the Russians and make a successful crossing into an American-controlled area gave most of us hope that similar good fortune would come our way. Notwithstanding the substandard accommodations, Judenburg was not a gloomy place. The Zionist leadership and the Jewish agency already in place on our arrival provided the camp with an atmosphere of optimism.

"You are the pioneers," we were told, "who will build a Jewish homeland for yourselves and for other survivors of the Holocaust."

There was a program for every night of the week. Just as in Budapest, here too classes were offered in Hebrew, music, and Jewish literature. All these activities, for which most of us were hungry, served as a distraction in addition to being of educational value. They helped us to forget for a while that we were still far from any place that we could call our home.

Within a week of our arrival I had the opportunity to take part in a variety show. My performance consisted of a song and dance duet, and a mimicry routine of British speech. I did not know English, except for a few isolated words. My imitation was inspired by listening to our aging British camp commander, whose speech sounded to me as though he were rolling a hazel nut between his soft palate and tongue. My imitation must have been fairly good, since the commander actually believed that I spoke English. At the end of the program he came over to me and made some comments that I took to be compliments on my performance. What saved me from utter embarrassment was my knowledge of "thank you," which I repeated several times till the commander left me.

I did the dance duet with a beautiful eighteen-year-old Romanian girl whose Hebrew name was Shoshana, meaning "rose." Shoshana had lost both her parents and many other relatives in the Holocaust, but she herself had been saved by a brave Christian family that kept her hidden from the Nazis. After liberation, a surviving aunt adopted her and the two of them came together to Judenburg. They had decided to go to Israel, where Shoshana intended to train for an acting career.

Besides an ebullient personality, Shoshana had a sonorous voice and was an excellent dancer. Our performance was a success. At the cast party after the show, Shoshana was showered with compliments and surrounded by handsome young men who were eager to keep her company. Nevertheless she chose to stay with me for the entire evening. We talked about our experiences during the Holocaust, and our aspirations. I returned to my room believing that she liked me and that we were going to be special friends.

When we met in the mess hall the next day, Shoshana invited me to accompany her to town after lunch. When I mustered enough courage to ask her for a date, she eagerly accepted. On that evening during Hebrew dancing I was the envy of many young men. We continued to see each other frequently, and everything seemed to be going well. Shoshana gave me the impression that our friendship was going to lead to the romance for which I had been yearning. A long time had passed since my puppy love with Lilly and my short friendship with Jera in Bratislava. I was now a young man ready to enter into a more mature relationship. For some three weeks Shoshana and I were inseparable. I was happy, never suspecting that my days were numbered and that my dear friend would soon look for new romantic adventures.

Shoshana's affection for me began to fade with the arrival of a new transport of fifty people from Eastern Europe, among them a fellow-Romanian who caught her fancy. For about a week she floated between handsome Leonica and me. Shoshana's inclination to spend time with Leonica combined with my jealousy to bring about our breakup. It caused me suffering, particularly when I saw the two of them together. But my misery was lessened by the fact that the Romanian's tenure with my flirtatious Shoshana was even shorter than mine. He lasted fewer than ten days. Leonica was succeeded by a Hungarian whose fate I did not even follow—by then I had virtually recovered from being jilted and did not believe that our short-lived romance merited a longer period of grieving. I bore Shoshana no ill feeling. I was in fact grateful for the good times we had spent together, since they had diverted my mind from refugee camp living.

Toward the beginning of September 1945, after some six weeks in Judenburg, we were informed that preparations were being made for about sixty of us to go to Italy within a few days. Though we would not need false identification papers as we had when we were fleeing from the Russians, there was still danger in crossing without legal documents, and we had to be careful not to be caught. Although the Berihah and the Jewish Agency had arranged with Italy for the entry of refugees, there was opposition from several countries to this essentially illegal exodus.

The British, in particular, who were in control of Palestine at that time, were against the Berihah's plan to bring Jews to Italy, since it was the jumping-off point from which entry into Palestine was constantly attempted and often successful. For a time, even the United States was against sending displaced persons to Italy or to Austria. And certainly, very little sympathy could be expected from the Austrians themselves, who just months before had been actively involved in the slaughter of Jews. Austria did in fact pose the greatest obstacle to our getting to Italy and was the most to be feared.

Given the fact that no one else really cared about what was going to happen to the few surviving Jews, our fate largely depended on the efficiency of our own organizations. Everything had to be well planned. Failure to get to the Italian side could spell disaster, since returning to Judenburg was out of the question. In fact, as we were about to leave the camp, a group was already waiting to occupy the room we had just vacated. Should we be caught, God only knew where the Austrians would send us. It was even possible that, if we failed in our attempt to cross the border, the Austrians might return us to the Russian zone.

We were driven in two trucks, and it was already dark when we arrived in the outskirts of Innsbruck. From there we walked in silence to the Brenner Pass, where we waited till midnight to begin the actual crossing. This time there were several children with us. They were wrapped in blankets and carried alternately by different adults, who would have to quiet them down should they begin to cry.

Fortunately it was a balmy fall night. There was enough moonlight for us to see the steep serpentine descent of one of the side passes of the Brenner, and the foliage was still thick enough for us to be hidden from the scattered Austrian guards. As much as we were assured by our guides that everything was going to be all right, one could see fear sitting on many faces. I too experienced intermittent anxiety, because the possibility of falling into Russian hands was always there. Despite my worries, however, I could not help but be moved by the imposing beauty of the Alps that seemed to reach into the heavens.

The descent was particularly difficult for some of the older people in our group. One could often hear moans and expressions of regret for having embarked on this difficult journey.

"*Ver hot dos gedarft hobben* [Who needed this]?" complained an elderly, dehydrated woman.

Because we had to stop so often to rest, our trek took about six hours. On the Italian side we were met by a new set of Berihah guides. They greeted us with many "*Mazel tovs.*" There were also several *carabinieri* (Italian border guards), whose presence at first gave us some pause, but we soon realized that there was nothing to worry about. Indeed, they were cordial as they led us to a guardhouse.

"*Acqua, acqua,*" proclaimed one young Italian carabiniero as he handed out glasses of delicious alpine water to our very thirsty group. This was probably the first time in a long while that a person in a uniform showed kindness to any of us. After a brief rest, we were taken by truck to the Udine railroad station. Here, too, the carabinieri displayed their eagerness to help the exhausted *profughi* (refugees), finding us a place to have breakfast before we boarded a train on our way to Cremona, the city of the famous violin master Stradivarius.

The Italian train bore no resemblance to those that had carried so many of us to concentration camps. Here we were treated to a separate car with windows through which we could see the beautiful Italian sky and picturesque landscape. Despite our exhaustion from the difficult crossing, the mood on the train was light-hearted. The young men and women sang Hebrew songs while the more tired older folk caught up with a lost night of sleep. "*Artza Aleinoo,*" a very happy Hebrew song whose few short lyrics tell about having come to Israel to plant and to harvest, was sung over and over again, each time with greater animation.

I could not share the mood of my fellow passengers and did not join them in singing. Perhaps it was because I could not identify with their dreams of being in Israel "to plant and to harvest." Instead, I walked into the corridor, where I leaned out through the open window and was fascinated by the panoramic view of the Italian countryside. Smelling the fresh fall air, I had the impression that this side of the

Alps was no longer polluted by Hitler's carnage. I enjoyed a sense of freedom that I had not felt for a long time. Almost throughout the entire trip from Udine to Cremona, I could see the Alps appear and disappear from view as though playing hide and seek. In that bucolic setting, cheerful and gloomy memories intermingled freely as though they naturally belonged together. I recalled my little village of Kustanovice, my childhood roaming the fields and playing happily with Mother. I thought of my poor mother's difficult life and death, of Samuel's tragic fate, and of the rest of my family that perished in the Holocaust. My musing was interrupted by a friendly *"Buon giorno"* from the conductor as he passed me. Preceded by the kindliest of smiles, he uttered several more Italian words that I did not understand, but which nevertheless gave me a sense of the beauty of the Italian language.

The Displaced Persons camp to which we were taken was one of many being established by UNRRA (United Nations Relief and Rehabilitation Administration), set up in 1943 for this specific purpose. The Cremona camp was located in what was once an Italian *caserma* (army barracks). It had been opened for refugees just a few weeks before our arrival, and the accommodations were just as undesirable as in Judenburg. Here, too, married and unmarried people were thrown together in one poorly lit room with virtually no privacy for anyone. But there was the difference that with more blankets available, we were all able to create separations between the beds.

The camp held about five to six hundred refugees. These were Jews from a variety of Eastern European countries and of diverse cultural and religious practices, running the gamut from Orthodox Jewry to secular nonbelievers, and a few who identified more with their national culture than with Jewish life. Some fifty of the camp's inhabitants, particularly those from Poland and Russia, were former partisans, among them a few women, who had managed to escape from German captivity. Some of them had fought their way out of ghettos and joined the underground which operated from hiding places in the forest. Most of their activities entailed raids against the Germans—blowing up trains that carried supplies and soldiers to the Russian front. These partisans were a new breed of Jews who radiated a sense of pride. They saw themselves as the future soldiers of the Hagana (precursor of the regular Israeli army), eager to fight for a country of their own.

Some of these former partisans inspired courage in future immigrants to Israel. But they also displayed behavior that reflected their former crude existence in the woods, making it difficult to live under the same roof with them. Their belligerent attitude toward those who were not of their caste created discord in the camp. Notorious for his coarseness was a thirty-year-old fellow who was known by his nickname, "Soldat" (soldier). Soldat billed himself as the leader of a small gang of former partisans who had fought with him in a Polish forest. He was a robust man with an angry face that looked as though he had trained it for such a pose. Hidden behind that angry face was actually a mild-tempered man. His soft manner was most apparent in the company of children, for whom he displayed a natural affection. From time to time, though, Soldat and his comrades would roam about camp and provoke fist-fights. It was as if these men suffered occasional attacks of hostility that they could not control. With the passage of time, however, Soldat and his disciples modified their behavior and learned how to live with their fellow Jews, seeming to have regained the part of their humanity that they must have lost fighting for their survival in the woods.

There was of course some discord between the various religious and nonreligious factions as well as between different nationalities, and many vociferous debates took place. The orthodox Jews referred to the rest of the survivors as renegades, *goyim* (Gentiles), suggesting that they should return to God, to *Yiddishkeit* (the Jewish way of life). The "renegades" called the observant ones fools for continuing to believe in a God that permitted the annihilation of millions of Jews.

Despite these polemics between the various believers and nonbelievers, there soon emerged in the Cremona camp a sense of community among them. Their common history of persecution, their recent tragedy at the hand of the same oppressor, and their hope of finding a safe haven united them all into a strange yet cohesive amalgam. This was most apparent during the High Holy Days, considered the most sacred in the Jewish calendar. On the eve of Rosh Hashanah, the men, women, and few children survivors made their way to a hall that was temporarily converted into a synagogue. As had always been the custom among Jews, they wished each other a healthy and a happy

New Year. The hall was filled to capacity, and the divergent loud opinions on politics and theology were laid aside, at least temporarily. The so-called Jewish *goyim* and the observant Jews were ready to pray together. Soldat, who by now preferred to be called by his Jewish name, Shimin, was also there with his followers. They looked repentant, as did the rest of the congregants. The single Torah that had been miraculously saved from Nazi defilement was pulled out of its makeshift ark. Once the cantor began the plaintive chanting of the evening's prayer, a spiritual silence pervaded that sanctuary, merging the entire congregation into one praying body.

The High Holy Days, in addition to their usual solemnity, were also permeated with intense sadness. For the vast majority of the refugees, this was the first time since the Holocaust that we were permitted to come together in a synagogue, makeshift though it was. Traditionally, families would be together there, but for us that was no longer possible. In the entire camp there was not one complete family. There were only fragments—a surviving mother who had miraculously saved herself and one of her children; a widower with two surviving boys; two brothers, as was the case in my family; a few cousins; or sole survivors from large families. It was on Yom Kippur, the Day of Atonement, that we were most poignantly reminded of our losses. On this day there is a special prayer called *"Yizkor."* *Yizkor*, meaning "remember," is recited in memory of the dead. Some of us wept audibly, others in silence, while we listened to the cantor's mournful chanting.

Despite the attendant sadness of the High Holy Days, the New Year brought with it a sense of hope, reflected, among other things, in the many marriages that took place. These marriages, along with births from earlier unions, gave one a sense of normalcy. My small family too was among those who were soon to experience the joy of a new Jewish life. My sister-in-law Lilly was pregnant, expecting to give birth some time in September.

Inspired perhaps by the New Year, a number of initiatives were undertaken by the Maskeeroot, our camp governing body. For one, they organized peaceful protests, demanding that UNRRA improve our living conditions. Also on the list of priorities was the need to engage as many as possible in some kind of work. Perhaps the most damaging aspect of D.P. camp life was the fact that several hundred people with a variety of skills were wandering about aimlessly without being productive. Before our petition for work, only a handful of people were employed, most of them in the kitchen. Within a few months, paying jobs were available in several other areas—office work, unloading incoming food supplies, and keeping the camp in good repair. As one of the lucky beneficiaries of this program, I landed work in the warehouse distributing dry rations to fellow campers. An infirmary was opened, which employed two full-time Jewish nurses from our ranks and an Italian doctor who visited the camp once a week. There was even in our midst an excellent dentist, who was very happy to return to his profession after several years of confinement in concentration camps, even though he had to begin his practice with a very limited set of tools and without a dentist's chair.

These improvements were welcome and made a difference in our daily lives. But the most significant change in Cremona came with the arrival of ORT. ORT—Organization for Rehabilitation and Training—was, and still is, a Jewish organization that had its start in Russia in 1880. The original Russian name translates as "The Society for Manual and Agricultural Workers Among Jews." It was founded by two Russian Jews, Poliakov and Zak, who successfully petitioned Czar Alexander II for permission to form the organization and to raise funds on its behalf. Enough money was donated to help needy Jews to

The ORT building in Cremona where D.P.s were trained for trades that enabled them to find jobs in their new countries.

Jay with his students doing gymnastic exercises.

acquire land and to teach them agricultural and vocational skills. Till about 1920, ORT operated mainly in Russia. Then it spread to other European countries and eventually to other continents. During my stay in Cremona, the United States and Canada were ORT'S most generous supporters. By the end of 1946, virtually every refugee camp in Italy, in Austria, and in Germany had an ORT setup with a variety of programs.

Our good fortune with ORT started in the spring of 1946, when about a dozen men and three women arrived in Cremona. Before the war, these people had been mechanics, electricians, tool makers, welders, and instructors in the operation of various types of sewing machines. Now ORT had given them extensive training in teaching vocational skills. The group was accompanied by two supervisors who began organizing the various shops, and about a half dozen of our own experts in various vocational areas were hired to join the ORT contingent. Several truckloads of machinery, some old and some new, were brought in. The camp was filled with excitement. A number of our men volunteered to help unload the trucks while others cheered as the different machines were carefully lifted off. There were drill presses, lathes, Singer sewing machines, carpenters' workbenches, lumber, blackboards, and many other items necessary to set up the shops and start instruction. A former basketball court was converted into a huge workplace with different vocational divisions. A camp meeting was called where the ORT offerings were presented and registration forms distributed. I signed up for the auto shop, eager to put on once more the mechanic's overalls that had always made me so proud.

No special encouragement or incentives were necessary for the eager applicants. The number of prospective students was so large that an adjacent tent had to be erected to accommodate all of them. The greatest enthusiasm for participating in the ORT program was displayed by those who before the war had been engaged in the very trades that were now being offered in Cremona. To be using their special skills again, even in a limited way, must have given them the feeling that they might soon return to a normal existence. Within a week the instruction began. The whirring of the sewing machines, operated mostly by young women, the hissing of the welding guns, the squeaking of the lathes, and the robust voices of the instructors filled us with aspiration, with a strong sense of usefulness.

Much was accomplished by ORT's presence, but much remained to be done. Ever since our arrival in Cremona, repeated attempts had been made by the camp's leadership to persuade the UNRRA people to organize a school for our fifty or so children. Although a Hebrew class was given at night, it was geared to adults and older teenagers. Our younger kids had been deprived of formal education. It was a question of converting some unused facilities to classrooms and budgeting a relatively small amount of money for books and other supplies. We had in our midst a sufficient number of former teachers who were willing to work without pay if necessary. There were in fact several rooms within one of the courtyards that would have been ideal for classrooms, but they were in very bad shape. In one case an entire wall was missing. Despite the fact that there were many eager craftsmen in camp who were willing to make the repairs, without money for materials they could not do it.

Irate parents, joined by other campers, organized a protest. They marched in front of the commander's office demanding that a school for the children be funded. I joined the protesters on impulse, but what followed turned out to be significant. Through my participation in the fight for a school, I discovered that being in the company of children had a special meaning for me. While the battle was still going on, I was moved to spend much of my free time with the little wanderers of the camp. I would gather them around me on a small playing field next to the ORT shop. Having had no formal education beyond fourth grade, I could not teach them subjects that should have been part of their early education. Instead, I resorted to telling them stories, teaching them songs, and playing athletic games with them. Soon our meetings grew into a daily affair. If by nine o'clock in the morning, come rain or come shine, I was not at our usual spot, my faithful friends came to my room to get me. Spending time with these young souls, miraculously saved from Hitler's henchmen, gave me a justification for being in the refugee camp, a raison d'être. I was happy in the company of these children. Somehow, life appeared much simpler in their midst than it was among adults. During the time that we sang and played, I learned many things. Most significantly, I discovered that children were prepared to give an abundance of love for a small return. It was surely as a consequence of getting involved with those kids that I was later drawn to the teaching profession.

It took about a month before our protest came to fruition. A budget was granted for teaching materials as well as for a small remuneration for teachers. Cement, lumber, and huge cans of paint were brought into the courtyard where the school was to be lodged. The work began. It was a delight to see the eagerness with which men and women set out to convert a ramshackle area into three attractive classrooms. In addition, one hitherto uninhabitable large room on the top floor was fixed up and made into a dormitory for the teenage girls.

A committee was formed, a kind of board of education that was to participate in the formation of a curriculum and the selection of teachers. Naturally, this process proved to be controversial, and resulted in a few debates. The handful of Orthodox Jews wanted their religious orientation included in the curriculum, whereas the more secular Jews—that is, those with Zionist leanings—insisted on the teaching of universal subjects such as science, math, and, of course, Hebrew, but not for strictly religious purposes. The disputes were settled. The majority won out. The school was formed along the lines of the secular education that existed at the time in Palestine or in non-religious kibbutzim. Of the half-dozen teachers, only one was of an Orthodox bent. He taught the Bible and traditional religious practices.

At the opening ceremony, I was praised for participating in the battle for the school as well as for having spent time with the children. But the real reward came when the head of the committee announced that I was going to be part of the staff, teaching gymnastics and supervising social events for the children. I was delighted and very proud of my new position, glad to give up my job in the warehouse.

The fact that we now had a school, combined with the other improvements, made life in camp less somber and more livable. Except for our accommodations and communal kitchen, Cremona was in some ways a microcosm of the ghetto life of Eastern Europe, with people becoming involved in all sorts of entrepreneurial activities in order to make life more bearable. For example, several managed to make contact with relatives in America and other places. As a consequence, they received packages containing items they could sell at a good profit to other Jews and to Italians in the town. Those who did not have connections with the West found other means of doing business. The most lucrative investment, although somewhat risky, was to negotiate an illegal crossing into Innsbruck, Austria, and buy cigarettes from the American GIs stationed there. Cigarettes, and a few other desirable items that one could acquire in Austria, if successfully brought to Italy, were sold at very high profits. There were in Cremona some two dozen men who engaged in this particular business on a steady basis.

The spirits of the young people in camp were further lifted when a number of athletic clubs were formed, among them a soccer team of which I became part. Soccer had always been for me not only a source of enjoyment, but an important distraction in time of trouble. As a teenager I often dreamed of becoming a professional player as a way out of poverty.

Chapter 14

A Near-fatal Accident

Two of my teammates had actually been professional players before they were taken to concentration camps. One of these fellows, Leo Kaganovich, played for a first division Russian team in Odessa before more than half of its large Jewish population was murdered by the Nazis. He and a former Romanian pro became our co-captains and coaches. Our British camp commander, himself an aficionado, took great interest in the formation of the team. He provided us with soccer boots and other necessary equipment. The Sports Club of Cremona generously offered us its stadium facilities and made us feel welcome.

Our coaches were demanding. They worked us hard, and we quickly became good enough to compete with Italian teams playing in the third division. Soon the camp commander arranged for us to play against neighboring towns, including several matches in Milan. We did very well in all of our competitions, and earned enough respect that we were invited to play friendly games against the second-division Cremona club. Our success also brought us the admiration of fellow campers, who became our fans and followed us to different playing locations. I immersed myself in the game, trained hard, and was rewarded with a permanent position as the team's undisputed center forward, or "striker." I became popular in camp and had a few of my own fans who frequently shouted from the stands during the games, "Micky, Micky." When I scored a goal, the shouting became louder and more prolonged. I was happy. Playing soccer again made me feel as though life were indeed beginning to run on a normal course.

While basking in my success, I never suspected that this sport I loved might accomplish what Hitler's persecution had failed to do. One Friday our team received a last-minute invitation to play the local club in preparation for their Sunday match. Given the generosity of the Cremona club, our coaches were happy to accept, and I, still hoping to be discovered as a future soccer star, was excited at the chance to compete against the team whose faithful fan I had become. Our supporters arrived in full force, including my brother Harry, who came to almost every game and took great delight in my success. Before the game, I even had a chance to chat with a few of my idols on the Cremona team.

After a short workout the game began. We did so well that at the end of the first half we were behind by only two goals—already a victory against a formidable team that was not about to show us any mercy—and we felt quite confident that we would at least not be trounced. About midway through the second half, with the score still the same, we were on the attack. Our right wing centered the ball. As I jumped high in the air to head the ball, one of the defenders, also in the air to head the ball, collided with me, hitting me with his knee in the lower part of my abdomen. I still managed to head the ball and almost scored a goal. When I fell to the ground, I felt severe pain but managed to walk off the field unaided. No one suspected that I was severely injured. The pain subsided for a few minutes, but just as I was about to enter the playing field the pain returned, and I had to remain on the sidelines till the game was over.

I walked the three miles back to camp with Harry and a few of my friends, stopping to get a haircut. By the time we got home, the cramps had become unbearable and I began to throw up as well. During the hour it took for an ambulance to get there, Harry stayed at my side trying to comfort me.

In the emergency room of the Ospedale Maggiore of Cremona I was diagnosed as having a ruptured intestine. After a more careful examination, Dr. Grignani gave Harry the bad news. It was his opinion that, because of so much activity after the injury and the spillage of intestinal contents, an operation held out little hope for my survival. I would undoubtedly develop peritonitis, an infection that was almost certainly fatal in those days. But Harry's pleading, combined with Dr. Grignani's compassion, did result in an operation. I remember distinctly the moment in the operating room when I was about to be given ether. Any release from the horrendous pain I had suffered from the time of my injury was a gift from God.

As the doctor anticipated, I developed peritonitis and was sure to die, barring a miracle. News of my condition spread throughout the camp and people gathered to pray for me. Among them was Soldat, the former partisan with a few followers who believed that prayer should be accompanied by action. Under his leadership, some hundred people stormed the office of the camp commander and demanded that a specialist be brought to examine me. They made it clear that they wouldn't leave the office till everything was done to try to save my life. "Enough Jews have already died!" shouted my fellow refugees.

The camp commander must have realized that these people meant business. He got on the phone and contacted UNRRA as well as the Jewish Agency in Milan. Within a few hours, the people were told that a specialist had been secured. It was Dr. Castiglioni of Milan, one of the best-known doctors in Italy who, years before, had been called in to operate on King Victor Emmanuel III. Dr. Castiglioni demanded that UNRRA provide him not only with transportation, but with security guards, because during the war he had been abducted by a resistance group in order to treat one of their wounded men.

Milan is eighty kilometers from Cremona. To save time, arrangements were made by UNRRA headquarters in Milan to bring Dr. Castiglioni to the hospital in Cremona. At seven o'clock on Sunday evening, I was awakened by the nurse. Harry, who had been at my bedside throughout my ordeal, told me that a special doctor from Milan was about to examine me. A few minutes later Dr. Castiglioni walked in, accompanied by Dr. Grignani and a nurse. Dr. Castiglioni appeared to be in his late seventies. He had large gray eyes and very bushy white eyebrows. After examining the chart and exchanging some words with Dr. Grignani, he started feeling different parts of my abdomen. I was conscious enough to search his face for a clue as to how well or how badly I was doing. There was nothing other than a gentle smile. In the discussion that followed between the two doctors, I was able to distinguish one word, *penicillina*, repeated several times by both of them.

Dr. Castiglioni had concluded from his examination that the only hope for my recovery was penicillin, the new drug that had just come into use in 1946 but was not generally available. He knew, however, that an American medical corps stationed in Bologna had the drug. He suggested that UNRRA contact the Americans and emphasized that anything beyond twenty-four hours would certainly be too late. There was of course the danger that normal bureaucratic procedures would not be fast enough to yield results. To expedite matters the Jewish Agency in Milan and the UNRRA officials themselves contacted the American medical corps. The usual American generosity prevailed. The request was granted. A small UNRRA van with two Italian drivers was immediately dispatched to Bologna, and by six o'clock on Monday morning I received my first injection. The penicillin worked. Within ten days the peritonitis infection was gone. The doctors ran into a few other complications, but they too were overcome and my health improved despite the fact that I was extremely debilitated. There was much jubilation in camp. I received many visitors, among them the soccer player from the Cremona team who had accidentally caused my injury and was deeply apologetic for what had happened. A lot of people sent flowers, as well as sweets which I was strictly forbidden to touch.

With all this attention, both Harry and Lilly were at last able to take a rest from their night and day vigils beside my bed. I cannot say enough about the splendid care I received from the doctors, the nurses, and the nuns. Suora (Sister) Angelica, who was particularly attentive, went so far as to take care of what she thought were my spiritual needs. Every morning at exactly six o'clock, the patients of Suora Angelica's ward were awakened for the chores performed by the nurses. The first thing on the agenda was morning prayer. Every patient had to sit up and join Suora Angelica in the benedictions. I, too, would have done so, had I known the words. As a gesture of respect for those praying, I sat up and listened in silence. Suora Angelica noticed the first day that I did not participate. After the praying was over, she came to my bed and repeated several times, "*Michele* [Italian for Micky], *perché non preghi* [Why don't you pray]?" She put her hands together as if in prayer to convey the meaning of her question. Before I could attempt an explanation, a benevolent smile appeared on Suora's face. "*Ah, capisco* [I understand]," she said in a remorseful tone, "*sei ebreo* [you must be Jewish]!" Suora Angelica wasted no time in finding a solution to my dilemma. On the following day she brought a well-fed, ruddy-faced Italian priest to my bedside. He opened an old prayer book and read to me in fairly good Hebrew several of the prayers that Jews repeat when they rise in the morning. I must have told this story a hundred times, and every time I do, I am touched. My hospital stay lasted long enough for me to learn the morning prayers in Italian. Although Suora Angelica no longer expected me to join the rest of the patients in this ritual, I did so to show my appreciation for her special Italian kindness.

By the time the peritonitis cleared up, my body was perforated from the intravenous feeding and the endless injections and, though I had enough strength to get off the bed and take a few steps with the help of the nurses, I continued to suffer from intermittent abdominal pains. The doctors expressed optimism about my progress, but I felt depressed, doubting that I would ever recover. I thought from time to time that I was doomed to the same fate as the rest of my family. What added to my feeling of hopelessness was the unexpected announcement that I had to undergo yet a second operation in five weeks to remove ingrown tissue from the area where the intestines were sewn. My poor brother was worried about my mental state, tried everything to cheer me up, but to little avail. Doctor Grignani was apprised of my mood and paid me a special visit on Friday afternoon. Half in German and half in Italian he explained to me how crucial it was to my recovery that I change my gloomy outlook. The doctor's visit gave me some comfort but it did not raise my spirits.

It was probably on the advice of Dr. Grignani that after breakfast on Monday morning Suora Angelica approached my bed pushing a wheelchair. She gave me a fresh robe and said, "*Abbiamo una sorpresa, Michele, vai a fare una bella passeggiata in giardino* [We have a surprise for you. You are going for a stroll in the garden]." A few minutes later I was introduced to the companion who was going to take me for my *bella passeggiata*. Signorina Laura Launi, a medical student who worked in the hospital as a part-time caseworker while attending the university. Signorina Launi was an attractive brunette with a noble face and penetrating blue eyes. She appeared to be in her early twenties and spoke fluent German, making it easier for us to communicate, given my limited Italian. Signorina Launi helped me into the chair and wheeled me to the garden. Being in the fresh air after my ordeal, I felt reborn. The garden was filled with recuperating patients in wheelchairs, supervised by nurses. We parked near one of the benches, away from the crowd.

As soon as we exchanged some words, it was obvious that Laura was well briefed about my case. She knew something about my work with the children and my experiences in the labor camps, as well as my medical condition. I was struck by her friendly disposition and her willingness to share with me some personal details. I learned that she came from a well-to-do Italian family which had suffered a great deal during the war years. Her father, a professor of chemistry, was among those who opposed Mussolini's regime and voiced his loathing for the Nazis. As a consequence, he lost his chair at the university. This, along with other persecutions, made life difficult for the family and caused the interruption of Laura's medical education. She had returned only recently to the university, supporting herself with the money she earned at the hospital.

Laura's natural empathy, which could be read on her face, made me feel comfortable in her company. Once she finished telling me about her family, she elicited similar information from me about my childhood, and as much as I was willing to tell her about my war experiences. She listened with interest as I spoke, never probing or appearing to analyze what I had to say. In addition to her sensitivity, she had a fine sense of humor and was an excellent raconteuse. As we spent more time together, she often fascinated me with funny stories of her boarding-school days and the pranks medical students played on each other. Laura's laughter was melodic and infectious, but I had to suppress mine to avoid pain from the incision.

Laura had yet another virtue. She was a natural teacher, and I took advantage of it. Every time she took me to the garden I received a formal Italian lesson. I was making such progress that we rarely had to use German, a language that I was happy to avoid at the time. It was clear that Laura saw her function not only as a clinician or caseworker but as a compassionate listener and friend. Dr. Grignani's remedy worked well. After several outings, I began to feel much better. I was happy; I could not wait to hear the click-clack of Laura's confident walk and be in her company.

The fifth week of my hospital stay was approaching. Harry was called in to discuss plans for my discharge and for my convalescence in anticipation of the second operation. Since a refugee camp was no place for recuperating from such a serious operation, other plans were already in progress. With the help of UNRRA, and mostly through the generosity of an Italian convalescent home, I would be taken to a villa located in Arona on beautiful Lago Maggiore. On a Saturday afternoon, after a short examination, Dr. Grignani told me I would be discharged the following morning, and warned me to be careful with my diet. He assured me that the forthcoming operation would be a comparatively easy one. Dr. Castiglioni would admit me to his private clinic in Milan, where the operation would be performed by his son-in-law, a well-known surgeon in his own right.

Sunday morning, Harry came to the hospital. Suora Angelica, who during the last four weeks had been like a mother to me, prepared me for departure. She gave me several medicines and instructed me to take them without fail. I said good-bye to my fellow patients. I was particularly sorry to leave behind my neighbor, Giovanni, who had often consoled me when I was in pain and helped me get out of bed when I was too weak to do so on my own. My last *addio* came from Suora Angelica, who said a prayer *sotto voce* as I was being led to the door. Though I was still weak, I was able to walk very slowly and slightly inclined toward the ground, with the support of Harry and one of the nurses from the ward. As I was about to be helped into the ambulance, I noticed with great joy my dear friend Laura who had come to see me off. "*Pensavi che ti avessi dimenticato, eh* [You thought that I had forgotten you, didn't you]?" she said. Just as the ambulance door was about to close, Laura smiled sadly and said quietly, "*Verró a trovarti fra breve; capito? Vengo al Lago Maggiore* [I will come to see you soon; do you understand? I'll come to Lago Maggiore]." I nodded my head in understanding. Throughout the entire ride to Arona I could not take my mind off Laura. I thought of the pleasant mornings I had spent in her company and regretted that I had to leave the hospital.

The convalescent home housed fifty DPs, the majority of them survivors of the Holocaust who were being treated in Italian hospitals for a variety of illnesses they had contracted in the camps—a few of them terminally ill. I was put in the same room with Géza, a middle-aged Hungarian Jew, also from the Cremona camp. He had already undergone two operations for stomach cancer and was waiting for a third.

Our room was large, with doors leading to a veranda. From its two panoramic windows you could see the vast expanse of Lago Maggiore, and beyond, the Swiss Alps rising above the nearby town of Stresa. The inside walls were decorated with frescos depicting hunting scenes and the ceilings with pastel-colored cherubim. The only items that were not in harmony with the rest of the decor in the room were the four hospital beds and the night tables.

The pleasure I derived from the beautiful grounds of the villa and the awesome view of the Alps must have contributed to the speed with which I gained the strength I needed for the forthcoming operation. Thanks also to the excellent care I received from the resident doctor, two nurses, and dietitian, I added some six pounds to my withered body in one week. The only thing missing from Lago Maggiore were those morning visits from Laura. I continued to think about her a great deal, hoping that she was going to keep her promise.

After that first week in Arona, Harry came to see me. He was glad to find me in good spirits and was surprised by how much stronger my voice had become. This was the first time since the injury that Harry appeared relieved about my condition. He brought regards from my fellow campers, soup that Lilly had prepared but which my nurse forbade me to eat, and the good news that he had found a place where he could do tailoring. An Italian seamstress was kind enough to allow him the use of her shop for a small fee, making it possible for him to undertake work and earn some badly needed money. This was particularly urgent because the baby was due any day. Other than a small ration of powdered milk provided by the camp, there was very little for a new baby, unless extra money was available to buy special food.

Harry and I spent Saturday together. It was wonderful to sit with him in the garden and have the strength to talk. In the four weeks I had spent in the hospital, it was mostly a one-way conversation, with Harry sitting at my bedside urging me not to use my weakened voice. To make me feel better, he kept assuring me that I would recover completely from my injury and be able to play soccer again. The time went by quickly. Unfortunately, Harry had to return to Cremona that night because he couldn't afford to stay over at a hotel. But he had a chance to see the doctor, who gave us a good report on my progress.

Sunday morning I was sitting in the garden with some of my fellow convalescents when an announcement over the loudspeaker summoned me to the office. The thought that it might be Laura made me walk faster despite some discomfort. To my delight, it was indeed Laura. We met in a long embrace. Her first words were, *"Michele, ti sono mancato* [Did you miss me]?" to which I responded with a very willing *"Si."* She noticed immediately that I had gained weight, and complimented me on how well I looked. Impressed by the beauty of the place, Laura suggested that I show her around. As we walked through the gardens, she gave me the latest news from Cremona. Among other things, she told me with great satisfaction about her new assignment as liaison caseworker between the hospital and the camp. This would bring her to camp several times a week to follow up on women with newborn babies as well as patients discharged after an illness. I was of course delighted, since it would give me the opportunity to see her from time to time.

From a bench in a lovely area of the garden right on the shore of Lago Maggiore, we could see the beautiful Alps. We chatted and joked, very much as we had at the hospital in Cremona, except that now Laura displayed a demeanor hitherto unfamiliar to me. She asked whether I thought she was pretty, occasionally held my hand as she spoke, and gave me penetrating looks. She seemed to want to tell me something but was having difficulty finding the proper words. I had mixed feelings about her behavior, thinking on the one hand that this signaled the end of our friendship, and hoping on the other hand that our relationship would blossom into the romance I longed for.

At noon Laura drove to Stresa to have lunch. She promised to hurry back, *"perche abbiamo ancora molto da parlare* [because we still have much to talk about]," she said in a half-serious tone. After lunch I went to my room to rest. When I awoke, there was Laura sitting beside my bed reading a magazine. I found it very comforting, even moving, to see her there. At her suggestion, we took some blankets and found a spot on the villa's private beach that was not surrounded by sunbathers. We sat for a while in total silence, both of us gazing in the direction of the mountains. She reached for my hand and waved it languidly a few times back and forth, then stopped and said almost in a whisper, "Michele, you must know by now that you are very dear to me." She paused for a few seconds and lowered her head. "Would it upset you if I told you that I have probably fallen in love with you?" She raised her head, passed her hand gently over my face, and looked at me inquiringly. I took her in my arms. What followed was our first kiss. I confessed to Laura how happy I was and how I had been praying our friendship would reach this point. Laura was elated with my response. She departed with the admonition that I not flirt with other girls and the reassuring, *"Sai che ti voglio bene, Michele* [You know I love you, don't you]?" The beautiful sound of this Italian sentence kept me dreaming and praying for her next visit.

Laura's declaration of love could not have come at a better time. It appeared that fate had sent my way not only a romantic partner but a devoted friend who might help me deal with many of the hardships that attended living in a refugee camp. A year had gone by since our arrival in Cremona. I was twenty years old, still occasionally haunted by Nazi nightmares, and facing yet another operation. Other than my brief encounter with flirtatious Shoshana, my social life in camp had been virtually nonexistent before I met Laura. For a while I belonged to a Kibbutz, but I soon became tired of singing the same songs and holding hands with other men while dancing the Israeli hora. I was essentially lonely. The few young women who had survived Hitler's horrors were not interested in me. They were eager to find a man, preferably with good connections in America, and get married. My age and the fact that I had very little to offer at that point made me a most ineligible bachelor. Other than my enjoyable work with the children, there were few other distractions. But I longed for more. I wanted to love and be loved, to live a bit of the life that would have been natural for a twenty-year-old under normal circumstances. It seemed to me on that Sunday afternoon that Laura's acknowledged affection would satisfy my hunger for companionship, alleviate my loneliness, and help me cope with the drabness of camp life. Although somewhat apprehensive about this new development, I was happy and did not care about how long our romance might last, nor what would ultimately come of it.

Just two days after Harry visited me, he called to tell me that Lilly had given birth to a baby girl and that both were fine. I shared my brother's deeply felt emotion. This new life was our small victory over the death and destruction that had befallen our people. The baby was going to be named Bertha after Lilly's mother, who had died in the Auschwitz gas chambers with her husband on the day of their arrival in May of 1944. I couldn't wait to be through with my operation and see with my own eyes our gift of life.

The day before I was scheduled to go to Milan to be checked by Dr. Castiglioni, I developed terrible cramps and began to vomit. It seems that, as anticipated, the intestinal passage had become too narrow and no digestion was possible. I was rushed to the clinic and the surgery was performed earlier than expected. Meanwhile, Harry was spending his time at the hospital in Cremona, where Lilly was recovering from giving birth. By Sunday, when Laura drove him to Milan, I was already able to get out of bed with the help of the nurse.

For most of the time that Harry spent with me, he talked about the baby. One could clearly see on his face the love he felt for his child. He attributed to her, as most parents do, all kinds of superlative qualities. She was of course the most beautiful child ever born in Cremona. "Micky," he said "you won't believe this, but Bertha already responds to my funny faces and smiles when I talk to her." He added jokingly, "You know, I think she understands both Yiddish and Italian." As if to humor my brother, Laura punctuated Harry's fantastic claims with an affirmative nod of the head, adding her own, more credible, praise of little Bertha, whom she had been visiting since her birth. As Harry and Laura were saying their good-byes, I was able to read on Laura's lips a slowly spelled out, "*Sai che ti voglio bene.*"

Although I was very well treated at the clinic, I missed the hustle and bustle of the large ward at Ospedale Maggiore, as well as Suora Angelica's attention. The fact that I was away from Cremona virtually eliminated the possibility of visitors. Other than a Signora Ponti, who spent the entire day with her father, who was dying in the next bed, I rarely saw people apart from the hospital staff. Signora Ponti must have realized I was lonely and made sure to keep me company from time to time. Here, as in many other places in Italy, humanity was poignantly exhibited. Signora Ponti's father died five days after my operation. After the funeral, she came to visit me every day for the remainder of my stay.

A week after Harry's initial visit to the clinic, he came to see me by himself. I didn't mind at all that he could stay only for a short while, because I could hardly wait to read the letter he had brought me from Laura. The moment he left I opened the envelope. It was as though I were opening a precious gift that I had been eager to receive for a long time. Although I did not understand every word, I understood its essence. Laura's letter contained many words of affection as well as practical wisdom. She assured me of her love, but suggested that we temper our relationship with some of the realities that surrounded both our lives. "Remember, Michele, your future is still uncertain. As for myself, I am a medical student with a great deal of work ahead of me and without any idea where I will end up once I become a doctor. This does not mean that we can't love each other, but I want to be sure that if our romance ends some day, it should not be with regrets. We ought therefore to allow our love to run its course and let fate make the ultimate decision." I was glad to accept Laura's reasoning because I was aware of my own unresolved future. I was still a refugee with neither a place to go, nor the possibility of remaining in Italy.

On my return to Arona I got a warm reception. Most of the patients I had left behind when I was taken to Milan were still there. I was housed again in the beautiful sunroom decorated with frescos and once more had Géza as my roommate. He was happy to see me and told me that his operation was postponed. The poor man did not know the truth about his condition. I learned from another patient that Géza's last examination had shown his cancer to be so advanced that an operation would not save his life. I spent a great deal of time in his company during my second convalescence, listening to yet one more tragic story of the Holocaust.

Before the war Géza was a farmhand. He was totally assimilated, and knew nothing about Jewish tradition. "The Germans," he said, "reminded me that I was Jew." Géza was married and had several children, none of whom had survived. Not knowing how seriously ill he was, Géza told me that as soon he recovered he hoped to go to Israel and resume his work as a farmer. But he died at Cremona within six months.

Unlike the first time, I was able to be more active within a shorter period of recuperation. Although I had lost weight, I no longer suffered from the cramps that had frequently plagued me. Among various activities, my favorite was joining my friends for boat rides to Stresa and the other beautiful towns situated on Lago Maggiore. I was of course longing to see Laura, but she was busy preparing for a very important examination at the university. She wrote me several letters which I reread whenever I felt lonely or unhappy. In her last letter, she wrote that the following Sunday she was coming to spend the day with me.

At nine o'clock, earlier that I anticipated, there was my dear Laura, wearing an elegant dress that revealed her graceful figure. Her hair was tightly pulled into a bun in the style of a ballet dancer. I walked in her direction as fast as my still unsteady legs would allow and, with more daring than on the few previous visits, I embraced her. Almost involuntarily, I emitted my own *"Sai che ti voglio bene."* My declaration was rewarded with a kiss and an *"Anch'io* [me too]."

Laura had a surprise for me. She had made arrangements for us to be taken by small boat to Isola Bella, a beautiful castle on Lago Maggiore. It was a clear, sunny October day without a cloud in the sky. Lago Maggiore looked like one vast blue mirror, with just a few ripples to suggest the presence of a gentle wind. In the distance the lake was dotted with sailboats, giving the impression that a multitude of butterflies had landed on its surface. Though our vessel looked like a gondola, it was propelled by oars. We were surrounded by similar boats whose passengers were singing. Giovanni, our "gondolier," was a friendly old man, eager to engage us in conversation. *"Amanti* [Lovers]?" he asked with a broad smile on his wrinkled face. *"Si,"* replied Laura without hesitation. *"Bravi, bravi, cantiamo allora* [Bravo, bravo, let us sing then]," said the old man, and started with the well-known *"Sul Mare Lucida."* Laura joined in. At Isola Bella we had lunch on a beautiful terrace overlooking the lake, where we were treated to the romantic music of two roving violinists.

At three o'clock we took a return boat. This time we had a less gregarious boatman, so Laura and I had a chance to talk about many things, particularly the events of the last seven weeks and our relationship. The beauty of Lago Maggiore, the lovely Italian songs coming from the boats around us, and Laura's display of affection made our trip seem like a chapter out of a romantic novel. Nothing like this had ever happened to me, nor could I have imagined during the war years that there would be a Laura in my life to make such an extraordinary day possible. When we got back to the villa, Laura insisted that I lie down to rest. We spent one more pleasant hour, with Laura sitting beside my bed holding my hand and entertaining me with her inimitable Italian humor. When the time came for my dear friend to leave, my disappointment was lessened by the knowledge that I was returning to Cremona within three days. In our last warm embrace for the day, Laura said in a quasi-commanding tone, "*Ritorna presto perché una ragazza ti aspetta con molte carezze* [Hurry back because a girl is waiting for you with many caresses]."

Time stood still during the three days before my departure. I was naturally eager to return to camp because I would see Laura, but that was not the only reason. I was genuinely moved and excited about the birth of Harry's baby and could not wait to hold her in my arms. And then, of course, there were my little students, to whom I had become very attached and whom I had not seen for such a long time.

When the nurse came to my room Wednesday morning and announced that I was going home, it sounded strange to me that she should refer to a refugee camp as my home. But she was right. The camp, with all its shabbiness, was in fact at present my home. Harry took time out from his work to accompany the jeep driver—the same one who some eight weeks earlier had raced to Bologna to get the penicillin. The driver greeted me and said in loud, cheerful voice, "*Ti ho salvato la vita, eh* [I saved your life. Isn't that so]?"

On our arrival, the jeep was surrounded by my little disciples and many other well-wishers. A short distance away stood Lilly holding Bertha. I rushed in their direction, embraced Lilly, and immediately took the baby in my arms. I looked at that lovely face and wept for joy and for sadness at the same time. I was happy with our small victory over Hitler but could not suppress thoughts of what had happened to the rest of her family—the baby's grandparents, aunts, uncles—and the one million children murdered by the Nazis.

Harry had been almost correct in his description of Bertha. She was indeed very pretty and seemed to respond with a smile to my funny faces, but he had exaggerated her linguistic talents. I spoke to her in both Yiddish and Italian, but the language she seemed to understood best was "googoo."

Chapter 15

Marking Time

It was decided that I should spend at least the first week of my return sleeping in the infirmary, with the freedom to visit my friends. I was supposed to be on a special diet, but the infirmary food still came from the camp kitchen, where it was invariably prepared with heavy grease, difficult for me to digest. Lilly did her best with the preparation of appropriate foods, but with no kitchen facilities other than a little electric stove, this was virtually impossible. Still, despite an occasional upset stomach, I was soon well enough to return permanently to the room I now shared with thirty-nine other people, and to stand once more in line for my meals like the rest of the residents.

Harry and Lilly were moved out of the main room after the baby was born, not so much to make them more comfortable as to spare the others Bertha's crying. They were given worse lodging in the drafty corridor at the entrance to the large room. The winter of 1946 was well on its way, making life under these circumstances more difficult. To make sure Bertha would not catch a cold, bathing her became a family project. Harry and I would hold a blanket around a barrel that we converted into a basin to contain the little warmth generated by a small electric heater.

At the beginning of December, I was well enough to return to my work with the children. In addition to doing gymnastics with them, I was now asked to put on shows for Purim and other Jewish festivals. Although I was not well enough to play soccer, a source of frustration, being back on the job and in the company of the children lifted my spirits considerably.

Laura and I managed to see each other at least twice a week, despite the fact that she was hard at work in the hospital as well as at the university. Although she came to camp twice and sometimes three times a week on official business, our rendezvous were always elsewhere. We both preferred it that way. Neither Laura nor I wanted to be the subject of camp gossip. But most of her friends knew about our romance, and I became part of their social circle. Her small apartment near the hospital became my refuge away from camp. On the evenings when she was off duty, she would fix a good meal for us. Pasta, which she could prepare in at least twenty different ways, was her culinary forte. Thanks to her delicious cooking I soon regained my full weight. When time permitted, we would go to a movie, take walks in the park, or go for a ride in the country in her small Fiat.

Laura also wanted to take me along for a weekend visit with her parents, who lived in a suburb about an hour from Cremona. I was reluctant at first, but after several imploring looks I acquiesced. She told me that her parents knew about her *giocatore di calcio cecoslovacco* (Czech soccer player) and were eager to meet me. She jokingly assured me that they understood the nature of our relationship and that this was not a preliminary visit introducing me to my future in-laws.

From then on, I spent many pleasant weekends with them. It was wonderful to be in a family setting, and to eat at an elegantly set table instead of standing in line for my meals with a mess kit. The Launis were most hospitable, and treated me with affection. Laura's father, who had by now regained his position at the university, was particularly attentive to me. We spent a great deal of time in each other's company. Although Laura had told him about my background and my Holocaust experiences, he wanted to know more. He listened with empathy to my stories and shared with me a few of his own unhappy experiences with the Fascist regime. It was in these conversations with Signore Launi that I learned a great deal about the fate of the Italian Jews under Mussolini, as well as about the heroic deeds of many Italians who had saved thousands of Jews from the Nazis. Signore Launi himself had served in the Italian antifascist underground and modestly told me about his own role in this humanitarian effort.

Over a year had passed since our arrival in Cremona. By now, a number of the DPs had formed connections as well as friendships with local families, some through business transactions, others for purely social reasons, a few through romantic liaisons, as in my case. Much of this was attributable to the sympathetic disposition of the Italians toward the camp inmates, the goodness of what is often referred to as *il cuore italiano* (the Italian soul). We were treated consistently with benevolence and respect, and I gained the friendship of several neighboring families. One in particular turned out to be very dear to me.

Signor Bruni worked with one of the drivers who delivered produce to the camp, while his wife worked in the office as a cleaning woman. Between them they earned very little. With five children to care for, they had a difficult time making ends meet, as was the case with many Italian families in those days. When I became ill, Signore Bruni approached my brother and offered to help in any way he could, including money. It was he who volunteered to accompany the driver to Bologna to get the penicillin that saved my life. While I was in Ospedale Maggiore, he often came to visit me during his lunch hour. His wife came on weekends, always with a bunch of flowers. When I returned from Arona, Signora Bruni would bring me her delicious soups, which she humorously referred to as *la zuppa che ti guarisce presto* (the soup that cures you fast).

Just before Christmas, when she came once more with her "medicine," she invited me to spend the holiday with her family. I was reluctant and made all kinds of excuses, but Signora Bruni's touching words made it impossible for me to say no. "*Guarda, Michele,*" she said, "*tu sai che non siamo ricchi. Vieni per Natale per favore. Si noi mangeremo soltanto pane tu mangerai pane con noi* [Look, Micky, you know that we are not rich. Please do come to us for Christmas. If we should eat only bread, you will eat bread with us]."

I will never forget that delightful celebration of Christmas in Cremona, so remarkably different was it from Christmases I had experienced as a child. In Kustanovice, we hid indoors on Christmas day in fear of that some anti-Semite would at any moment break a window, pour out obscenities, and accuse us of having killed Christ. Signora Bruni, on the other hand, knew that I was a Jew and was happy to have me at her table.

Life in camp continued to be more or less the same. Our living quarters were as crowded as ever, with about forty people sharing the inadequate washroom and toilet facilities. We stood in line sometimes as long as a half hour for the substandard food served to us. Although Italian winters tend to be mild, Cremona, in the northern part of Italy, had its share of cold weather, and the fact that we had no heating facilities made the winter months difficult, particularly for the young families with children. The one additional blanket issued for each cot did not solve our problems.

With the passage of time, the earlier cries for improvements in our living conditions died down, and most of us suffered quietly, pretty much resigned to our circumstances. UNRRA had apparently done all it was going to do for us. As for the hope of finally moving on to our desired refuge, this too remained unrealized for most of the campers. The papers of many DPs were being processed by relatives to bring them to places like America, Australia, and Argentina, but so far just a handful had succeeded in leaving Italy. Ironically, the German quota enjoyed preference, which actually meant that former Nazis had a better chance for emigration—particularly to Argentina—than their victims.

Those who chose to go to Palestine bore the greatest disappointment, since the British, who were in control, kept rescinding and reinstating the quota for legal immigration until it was finally halted altogether. This forced the Zionist movement, led during that time by David Ben-Gurion, to resort to *Aliyah Bet* (illegal immigration), which was fraught with danger. Some illegal ships succeeded in getting to Palestine, others were intercepted. Most of the people caught on these vessels were sent to Cyprus, where they lived under far worse conditions than in the DP camps. The majority of these captives had to wait for almost two years before they finally got to the Promised Land. A few were sent back to their respective DP camps to face an uncertain future.

It should have followed, from all the hardships, that these souls scarred by the Holocaust might give up hope, become despondent, and be indifferent to each other's plight. But in Cremona, as in other places and in other times, adversity tended to strengthen the Jewish people and to unite them. Our Cremona survivors, too, were able to sustain their hopes and their humanity against difficult odds. The importance of *Tzedakah* (charity, or justice), one of the 613 *mitzvoth* (commandments) in the Torah, was upheld even in refugee camps. This was displayed particularly toward the children, that tiny remnant who had come through the Nazi ordeal. While the rooms for the adults were for the most part without heat during the cold weather, fellow DPs collected money and bought electric heaters for the school dorms and for a few of the rooms where small children were housed. There were many other manifestations of charity and good will on the part of this varied collection of humanity living in crowded quarters. Just as in their recent past in concentration camps, they found a way to live together, to form faithful friendships, and to make life more tolerable. I too found a dear friend who had a marked influence on my life.

In the cot next to mine was Henry Gelberman, a young man from the Czech town of Berehovo, just thirty kilometers from Mukachevo. Henry was twenty-seven years old and the sole survivor of a large family, except for an uncle in Chicago who had managed to flee in time and was eager to get his nephew to the United States. Henry came from a background of affluence. He had attended the university and was well educated in both Czech and Hungarian. He was a very bright man, an excellent mathematician, and spoke fluent English, French, German, and Italian. Before the Holocaust, Henry had aspired to become a teacher on the gymnasium level.

Henry was a gloomy person by nature. The loss of his family, his fiancée, and his own experience with concentration camps, brought on occasional moods of depression. Henry had a very sharp wit. He tended to be impatient, critical, and even rude, particularly with people who did not know what they were talking about. He did not suffer fools gladly and, as a consequence, had a very small circle of friends. Nevertheless, he did have admirers, mostly people who respected him for his knowledge. Those of us who knew him well understood that behind his arrogance was a kind-hearted human being ready to help others. Because of his excellent knowledge of English, many people called on him to assist them in corresponding with their relatives in America and other English-speaking countries. Henry must have filled out hundreds of applications for visas, passports, and other documents. His job in the camp commander's office put him in a position to do other favors for our refugees, like making long-distance calls to the United States in search of relatives. For none of these services would he accept money or gifts.

My friendship with Henry began during the days when I was still playing soccer. Since he was totally uncoordinated when it came to sports, I think he became a fan in order to enjoy vicariously what he himself was not able to do. It was clear from his occasional compliments that he admired both my athletic talents and the fact that I was so devoted to the children. Though Henry was not given to effusive display of affection, he appeared pleased that we had struck up a friendship despite our contrasting educational backgrounds. During my illness, Henry often came to see me in the hospital. When I was recuperating, he occasionally got me meals from the kitchen so I wouldn't have to stand in line. He also accompanied me from time to time for my checkups at the hospital.

Among Henry's many talents, I particularly admired his linguistic knowledge, and I hoped that some day soon I too would possess such skills. I greatly valued our friendship and saw him as a mentor from whom I could learn a great deal. I constantly sought his advice on how I could realize my long-standing dream of acquiring an education. It took persistent pleading before Henry consented to give me lessons in his favorite language, French—for a price. To supplement my meager earnings from the school, I was giving ballroom dancing lessons to a group of young people from the camp. Henry, too, wanted to learn how to dance but under no circumstances would he join a group. Keenly aware of his lack of coordination, and wanting to hide it as much as possible, he insisted that I give him private lessons in the evening in his office where no one could see us. He would not even permit me to bring along the young lady who assisted me.

Henry was by far the most awkward person I had ever taught. Deprived of my assistant to act as his partner, I had to suffer the pain inflicted on my toes by Henry's clumsy steps. Only my desire to sustain our friendship and to continue to learn from this bright man made me go on with the almost impossible task of teaching Henry to dance. My perseverance paid off; after four weeks of instruction, Henry was able to do several dances and muster enough courage to ask a girl onto the floor.

As for my French lessons, Henry turned out to be a dreadful teacher. He was impatient, and sometimes even insulting, when I did not understand something or when an explanation had to be repeated. I was simply not fast enough for Henry. When I could no longer bear his teaching methods, I continued to study French on my own with just occasional help from him. Despite his irascible nature, Henry served in the long run as an inspiration to me. I learned a great deal from him, notwithstanding his unappetizing approach to teaching.

Having heard so much about my morose friend, Laura was eager to meet him. She suggested that I bring him along for dinner in her apartment. The date was set for a Saturday evening, and Laura invited a few other friends, among them a brunette about Henry's age. The evening was a success, except for the fact that Henry did not particularly like Laura and the brunette definitely did not like Henry. She thought he was arrogant, and certainly too rotund for her taste. As a consequence of Henry's feeling toward Laura, which I never revealed to her, every time I was about to go to see her, Henry would be annoyed with me. He would have preferred that I join him in his favorite pastime, frequenting pubs, drinking beer, and chasing women.

In February of 1947, as winter was drawing to an end, I was hard at work on the Purim festival play with my schoolchildren—the story from the Book of Esther in Yiddish. I decided to incorporate several dance numbers in the scenes that depicted the court of King Ahasuerus and his Jewish wife. With the help of the older girls of the school, I choreographed the dance pieces and designed the costumes. The ORT seamstress provided us with the materials and the tailoring, and the boys built and painted the scenery. Maestro Sterzati, a handsome middle-aged Italian gentleman who gave guitar lessons to our children free of charge, provided the music for the entire show. For weeks, our after-school hours were filled with excitement. The social hall hummed with the pleasant sound of the children—the dancers rehearsing in one corner, the actors in another, and on the stage, their faces smudged, the painters preparing the scenery. One could not help being caught up in the enthusiasm and the joy displayed by the children and feel like a child again.

The play was scheduled for two performances, one on the eve of Purim and one on Purim Day. An hour before the first show the hall was already filled, not only with parents and other folks from camp, but with some of our Italian neighbors. Maestro Sterzati's entire family was there, and my special guest, Laura, who would not have missed the show for anything in the world.

Before the play began, Maestro Sterzati gave a synopsis of it for our Italian visitors. He made some moving comments about his work with the children, and about the significance of Purim as a symbol of victory for the Jewish people, not only over the tyranny of Haman, but over all the other oppressors. With visible pain on his face, he made reference to Mussolini, Italy's contribution to the nightmare of the Holocaust.

The show was a success, as children's performances always are. There were many curtain calls, and I was very happy to be in the midst of the little souls who bowed to the repeated applause and the shouts of bravo. Both the camp commander and the head of the Maskeeroot expressed special thanks for our work. Laura, throwing caution to the winds, gave me a big hug and congratulated me. The children were so excited that the parents, or in many cases their guardians, could not get them out of the social hall. I learned later that several of my performers refused to remove their makeup and that some of the dancers insisted on sleeping in their costumes.

The second performance was just as successful. Doing the Purim play and being back at work in full swing gave me great satisfaction. What added to the enjoyment was the fact that Dr. Grignani assured me that I was in good physical condition and no longer had to be concerned about doing strenuous activities with the children. Although he advised me not to play soccer with the team for a while, I could play it with the children.

Everything was going well except that I was making no progress in finding sponsors to help me get to America, or anywhere else for that matter. At this point, Harry and Lilly were already assured of their visas to the United States, but any chance of my getting papers through Lilly's family had failed to materialize, and I knew of no other source. My friend Henry showed great concern for my plight and reproached me for not trying hard enough to escape from what he called "the confounded refugee life." As a consequence of his urging, and with his help, I wrote to several Jewish agencies and educational institutions in the United States, but nothing came of it other than letters of regretful rejection. Agencies like HIAS (Hebrew Immigrant Aid Society) would help in those days only if relatives in the States were willing to foot the bill for the immigrant. Ironically enough, I received a letter from a Hasidic yeshiva that would try to bring me to America provided I was observant enough to dedicate my life to an austere adherence to Torah. This was certainly not what I was looking for. As disappointed as we both were about the rejections, Henry would tease me from time to time about having missed the opportunity to become a Hasid.

Henry and I knew a few people who had no relatives in America and were attempting to secure immigration papers from individuals not known to them. They would obtain addresses of American Jews, write them about their hopeless situation, and pray that some good might come of it. Part of the deal was to assure the recipients of those letters that the DPs would send money to cover legal fees, passage, and other expenses that were necessary to get them to America. One young couple I knew managed to find a willing sponsor and received their visas within six months.

It was Henry's idea that I think of trying this method. There was of course a huge obstacle in my way, namely, the lack of the kind of money that was necessary for such a project. But Henry had a solution for that. One of the most lucrative ways to make money on a one-shot deal was to join a group of entrepreneurs who made trips to Innsbruck, Austria, where they bought cigarettes from American soldiers that they then sold in Italy. The amount needed for this purpose was not very large, and one could at least quintuple the investment. Henry suggested that if I combined my bit of savings with what I could borrow from Harry, he would take a chance and lend me the rest. This was of course an illegal operation. If we were caught at the border, not only would the merchandise be confiscated but a possible jail term imposed. There was, in fact, a young man in camp who had been captured and kept for four weeks in an Austrian jail. There was also the very difficult physical task of crossing the Alps and having to brave the severe cold.

Although Henry's plan was well-intentioned, the idea of being involved in such an enterprise did not sit well with me. I would have liked to earn money in a nobler way. I thanked Henry for his willingness to risk his own savings and invented all kinds of excuses to avoid making such a trip. Neither my protestations nor my excuses proved of any consequence in the face of Henry's genuine concern on my behalf; eventually, I yielded to his plan.

We contacted a young man named Mottek, a former partisan,

known to be an excellent guide across the Brenner Pass to Innsbruck. He ran two trips a week, and told us that the round trip would take only three days. Since the camp's school was about to begin its ten-day Passover recess, I did not have to worry on that score. I chose to join a midweek group so as to make it easier to hide my absence from Laura. At this point I did not care how dangerous or how difficult my expedition was going to be. But I hoped that Laura would never find out that I had consented to this scheme, fearing that if she knew what I was up to, it might damage our relationship. I was going to be the only novice on this expedition, the other four fellows had done this many times before. I was told to bring along food, a knapsack in which the cigarettes would be carried, and an extra set of clothing.

Tuesday morning five of us, accompanied by Mottek, walked to the Cremona station and boarded a train that took us to Brennero. By late afternoon we made our way on foot to the Brenner Pass where we waited till dark to begin our steep climb toward Innsbruck. Although in some parts of the Alps the snow was already beginning to melt, most of the road was still covered with deep drifts that made our crossing extremely difficult. Mottek, who appeared mild-mannered in camp, turned out to be a demanding taskmaster, showing no pity for those of us who complained about being tired. The crossing took five hours. By the time we got to the Austrian side, most of our clothing was torn to shreds by rocks and shrubs. I understood why we had been told to bring a spare set. Arrangements had been made for us beforehand to spend the night at an Austrian farmer's house. In the morning, after making ourselves presentable, we went into Innsbruck. Under Mottek's guidance, we completed all our transactions by noon. But we had to wait till dark again before we could begin the return journey.

We stored our knapsacks and went into town in separate little groups to have lunch. I was paired with Mottek. As we walked around the center of town after lunch, I noticed a familiar face coming toward us. Within seconds I realized that this was the high-ranking Hungarian Nazi officer who had kicked me about in Csepel during lineup. I remembered his name, and called out, "Almási!" Almási did an about-face and started running.

"Mottek, Mottek," I cried, "that was a Nazi who I recognize from forced-labor camp." Mottek and I ran after him, but we lost him in the crowd. We approached a police officer who stood on a round platform directing traffic. I told him we had just seen a Hungarian Nazi and that we wanted help chasing him down. The officer gave us an irritated look and said in a loud, angry tone, "*Ich kann nichts tun* [There is nothing I can do]." The fact that we were in Innsbruck on an illegal mission made it impossible for us to press the issue, and we gave up.

It was frightening to see the face of a sadist who had humiliated me and who I was sure was responsible for many deaths. For a while I felt as though the danger I faced in Hitler's camps was not over, that the Nazis were still around and ready to resume their horrors. The angry and loud "*Ich kann nichts tun*" of the gray-headed police officer, and his indifference to our appeal for help, made me wonder if he, too, was and still might be a soul brother of Almási.

Crossing the Alps from Austria to Italy was considerably easier despite the fact that my knapsack was well-loaded with Lucky Strikes. The downhill trip took only three hours, but at Brennero we had to wait over two hours for our return train to Cremona. To play it safe we did not stay in the waiting room but outside the station, where we had to endure the bitter cold. Once on the train, the risk of being caught was minimal. As soon as we arrived at the camp, the dealers, who had their steady Italian customers, paid me the going rate for my merchandise. As predicted, I made five times the amount of my investment, repaid Harry and Henry, and was left with a profit of fifty American dollars, a respectable sum of money for those days but certainly not enough to pay for the expenses I would need if I found a sponsor.

On my return from Innsbruck, I found several people in my room feverishly engaged in cleaning their little sleeping areas in preparation for Passover, which commemorates the escape of the Hebrews from Egyptian bondage. This was the second Passover since our arrival in Italy. During this festival, it is prohibited to eat foods prepared from products that ferment, such as wheat, barley, rye, oats, and rice. Since the ingredients that were necessary for the celebration of the Holiday were not available, those who were strict in their observance lived for the eight days mostly on potatoes and *matzo* (unleavened bread) that we received from the Jewish agency in the United States. The Seder, the traditional evening meal that is supposed to be a joyous occasion with an abundance of food, was celebrated with an almost empty table and very little to be happy about. We had a separate Seder for the schoolchildren where the lack of the customary plenty was well camouflaged with traditional songs and some specially prepared sweets.

In May 1947, Harry, Lilly, and Lilly's sisters received notification that their visas were granted, with a departure date in mid-July. Except for passing a medical examination, they were now assured of going to the United States. I was of course glad for all of them but quite unhappy about my own uncertain future and the prospect of having to separate from my only family. Harry reassured me that as soon as he got to America, he would find a way to bring me over.

Henry continued to help with my search for a sponsor, but nothing productive came of it. I did receive, through a Canadian contact, a letter and several photos from a twenty-six-year-old woman who was interested in meeting a young man for the purpose of matrimony. There were in fact several instances in camp where women from the United States and Canada came to Cremona and returned with husbands. The letter made me very sad. It was not so much the appearance of the woman nor her age that repulsed me, but the very idea that, for the possibility of liberating myself from a refugee camp, I might have to make such a compromise. Though some successful marriages probably did result from such arrangements, it was not for my sensibilities, particularly at this point in my life when I was enjoying the romantic company of Laura.

It was now early June, and the school year was coming to an end. After many unsuccessful requests, the school was finally granted food and transportation to reward the children with an excursion to Isola Bella, the scene of my precious day with Laura. It was delightful to see the excitement of the children as they were hoisted onto the trucks. It was a real treat for the kids, who were essentially confined to the camp and rarely had a chance to see the outside world. No matter how sympathetic the Italians were to our plight, we were still refugees whose borrowed territory was the *caserma* and not the city of Cremona itself. Our children were not forbidden to leave the camp, but the fact that they had so little in common with Italian children, including the language, made contact difficult.

Although the school year was officially over, I continued to work with them, organizing all kinds of games, including a soccer league, that the youngsters enjoyed very much. Also, in anticipation of Bertha's approaching departure, I devoted most of my free time to being with her. I wanted to be sure that if fate should separate us I would have a well-engraved memory of this gift to us. Bertha was a very happy baby. When I was in her company, it was as though I were a father, an uncle, and a child at the same time.

July came quickly, sooner than I wanted it to, and with it the preparation for Harry and Lilly's departure. On the appointed day we got on the train for Genoa with several other families from our camp. Harry and Lilly anxiously proceeded to the American embassy, where they and the baby were to undergo a thorough physical examination. I distinctly remember Harry's preoccupied, pale face. Holocaust survivors, having lived under such horrendous conditions, always ran the risk that they might have acquired some illness that would impede their admittance to the United States. We knew that, even with visas in hand, many were barred as a consequence of imperfect health.

The American embassy was surrounded by hundreds of immigrants nervously waiting to get into the building. When our turn finally came, after three hours in line handing the baby from arm to arm, the entire family passed the examination. The four of us spent the night in one room, in a cheap hotel right on the dock. We were constantly awakened by the noise of the loading and unloading of cargo that went on around the clock, while Bertha "slept like a baby" through the entire night despite the deafening clatter.

The following morning we walked to where the aged *Marina Perch* stood, already crowded with passengers who had been picked up at another port. Those who were now waiting to squeeze aboard formed such a long line that it took about an hour to get to the entrance. My family's turn came and it was time to say good-bye. Once more Harry assured me that one way or another we would soon be reunited. Harry and Lilly found a spot on the deck from where we could, with tears in our eyes, wave to each other as the ship pulled away from its moorings. I was unhappy that, after so many years of wandering, I could not be on that ship with my brother and his family on the way to the country I so yearned for.

Back in Cremona, Henry tried to divert me from my gloomy state by suggesting, among other things, that we get drunk, a remedy he often used during times of ill fortune—and in times of good fortune as well. As in the past, I assured Henry that I was going to be fine without his prescription. Henry was a dear friend, but he did not know how to console me.

The next day I visited Laura who, better than anyone else, understood the hopelessness I felt with the departure of my family for America. From her I got not only a fine meal, but the commiseration I badly needed. She had always known how to cheer me up when I was especially despondent. This time she arranged for a week's vacation at the country home of her parents. Being away from camp and in Laura's company distracted me from my worries—certainly a better remedy for my melancholy than getting drunk with Henry.

When I returned, I learned that Henry had found new ways to make contacts for potential sponsors. One of the fellows in camp who was also trying to get to the States suggested that we use the names and addresses in the advertising section of the *Forward*, a Jewish newspaper published in New York. Using this method, he had succeeded in finding a compassionate Jewish family which was now in the process of getting him a visa with no cost to him other than the eventual ship passage. We tried our luck, but out of the ten letters we mailed only one family responded—with great sympathy for our plight and with a ten dollar contribution. This was not as good as a visa, but certainly not a total loss in my financial predicament.

Finally I received the long-awaited letter from Harry. The ten-day voyage on the *Marina Perch* had been terrible. Everyone, including little Bertha, suffered from seasickness and from the awful food that was served on the ship. The good news was that Lilly's cousin Eugene had already rented a small apartment for them on Herzl Street in Brooklyn. It was, to be sure, in a very poor neighborhood, but good enough for my brother, who had no money and did not want to put a further financial strain on Lilly's relatives. As humble as the apartment was, both Harry and Lilly expressed delight at finally having privacy, and a bathroom of their own where no one would knock on the door asking them to hurry up. Just as encouraging was the news that Harry was able to start working within a few days of their arrival.

The demand for tailors was so great that he even had a choice of jobs.

In spite of Harry's investigations, the prospects of finding a sponsor for me were not very good. It was now two years since my arrival in Cremona and it looked more and more as though getting to America was a futile dream. Our once-overcrowded camp was becoming less and less populated. From my room alone, almost half the people had already left, either for Israel, Canada, or the United States, while others awaited departure with visas in hand. Seeing so many empty cots brought on feelings of anxiety. I feared that soon I was going to be the only one left in that room with no place to go. Adding to my distress was the fact that in the fall Laura was to begin classes at the University of Bologna, which would considerably limit our chances of being together. Despite Laura's comforting words, I felt as though everything was crumbling before me. I had to find a way out of this limbo.

The refugees who remained were, for the most part, those who were waiting to go to Israel. With their strong Zionist orientation, they attempted to influence the rest of us to consider Israel as a refuge. Given the apparent hopelessness of my emigrating to the States, I too began to think seriously about the possibility of going to Israel, despite the fact that life there was particularly tough for new arrivals. They often lived in tents in remote parts of the country far away from civilization. The devoted Zionists were prepared to endure this kind of life just so they could be in the Promised Land. I was hoping for something better.

I spent many agonizing hours vacillating between the remote hope of eventually getting to America and the more likely prospect of getting to Israel. I naturally turned for advice to my two dear friends, Henry and Laura, though never at the same time! Henry, who had succeeded in making his own arrangement to go to America, was opposed to my considering Israel as a refuge. He still held out hope that I would manage to find my way to the United States. Poor Laura could give me no advice in this matter. As much as she wanted to perpetuate our relationship, my happiness took precedence over her desire for me to remain in Cremona. Laura, more than anybody else, was keenly aware that I had made an irrevocable decision to become a teacher. This dream could not be fulfilled without my obtaining an education.

Perhaps Israel might afford me the opportunity? I knew that Israel was now fighting a war and was more likely in need of soldiers and hard-working men and women than in future teachers.

Still, since I could not count on getting to America, I joined a kibbutz that anticipated being called to Naples, the base from which illegal ships took off whenever the time was propitious. My decision to try for Israel was of course not carved in stone, nor was joining the kibbutz a firm commitment. I was still hoping that Harry would come up with a sponsor. But I felt that I should stop relying on miracles alone. I had to make at least a symbolic step to prove to myself that I was not possessed by inertia.

The school year began for our children. Here, too, it was obvious that many families had left camp. The school population was considerably reduced, and those children who remained appeared restless, many of them upset by the recent departure of their classmates. They too must have felt that what was once a vibrant place was now listless, and were as anxious as I was to leave camp for a more permanent place. Within a month after I joined the kibbutz, Aliyah Bet was almost completely halted. In fact, a few of my friends who were taken to Naples had boarded a ship that was detained in port. The poor fellows returned to Cremona devastated. The news of ships being caught and refugees returned to their camps drove many people to despair. There were of course a few happy families who were waiting for imminent departure to America and other destinations. But for the most part those who were still bogged down in our camp were beset by gloom and hopelessness, I among them.

Chapter 16

On the Way to America

Just when everything looked bleakest, a most fortuitous event took place. One of my dance students came with great excitement to tell Henry and me that he would be leaving for America in a few weeks. He had an uncle there who sent papers not only for him but for others who were not relatives. He said casually, "Micky, I'll give you Mr. Newman's address. He is a very generous man. Perhaps he will help you." His tone implied that he did not believe this was actually going to happen.

We quickly returned to our room. Henry always spoke very fast, particularly when he spoke Hungarian, but this time he was so excited that he began to stutter. "C-c-c-come on, c-c-c-come on, dummy," he said impatiently, "we must send a letter immediately." We wrote briefly about my childhood, my experiences with the labor units, and the refugee camp. Henry insisted I say nothing about my intentions of becoming a teacher. With every sentence Henry nervously said, "No, no, this is too bland; let's be more dramatic; let's move the man." The final draft was a dramatic but sincere account of my situation. We emphasized that Mr. Newman's only out-of-pocket expense would be the five-dollar application fee for the visa, which I would repay. I would pay for my passage as well as for all other expenses. The fact that my name had been registered on the quota for the last two years would save him the trouble of visiting the immigration office to expedite my processing. As for my capacity to earn a living, we included in the letter that I was an experienced mechanic, assuring Mr. Newman that in no way would I be financially dependent on him. We included Harry's address and telephone number in case he wanted to discuss the situation with him.

We sent the letter by registered airmail and were told that it would most likely be in Mr. Newman's hand in three days. Henry even had the foresight to make a long distance call to my brother in Brooklyn, which cost us nothing because of his employment in the commander's office, not a small advantage, given my financial state. I related the good news to Harry; he was elated by this fortunate development. I suggested that he call Max Newman within five days. What follows has been retold so many times by both my brother and Max Newman that I can recall every detail as if I were there.

Harry did not have to wait the five days. Mr. Newman phoned as soon as he received my letter and invited him to come to his house the following Sunday. Harry, who was unfamiliar with the Bronx, had a hard time finding 207 Post Avenue, but finally reached the house and was welcomed by a short, cheerful-looking man. "It must be very cold outside," Max Newman said. "You look so pale. Esther," he addressed his wife, "let's give this man a hot cup of tea." All this in Yiddish, not only because Harry's English was still limited, but because Max loved to speak *mame loshen* (the mother tongue).

"I read your brother's letter," he said to Harry. "I want you to stop being anxious about Micky's coming to join you. I'm going to send him the papers. You see, forty years ago another man sent me papers. And I am doing the same for a few Holocaust survivors. I am very grateful to God that I have been able so far to bring to the States seventeen people. I have a delicatessen store. All I had to do, was to sell a few more pastrami sandwiches to bring to America my fellow immigrants. I think I can afford one more person, so we will make your brother number eighteen. You know that number eighteen, *chai*, has a special meaning for us Jews; it is the symbol for life." Max's unassuming monologue was capped with a "*le chaim*" (to life) and a glass of schnapps that he finished in one gulp while Harry had to struggle to drink just some of it so as not to offend his host. "Now," said Max Newman, "let us get to the information I will need to start things going." He led Harry into the kitchen, and the process of my liberation from refugee camp began.

How extraordinary that a conversation with a casual friend from camp should have led me to this generous man for whom I had been searching desperately the past two years. It is difficult to describe the exultation Henry and I experienced when we received the telegram from Harry with this overwhelming news. We knew that it did not mean I was going to America tomorrow. In fact, given my past disappointments, I did not rush to celebrate. However, I had taken the first step on the long journey to a new home and now had a reason to hope.

It was the beginning of November and Laura was hard at work at the University of Bologna. I called to give her the good news. She was of course happy for me, but I could tell from many of her questions that she would have liked my departure to be delayed. I assured her that it would take three months or more before I would actually leave. When I met her at the train Friday evening, she held me in her arms for a long time. It was as though we were already saying our final good-bye. We spent part of the evening by ourselves. Laura's mood was ambivalent. She spoke with enthusiasm about my beginning a new life, but always with a subdued sadness about our eventual separation. She urged me to continue studying English and not to give up my aspiration to become a teacher. "You see, Michele, fate decides things for us, and fate is probably right. But why am I talking this way? After all, we still have a great deal of time to spend together." Later that evening Laura's friends came to the apartment to share in our celebration. On Monday Laura returned to Bologna.

Discouraged by Henry's teaching methods, I decided to study English on my own. He helped me by making phone calls to bookstores all over Italy to find a Hungarian-English grammar. He found one in Rome, and suggested that while I was there I should also buy some books on math. Having worked with me, he was probably the only person at the time who knew that I had no formal schooling beyond fourth grade, and he felt that mathematics was crucial to resuming my education. Henry wrote out a round-trip ticket, and I was off shopping. My purchases left me broke. I still have the grammar book, thanks to which I was able to make some progress with English, but I had a hard time with math; fractions were not my cup of tea.

In addition to continuing to work with the children and studying math and English, I joined a drama group conducted by a professional actor-director who had worked in one of Warsaw's Jewish theaters before the war. After two weeks of workshops, and the opportunity to appear in several Yiddish plays, I was bitten by the acting bug.

Within a few weeks of Harry's visit to Max Newman, my application was sent to the Office of Immigration, and my chances of getting a visa appeared to be good. Now I had to start thinking seriously of finding ways to get money for passage. My profits from the cigarettes brought from Innsbruck had by now been spent. Once more Henry was the driving force behind my effort to find a sponsor to pay for my passage.

We wrote mostly to Jewish organizations in the United States and Canada, but nothing was forthcoming, not even a few ten-dollar donations like those resulting from our previous campaign. Several of our respondents suggested, some with annoyance, that there were organizations set up for the purpose of taking care of refugees, such as HIAS or the JDC (American Jewish Joint Distribution Committee). We knew about these, but we also knew by now that HIAS gave money only if there was a sponsor in the States who would reimburse them.

In the middle of December, in the same mail as one of the rejection letters, I received notification from the U.S. Immigration Service that a visa had been granted with a possible departure date in February 1948. This was contingent on whether all my other documents were in good order and on my successful passing of the medical examination that would take place in January. Henry and I were thrilled at my good fortune, but worried about my failure to get passage money. "Micky," Henry said imperiously, "you are going to Rome. First try the HIAS. Most likely they will reject you, but you have nothing to lose. If they do say no, you must then go to the JDC. I don't want you to come home without a ship ticket."

I arrived in Rome at night with barely enough money for two meals, and with no place to stay. Since I could not afford a hotel, I spent part of the night in the corridor of a building until I was chased away by the concierge. Fortunately, the December nights in Rome were not cold, and I went to sleep near the Trevi Fountain to the soothing murmur of the tumbling water. By seven o'clock in the morning I was already standing in line in front of the HIAS office with some two dozen other refugees, waiting nervously for my turn. Hours later, having repeated my story in office after office to no avail, I left, thoroughly dejected.

With the last few lire in my possession, I bought a plate of spaghetti and then went to the office of the JDC. The building was surrounded by petitioners and it took three hours just to get inside. Here I was treated more cordially than at HIAS, but as soon as the caseworker learned of my brother and Max Newman, she suggested that I ask one of them for passage money. Despite my explanation of the circumstances, she dismissed me politely but firmly.

I returned to Cremona feeling hopeless and depressed. Everyone in the room was asleep when I arrived at midnight. Henry awoke and whispered, "Well, Micky, I bet you have good news." I told him I had returned empty-handed. He jumped out of his cot, put on his pants, and motioned with his hand for me to follow him to his office. I gave him a blow by blow description of what had happened in Rome. "Micky," he said, "you were probably not emphatic enough." He raised his voice. "You still don't understand that the world doesn't function to help the meek. You are not going to get anywhere with gentleness. These fellows will grant you nothing just for your politeness." He paused and checked the train schedule. "Now listen. There is a train at five o'clock in the morning. I will write out a ticket. I want you to return to Rome and go back to the JDC. They are still your only hope. Be forceful. If that doesn't help, cry; be dramatic; show them your acting ability, and make sure you see someone more important than a caseworker!" I wanted to delay my return by at least a day, but Henry would not allow it.

Back in Rome, while standing on line again for several hours at the JDC, I met a young woman who was there on a similar mission. She suggested that I ask for Mrs. Elkin who was in charge of one of the offices. When finally, with great difficulty, I got in to see her, I followed Henry's instructions and, warming up to my assignment, made full use of my acting talent, shedding genuine tears.

Mrs. Elkin was herself a survivor of the Holocaust. Unlike most of the people I had seen before, she showed sympathy for my plight and was eager to help. Fifteen minutes into our conversation, she concluded that there was a good chance of her getting the passage money for me but suggested that I continue the search for another source just in case she did not succeed. She anticipated that she could let me know one way or the other within two weeks. I returned to Cremona exhausted, eager to tell Henry the promising news. He was overjoyed and puffed up with pride to learn that his advice had borne fruit.

Laura came home for the Christmas break, and I spent several days with her family. As always, her parents were hospitable. Signore Launi jovially admonished me that if I became a millionaire in

America I should not hesitate to share some of my wealth with the family. As for Signora Launi, I had the impression that she was sorry Laura and I were going to separate. Several times in the past she had said jokingly that she would like to have a son-in-law just like me. At a New Year's Eve party, my Italian friends wished me well in anticipation of my departure for America. Before Laura returned to Bologna, she assured me that she would come back to Cremona before I was to leave for America.

The reply from Mrs. Elkin for which I was impatiently waiting finally came in the form of a letter. It said that a ticket was being prepared and that I must come to Rome at once to fill out the necessary papers. According to the Immigration and Naturalization Service, I would be eligible for departure around February 8, provided I passed the medical exam. Now all I had to worry about was that the doctors might find a disqualifying health problem resulting from my soccer injury.

Henry lost no time in making out yet another train ticket. I was off once more to Rome, this time with considerably less anxiety. Letter in hand, I no longer had to stand in line with the rest of the anxious refugees who encircled the large building. Mrs. Elkin received me with a warm smile that showed her satisfaction with having been able to help me. She said I was going to sail from Naples, on the SS *Marina Perch*, the very ship that had carried Harry and Lilly across the sea. She added with a smile, "It's not a luxury liner, as you will discover for yourself, but young travelers can take it. I'm sure you won't be too uncomfortable." After the various forms were filled out, we spent some time talking. Mrs. Elkin sent me off with some encouraging words about the opportunities to become successful in America. "Should things go well for you," she concluded, "don't forget that there are still thousands of refugees less fortunate than you. Help them as soon as you can."

The train ride back to Cremona seemed longer than ever. I couldn't wait to show Henry the ticket to America that I held firmly in my hand throughout the trip. When I got to the camp, I ran to my room with arms stretched high in the air waving the ticket as though it were a flag of victory. In the middle of January, I was on my way to Naples for my physical. I brought along my Hungarian-English grammar with the intention of doing some studying, but I was too worried about the examination to concentrate. Sitting across from me on the train was an unshaven, poorly dressed, tired-looking Italian man of about forty. He glanced at me from time to time with sunken red eyes, as though he was eager to start a conversation. After a while, he pulled out a cloth kerchief in which were wrapped a piece of cheese and slices of bread. This time he looked directly at me and said quietly, *"Volete favorire* [Would you like to help yourself]?" He held the open bundle out to me, and urged, *"Dai senza vergogna* [Come on, don't be ashamed]." Though I was hungry, I did not want to deprive him of his skimpy meal. After more urging, I accepted a slice of the bread and some cheese. This was soon washed down with the red wine that we both drank straight from a grubby bottle.

The meal was followed by formal introductions. I learned that his name was Pietro Panini, and that he was a farmhand from the outskirts of Naples. Whenever he could not find work in his area, he would travel to other towns in the south to earn some money. He was now on his way home after a one-week absence. I told him about myself as well. Other than the fact that the foul smoke from his hand-rolled cigarette drifted in my direction, I was happy to have such a congenial traveling companion.

At around eight in the evening, as we were nearing Naples, Pietro asked me where I was going to spend the night and whether I would like to have a meal at his house first. I replied that I planned to go to the port where another refugee had told me there were many comfortable benches near the water. Pietro let loose a torrent of words, speaking so fast I could barely understand him. "You will do no such thing. What do you want, to be killed by some thief? You are coming home with me!" I was very relieved, and eagerly accepted his offer because I had heard of the area's bad reputation and was really frightened at the thought of going there.

As we entered Pietro's small two-room house, Pietro called out cheerfully to his wife, *"Angelina sono qua; abbiamo un ospite* [Angelina I am here; we have a guest]," and added laughingly, *"Metti un po' più d'acqua nella zuppa* [put some more water in the soup]." The soup and the rest of the meal were delicious and served with a generous Italian heart. After dinner they opened a folding cot for me in the children's room. I slept well and for some eight hours I was able to forget all about the checkup that had been causing me so much anxiety.

I was sent off to the embassy with a rich serving of polenta and the good wishes of the entire family. At the end of the extensive half-hour examination, the doctor told me that as a consequence of the two operations there remained a slight opening in the abdomen, an incisional hernia, that must eventually be corrected by surgery. After another half hour of waiting alone in the tiny room, worried to death while the doctor consulted with a colleague, he returned with the good news. "You are lucky," he said. "We have decided to pass you for entry, but you must promise that you will have the surgery soon after you get there. We want you to know that according to strict rules we should have rejected you." He warned me that until the surgery was performed I should not lift anything heavy. My jubilation was only somewhat diminished by the prospect of facing yet another operation that might limit the kind of job I could take on in America.

It was now definite that I was to sail on February 8, arriving in New York a month before Henry was scheduled to leave—a reversal we had never anticipated. When I called Harry, he could barely talk for happiness at the good news. He told me that he had spent many sleepless nights worrying about me and feeling guilty about leaving me behind. My normally grouchy friend Henry was listening in to our conversation, smiling and glowing with pride, and rightly so. I cannot imagine how I could have managed without his unflagging help.

Laura would have liked to come home, but could not afford to miss her classes. At her suggestion, I went to Bologna for three days even though we could not be together as often as we wanted. Nevertheless the time we spent in each other's company was precious. Laura was particularly tender; she consoled me about our separation and gave me several reasons why going to America was my only way out of refugee existence.

My last week in Cremona was taken up with fulfilling immigration service requirements, such as getting injections and filling out papers. I tried to spend as much time as possible with the children, preparing them for my departure. I knew they would be as upset as I at our separation. To console them, I told them they would be leaving the camp soon and that we might see each other in the United States. My work with them had given me the strength to contend with many difficulties, especially my illness. I will always treasure those two-and-a-half years I spent with them.

Laura came back three days before I was to leave. We spent Saturday and part of Sunday hidden from the rest of the world. Although we had anticipated and rehearsed our eventual separation for a long time, the final leave-taking was very painful for both of us. We reminisced about the wonderful times we had had together and fantasized about the possibility that fate would bring us together again. We would not forget each other; we would write—all these promises were small consolation in this last hour before our parting. I accompanied Laura to the train station when she had to return to Bologna for Monday morning classes. The train arrived. We exchanged our last embrace. I held her hand in a firm clasp till the last moment and reluctantly let go when she was obliged to get on the train. As the train pulled out of the station, I ran after her car to the end of the platform trying to capture one last glimpse of her face.

By now all the people in my room and many others in camp knew that I was leaving for America. Some brought letters they wanted me to mail in the United States, and others were sending messages to relatives and friends. On Monday morning I said goodbye to the Bruni family, who had been so devoted to me and whose delicious soups had often saved me from having to eat the camp food.

In a friendly gesture, the camp director arranged for a truck to take me to the station though, with my small valise, I could have walked there easily. My last hour in camp was spent running from room to room saying good-bye to my fellow refugees. While I waited for the truck, I was surrounded by well-wishers. Some looked happy, probably in anticipation of their own imminent departure; others looked as if they had been forgotten by the rest of the world. The children, too, came to say good-bye and give me their hugs and kisses. I wished I could take them all with me; in a sense I would. As we were pulling out of the camp, I was leaving a place where a host of people and events had profoundly affected my life. Although, I was on my way to a new country, to the golden land, a permanent home, I felt that in leaving Cremona I was uprooting myself. I hoped ferverently that it would be for the last time.

Henry accompanied me to the station. As I was about to board the train, I tried to thank him for all he had done for me but he stopped me after the first expression of gratitude. "You probably did as much for me as I did for you," he murmured. "Who else but you would have taught a bear like me to dance and tolerated his unpredictable moods." We embraced and made a date to meet in New York on his arrival, some time in March. Henry made one more attempt to offer me some money. I refused adamantly, claiming that I had enough until I boarded the ship. Not true, but the pride instilled in me by my mother always prevented me from accepting charity even if it meant hunger pangs. Exhausted from the emotions of the last few days, I would have liked someone to talk to about what I had left behind. Alas, most of the people on the train were asleep. I, too, fell asleep and was awakened two hours later by the shouts of the train vendor who was loudly advertising his prosciutto sandwiches.

We arrived in Naples at eight in the morning. I ate breakfast for my last few lire and, carrying my small suitcase, walked to the other end of town. The waterfront was mobbed. Porters, pushing their carts loaded with suitcases and packages, shouted "*Attenzione!*" as they carelessly cut their way through the crowds. With great difficulty I found the place where the *Marina Perch* was anchored. In front of the dock, hundreds of people sat or stood amidst their meager possessions. The vast majority, it turned out, were Italians, mostly from Sicily, emigrating to America. Only some three dozen or so were Jews.

Mrs. Elkin was right. The *Marina Perch* was not a luxury liner. It was in fact a rundown old vessel making its last few voyages. It was so overcrowded that some people didn't even have assigned sleeping quarters. My ticket entitled me to the cheapest berth, in the lowest part of the ship right over the engine room. The "bed" was suspended at the four corners by yard-long heavy chains, a kind of iron hammock. When the sea was turbulent, the beds swung furiously in every direction, so that several times during the trip my neighbor and I collided and fell out. We soon realized that we were better off sleeping on the floor where we would simply roll back and forth during rough weather.

The food was so bad that even I, who had often subsisted on an inadequate diet, was barely able to eat any of it. Had I been able to afford it, I could have bought better meals at the canteen. Richly compensating for the poor food, however, was the cheerful atmosphere. On different parts of the deck, groups of Italian merrymakers entertained each other as well as the onlookers. It was not unusual during the course of a day to listen to Sicilian and Neapolitan songs as only the Italians can sing them, the bel canto of a melancholy Italian tune, or an aria performed by a respectable amateur baritone. One might also join in the vivacious tarantella and other dances to the reverberating accordion of Pepino, who was after a few days the most popular young man on the ship.

For a change from these diverting performances, one could simply stand on the deck and observe the impressive workings of nature—the beauty of the sea, the changing hues of the water, the playful porpoises, and the colossal waves that from time to time tossed our ship about. This was the first time in my life that I had the opportunity to see such breathtaking natural marvels.

Although still feeling bad about my separation from Laura, I began to look ahead with anticipation toward my new home and to joining my family. But I was anxious as well about a number of things. Foremost on my mind was the fact that with all my good intentions I had not studied enough English. The constant running around for documents and working with the children almost to the last day before my departure, had left me very little time. I was also concerned about getting a job as soon as possible so that I would not have to depend on anyone for assistance.

My wandering through the ship led me to a small group of Jewish men and women who huddled in a corner of the deck near a vent that supplied them with warm steam. All of them, in one way or another, were victims of the Holocaust. They gathered at the same spot, some for morning prayer and others simply to find companions with whom they could share their hopes and sorrows. Among them was Rachel, a Romanian woman in her late twenties, who had miraculously survived the death camp at Birkenau. When she searched for her family, she found only her sister's two young girls, aged nine and eleven, who had been hidden in a Catholic convent. The older girl still remembered some of her Yiddish but the younger child no longer spoke it. Rachel told us how difficult it was to persuade the younger child that she was Jewish and that Jews have their own prayers which do not include crossing themselves.

Being naturally drawn to children, I spent some time with the two girls almost every day listening to their stories. Chanele, the older girl, told me that when they were first brought to the convent she missed her parents very much and cried a great deal. But the mother superior and the other nuns were so kind to them that she stopped crying. The little one, Perele, told me that she did not cry much, because she knew that her mommy and her daddy would soon come back. She now believed that she was going to meet them in America.

The only other surviving member of Rachel's family was an aging aunt in America who sponsored their immigration. Rachel was obviously devoted to the children. She referred with great pride to the fact that the two girls called her Mama. "You see, I am now a mother *un boich veituk* [without having had labor pains]," she said with a wry smile, "*Ich will fon sei vider Yiddishe maidlech machen* [I want to turn them back into Jewish girls]," she added. The day before we were to disembark I saw for the last time this fragmented family. I said goodbye to Rachel and to the children and was rewarded with a kiss by the little girls. I prayed that the ordeal they had endured would not come back to haunt them and that they would be able to overcome the harm done to them.

On February 16, the morning of our arrival, the Jewish contingent met in the usual spot. But this time, there were no more sad stories. The mood was jovial, everyone anticipating with great excitement his entry into America, the *Goldene Medina*. One of the young men took out of his pocket a worn-out sheet of paper with a picture of the Statue of Liberty, explained its history, and read with great solemnity part of the inscription on its base.

About an hour before we were to dock, an announcement was made that we should start preparing our luggage. After an exchange of addresses and good wishes, our group broke up, later to join the rest of the passengers, who lined the railings as though linked to each other, a living chain. As we passed the Statue of Liberty, people tossed coins and hats in her direction. I managed with my sketchy English to read the first few lines inscribed at the lady's feet. Standing on an elevated part of the deck, Pepino played his accordion lustily, and the singing and dancing continued until the ship was fully docked and ready to pour forth its hopeful human cargo.

PART TWO

THE GOLDEN DOOR

Here at our sea-washed sunset gates shall stand
A mighty woman with a torch, . . . and her name
Mother of Exiles. From her beacon hand
Glows world-wide welcome; . . .
". . . Send these, the homeless, the tempest-tost to me
I lift my lamp beside the golden door!"

Emma Lazarus, "The New Colossus"

*Lines from sonnet inscribed
on base of Statue of Liberty*

Chapter 17
_____

A New Beginning

Was there any unanticipated circumstance that might prevent my entry to the United States? If not, would my dreams be realized in this new, unknown world? Was I prepared to face the many daunting challenges which would no doubt confront me in my pursuit of these dreams? Or was I leaving myself vulnerable to more disillusionment and failure? These were among the many questions that plagued me during the half hour I waited nervously in line to have my papers processed.

My voice trembled as I responded to the questions posed in German by a severe-looking customs official. To my great relief he passed me through with a noisy application of rubber stamps to my various documents and a brusque, "Good luck."

Two welcome encounters quickly eased some of my anxieties. The first was with a representative from the JDC who approached me as I walked toward the gangplank. He said he was there to take me, along with a few other new arrivals, to a hotel where I would be given room and board till I could get a job and live on my own. The second, after I disembarked, was with my sister-in-law, who was excitedly waving her hands and calling my name from behind a railing. It was a very emotional and happy meeting, despite my disappointment that Harry had been unable to get off from work and I would not see him until evening.

Lilly and some others were permitted to get into the minibus to accompany their newly-arrived relatives to the hotel. The winter of 1947-48 ranked among the most severe of the twentieth century, with several particularly heavy snowfalls, one of them just a few days before my arrival. Traffic moved at a crawl, and it took us over an hour to get from the 42nd Street pier to 103rd Street and Broadway where the Hotel Marseilles was located. It was a penetratingly cold day, and the city looked somber, but nothing in my dreary surroundings could dampen either my elation or a sense of freedom beyond any I had ever experienced before.

At the hotel yet another surprise awaited me, my sponsor, Max Newman, who immediately picked me out from the group because he had a photograph I had sent him from Cremona. He embraced me and repeated several times, "*Se zol zein mit mazel, mein zeen* [Let it be with good luck, my son]," a phrase my mother had used often. Mr. Newman was a stocky man in his mid-fifties, with a kindly face, and smiling eyes that were partly hidden under his huge dark eyelids. "Where is your winter coat?" he asked, alarmed. "You will freeze in this cold weather! Perhaps you don't have one," he whispered in my ear. "Tomorrow I'll take care of that."

Max Newman accompanied Lilly and me to my tiny room. As soon as I had deposited my few belongings, he insisted, despite my polite protestations, on taking us to a restaurant for a good Jewish meal. As we walked out of the hotel I saw for the first time in four years, on the window of a butcher store a sign, KOSHER, written in Hebrew letters, as well as others in Yiddish. At the sight of this flourishing Jewish life untouched by Hitler, I was filled with joy and sadness at the same time.

The delicious food was the best I had eaten since my mother's cooking. This was no reflection on Laura's culinary skills and the wonderful meals I had with her family, but there is something about one's own ethnic food that, if only for sentimental reasons, cannot be rivaled by any other cuisine. The conversation at the table was filled with optimism. Max Newman was very hopeful about my future and predicted jovially that I was going to become "a millionaire in America." We also learned that Mr. Newman came from the same area of the Carpathians as my mother and had known some members of our family before the Holocaust claimed them. When we parted after lunch, he reminded me emphatically, not only that he was taking me shopping for a coat the next day, but that he wanted to be the first person to show me around New York.

Finally, Lilly and I were on our way to Brooklyn. Going down into the subway for the first time was a strange experience—a descent into the underworld, an oppressive darkness that I did not associate with the liveliness and beauty of the city itself. I breathed a sigh of relief when we got to the part of Brooklyn where the train emerged from under the ground. Throughout our trip, Lilly did not stop talking about little Bertha. I could not wait to hold her once more in my arms and plant a hundred kisses on her.

We made our way from the station through huge snowdrifts to Herzl Street in Brownsville, a poor neighborhood even in those days. The building where Harry and Lilly lived was in a disappointing state of disrepair, and I was shocked to see the mounds of garbage piled up in the street. This was America where the streets were supposed to be paved with gold. The neatly furnished little apartment was a welcome relief after the trash-filled sidewalk.

There at last was little Bertha. When she saw me, she willingly left her Aunt Helen's embrace as I extended my arms to hold her, and she displayed the same affection for me as in the past. At the urging of her mom, I got my first kiss, followed by a few more on her own initiative. Despite the excitement I had already experienced, seeing that child was still one of the highlights of the day.

The reunion with Harry crowned it all with mutual joy. Finally, I had made it to America after so much suspense and uncertainty about whether we would see each other at all for years to come. This was a cause for celebration, and a surprise gathering had been arranged in honor of my arrival. Lilly's sisters and their husbands, Harry's friends, and a few eligible young ladies from the building were all there to meet "the greenhorn" so often talked about in the family.

It was indeed a fine first day in America, a happy beginning of a new life. Harry wanted me to stay overnight, but I felt adventurous and had him walk me to the subway. I was a little anxious about getting lost, but I had no trouble finding my way to the Hotel Marseilles. It took me a long time to fall asleep, for my thoughts wandered toward the recent past, and my happiness at being in America collided with the regret of having had to leave Italy. I longed more than ever to see and to caress Laura's face. I wanted to tell her that I loved her and that I was not as ready as I thought to accept the parting that fate had decreed for us.

After breakfast the next morning, Mr. Newman came to take me shopping. I tried to persuade him that I would very soon be able to earn my own money and buy all the things I needed, but he would not hear of it and took me by taxi to a clothing shop on 42nd Street. The storekeeper greeted him with, *"Noch a greener,* Max [One more greenhorn, Max]?"

"Yes," Max responded proudly, "this one is number eighteen." And turning to me, "You see, Micky, I've been here before a few times." The clerk had me try on several coats as Mr. Newman circled around me to check whether the fit was perfect. We finally found one to his liking and, I must say, to mine as well. It was the most beautiful coat I had ever had. "Chaim Yankel," Max said to the clerk, "show us some nice scarves," and, to me, almost apologetically, "Micky, my boy, you can't wear such a nice coat without a warm scarf."

When we finished shopping, Mr. Newman took me to the top of the Empire State Building—so remarkably delicate despite its enormous height. It was overwhelming to see the seemingly endless expanse of the city, as though only the horizon bounded it. Black smoke belching from factories across the river contrasted with the gleaming white snow in Central Park in the near distance. Ant-sized cars crawled through the crowded streets below.

Then my guide showed me the Chrysler Building, the 42nd Street Library, and many other landmarks. By noon my neck was stiff from looking up at all the magnificent skyscrapers, far more striking than any I had seen in Rome, Milan, Naples, or Vienna. I was impressed not only by the beauty of this unique city, but by the variety of humanity I observed as we walked through the busy streets.

Next, Mr. Newman took me to one of his delicatessen shops, in Greenwich Village, where he introduced me to his workers, obviously proud of his newest protégé. Over a lunch, he told me how hard he had worked to finally have several such stores, each one more impressive than the other. "Micky," he said, "this is what America is about. I too came to this country with just a few pennies to my name. The answer is hard work. If you will work hard, I am sure you will have things that you never dared to dream of." I left the delicatessen well fed, not only with pastrami, but with the kind of paternal care I had never experienced. Like others who did not have this kind of father, I was forever in search of one.

When I returned to the hotel in the afternoon, I saw a notice in the entrance hall looking for a part time dishwasher and general kitchen worker. I immediately went to see the manager and got the job. I was to work four hours every morning for seventy-five cents an hour, plus one meal that I did not need since the JDC was providing me with food for the time being. The work was very hard, the environment was extremely stuffy and dirty, and it was not unusual to see rats running through the area.

Fortunately, I did not have to spend more than a week there. A caseworker came to inform me that the committee had found a job for me as an electrician's helper in Brooklyn, and I was to start work on Monday. I would have preferred to resume work as a bicycle mechanic, but since such a job was not available, I was glad to get out of the kitchen. This job also meant that I would no longer need help from the JDC.

With the ten dollars that Harry forced on me, I was lucky enough to find lodging on Herzl Street, very close to his place, for five dollars a week. There was barely enough space for a single bed in the tiny room. The toilet in the hall, which was shared by several tenants, had a cold-water sink but no bathing facilities, and it was so dirty that I avoided using it as much as possible. The landlady, however, permitted me to use her bathroom once a week if I promised not to use up too much of her hot water.

On Friday night I was invited to my brother's house for dinner. Lilly's sister Helen and her husband were there as well. In this familial setting, the smell of freshly baked challah, the flickering candles, the blessing of the wine, and the familiar Hebrew chants took me back to the days when Mother was still alive. I wished she could have been there to see her vivacious granddaughter dancing, singing, and hand-clapping as I held her on my lap.

On Monday I started my job, knowing that, since I was not a union member, my promised $25-a-week salary for an eight to nine hour workday was half the regular rate. My boss, Mr. Ruben, did not have a shop, but operated from the basement of his house, employing only one so-called journeyman electrician. Each morning, we would load up the station wagon with tools and different size ladders and drive to the work site. Mr. Ruben's work consisted almost exclusively of repairs, usually the restoration of electrical lines in burned-out buildings or old tenements, jobs which a well-established electrician would not touch.

Having to work in the filth and soot left over from a fire, with no place at home or at work to clean up, I decided that this was not going to be a job of long duration. Besides, it was obvious that I would not be able to use the skills I had learned with ORT in Cremona. Mr. Ruben did not need an electrician's helper, but someone to clean up and to carry a very heavy toolbox. I made up my mind, however, that I was not going to leave a bad job until I found a better one. So I stuck it out for six long weeks.

I did not allow my dissatisfaction with the job and my shabby lodging to distract me from my yearning to learn English as quickly as possible and get an education. This was one of the primary reasons for coming to America, and it took precedence over everything else in my life. Within a week of my arrival, I discovered P.S. 149, located on Sutter Avenue in Brooklyn. Unlike many other places in the world, this generous country offered free English lessons to immigrants. I attended classes three evenings a week with Mrs. McAffrey, a devoted teacher. She spoke a variety of languages, including Yiddish. It was not unusual to hear her explain a point of grammar in Italian or Yiddish flavored by her lovely brogue.

Grammar and vocabulary were not hard to master, but there was a lot of confusion over common expressions that Mrs. McAffrey used routinely without realizing that our literal minds might misinterpret them. If she said, "Look up when you speak to me," we did not realize that she meant we should look at her and not at the ceiling. "Look it up," though, referred to consulting the dictionary, and "Look out" meant to be careful rather than to gaze out the window. When she told us to write a "composition," I thought she was referring to music.

Nevertheless, I did well enough to become convinced that I had an aptitude for languages. In about seven weeks I was making such good progress that Mrs. McAffrey insisted I switch to a more advanced class offered at Thomas Jefferson Evening High School. Following her advice, I registered there not only for English but for other courses that eventually would be credited toward the high school equivalency diploma I was determined to achieve. Thanks to this caring teacher, and the unique American educational opportunity, what was once a hope was slowly becoming a reality.

During the same period I got a new job with the William Seidler Company on Broadway and 24th Street in Manhattan, which produced ladies' skirts and blouses on one large floor and stuffed toys on another. I had a variety of responsibilities. In the morning I worked like a longshoreman, hook and all, delivering huge bales of cotton to the three rooms where the toys were manufactured. In the afternoon I operated various sewing machines that made parts of the skirts and blouses, and did some pressing as well. These skills came from Mother's patiently showing her curious little boy how to work her old Singer as well as how to iron the most complicated pleated skirts.

The working conditions were as poor as they could be within the framework of legal requirements. While the place was not a firetrap, as "sweatshops" had been in earlier years, the air was hot and stuffy, the din of the machines was nerve-wracking, and the hours were long. But at least it was clean—a most welcome change from working on filthy burned-out buildings.

Another blessing of the new job was the $28-a-week starting salary, with an $8 raise within two weeks, that permitted me to move to a larger furnished room in a family's apartment on Pitkin Avenue. Though I shared the bathroom, I could shower every day, a luxury I had not had in all the years in DP camp or on Herzl Street. The most unexpected and most cherished benefit was being just a few blocks from Washington Irving High School. I was now able to register for two more courses, biology and elementary algebra, that Thomas Jefferson did not offer in night school. This brought my class attendance to five evenings. It was difficult to work as many as ten hours a day and study as well, but since I had no social life to speak of, other than visiting my family and writing letters to Laura, I had enough time to dedicate myself to my books, even beyond what was required.

I was lonely, but I could not bring myself to try to date girls while still suffering the loss of Laura. In addition, my earnings did not permit me the luxury of spending the kind of money required for dating in America. I learned that lesson the hard way. I had in fact become friendly with a young lady at school, who within a week of our acquaintance invited me to her prom at the Essex House, across the street from Central Park in Manhattan. Not realizing that a prom in America was an elaborate affair, I accepted. This event, a completely alien ritual to me, relieved me of two weeks' salary, an extravagance I could ill afford. Of all the cultural shocks one suffers coming to a new country, this was a major one for me, probably a .7 on the Richter Scale. In the milieu I came from, there were no proms for which you had to rent special evening attire and share the cost of a limousine. In Europe, the end of school was celebrated with a dance that required a minimal outlay of funds, followed by a leisurely walk in the park or on the main boulevard.

My forlorn social life and my loneliness paid off handsomely. My studies were going surprisingly well. The Grand Army Plaza library became my refuge. And at home, my antique-looking radio served as a companion as well as a source for learning English. I would listen to broadcasts, write down the new words, look them up in my well-worn English-Hungarian dictionary, and memorize them. I attended classes at both schools continuously every night of the week, even during the summer.

Just a year after my arrival, I had accumulated a sufficient number of credits to be close to high school equivalency. Mr. Aaroni, a teacher at Thomas Jefferson who had shown an interest in me, suggested that after the coming spring and summer sessions, I should start thinking about entering evening college as a non-matriculated student. It was hard for me to believe that such a step might soon be possible. Despite the daily hardships, I was happy with the progress I was making, for I now felt that I had begun to build a permanent life for myself, no longer fraught with repeated uprootings.

Laura's letters were becoming fewer and fewer. For a good while our correspondence had been filled with mutual expressions of affection. At about Christmas time her letters, while still loving, began to take on a less romantic tone. I had anticipated that this change was going to happen sooner or later. Laura revealed to me that she had met a young man who meant a great deal to her. The letter was replete with comforting words that showed sensitivity and concern about causing me disappointment. "Fate's decision to end our romance," she wrote, "should not end our friendship. I know that in some special way we will always love each other." She suggested that we continue our correspondence. What made me accept Laura's revelation with equanimity was the thought that our romance came to an end, not with recriminations, but with the confirmation that we had loved one another.

Along with the sadness that attended our final breakup, I felt a sense of relief, a sense of liberation from my own self-deception that by some miracle Laura and I would one day be able to pick up where we had left off. It was time for me to emerge from my delusion, to begin a more active social life and meet someone who might alleviate my loneliness. There were certainly enough advisers to urge me on. Harry, Lilly, Mr. and Mrs. Newman, and my landlady all came up with eligible girls who were also recent immigrants for the most part.

After a few such attempts at socializing, I realized that going to dances attended exclusively by other foreigners, most of whom spoke only Yiddish, was not really what I wanted. Not out of snobbery, but out of practical considerations, I was eager to associate as much as possible with American young people, to improve my English and to become part of my new world rather than live isolated from it.

On a Saturday in March of 1949—after a few dates with American girls, one of whom was forced on me by my landlady—I saw an elegant yet athletic-looking girl on the public tennis courts of a Brooklyn park where young people gathered and, between games, socialized. There were several attractive girls among those gathered, but Shirley's European looks appealed to me and her deep-set brown eyes beckoned me, though not intentionally on her part; she did not even notice me. I was hoping that someone would introduce us. Since no one did, I mustered up the courage to approach her on my own. We talked for a while and played some tennis. Although I enjoyed the tennis with this energetic, enthusiastic player, I enjoyed more watching her slender figure and shapely legs as she ran to retrieve and return my shots. Towards the end of the afternoon, I asked Shirley whether I could accompany her home but she had other plans. It took several efforts on my part before I was able to persuade her to go out with me.

Shirley was my age, a college graduate and a teacher of English in the secondary school. Who would have believed that, quite by accident, I had met a girl to whom I was so attracted and who turned out to be the ideal person for me, an English teacher! And here I was struggling with the English language. Shirley told me that my English was surprisingly good and suggested that I never improve so much that I lose my accent. I was sure that I would make progress in English and, I hoped, in our romance if our relationship continued.

My hope was fulfilled; after a short courtship Shirley and I decided to marry. In retrospect we were impetuous; there were practical reasons to wait, but we were young and in love.

There were a few obstacles along the way. Shirley's parents were very much opposed to her going out with, much less marrying, an immigrant who was about to begin his college career while she was already a teacher. It is a standard joke that Jewish families—and I suppose others aspiring to middle-class status—would like their daughters to marry a doctor, a lawyer, or someone in the so-called higher professions. Shirley's parents were no different. They did not know how determined I was to pursue my education and reach my goals. It was quite natural for them to hope that their intelligent, attractive daughter would marry someone with a more certain economic future than mine was at the time.

Both Shirley and I preferred not to have an ostentatious wedding. We chose instead to have a simple ceremony at the home of the rabbi, attended by the immediate family and a few close friends. Shirley and I moved in temporarily with her parents. Their objection to our marriage posed hardships for both of us, but it was I who bore the brunt of being rejected. It was difficult to live with the notion that I was considered unworthy of being their son-in-law. Notwithstanding the occasional unpleasantness, I continued my studies with determination, inspired by my wife's own resolve to help me realize my dreams.

In the fall of 1949 I entered the evening school at Brooklyn College as a semi-matriculated student. To become fully matriculated, I had to finish my high school equivalency, pass a foreign language examination, and maintain a B average in the first fifteen consecutive credits taken at the college. To get me started, Mrs. Geesis, the chief registrar, generously guided me through the maze of paperwork required for enrollment. Now I would be taking American history and English at the college, and two courses at the high school, a demanding undertaking after ten hours of sweating in Seidler's factory.

With great excitement and many misgivings I waited to attend my first classes. How was it actually going to be? Had I all this time been living an illusion that I was capable of getting a college education? Did I really possess the ability required for this daunting task? On the Tuesday of my first evening class, Mr. Seidler let me leave the factory an hour early. After waiting all those years for this chance, I was so anxious to be on time that I got to the campus at five o'clock for the six-thirty class. Those who attended Brooklyn College in my era probably remember the beauty of its Georgian architecture which has since been camouflaged by the many modern buildings that now crowd the campus. I sat on a bench with my faithful companion, the English-Hungarian dictionary, and a notebook in hand, looking at the beautiful bell tower of the library and listening to its soothing chimes. Surrounded by those imposing buildings where so much learning was taking place, I had a feeling of hope. Everything seemed well with the world and I knew I was going to succeed in my daring venture.

In Boylan Hall I waited outside the classroom door for the previous section to be dismissed, and was the first student to enter. Nervously I gave my name to the instructor, who checked it off on his roster. Soon the class was filled with young men and women who, unlike me, walked nonchalantly into the room. The teacher gave us an outline of the course in American history and the title of the text we were going to use. Other than a few strange expressions, like "whigs" referring to people rather than hairpieces, I was pleasantly surprised to find that I had no difficulty understanding the lecture.

Everything was going well in my English class too, until Mrs. Davidson began to discuss *A Portrait of the Artist as a Young Man* by James Joyce—not a fortuitous start for an immigrant struggling with the English language. I nevertheless felt that through hard work I would be able to overcome my disadvantages, and left both classes feeling confident that I would be able to cope.

Adding immeasurably to my happiness at the end of the semester was a most joyous event. My wife gave birth to a robust eight and a half pound baby boy, whom we named Jason Frederick after my mother, by taking the initials of Yitta Feiga. Jason's birth belonged to the same category of miracles as that of my niece—both were children born to Holocaust survivors who had many times looked at the face of death.

But Jason's arrival had much more than a symbolic meaning. If time had not been enough to heal my in-laws' disappointment over our marriage, the arrival of their grandson certainly did. There was a palpable change in their attitude toward me, making life much easier for all of us. Both my in-laws were devoted to the baby, and Shirley's mother was available to take care of him whenever we needed her.

Jason's birth was followed by a succession of other happy events. At the end of the 1950 summer session I learned that I had successfully completed the required admission credits with better than a B average. I had become a fully matriculated student, thanks not only to my own perseverance but to Shirley's help with my studies. As a result of my academic achievement, I was named one of the most outstanding foreign students and placed on the Dean's List. All the exhausting work had paid off, not to mention the anxiety accompanying those dreaded final examinations which I was barely able to finish on time, and the running to the mailbox with trepidation to find out the marks on which so much depended.

My honor gave me the opportunity to show the Newmans my gratitude. At a reception for the students who had made the Dean's List, each one was allowed to invite a special guest in addition to members of the family, and I chose Mr. Newman. If ever one wanted to see a proud face, looking at my benefactor would certainly have provided that sight.

Completion of the requirements for my high school equivalency made my work at Brooklyn College so much easier that I could enjoy the luxury of attending classes only three nights a week. And the fact that I was permitted to take courses in foreign languages, my strong suit, considerably tempered my earlier anxieties about examinations. To top it all off, I felt more comfortable on campus because I now had the opportunity to participate in school activities. Dr. Holtzman, our dedicated Russian teacher, who eventually became my devoted mentor, recruited me for the Russian Club where I met some wonderful people who were to become lifelong friends. Under Dr. Holtzman's leadership, the Russian Club was the most active in the school and always complemented our class work with solid activities. When we read Gogol, Gorky, or Tolstoy, the Russian classes would put on a play, with almost professional standards, to which the entire school was invited. In the course on Russian culture, the students performed variety shows with music, song, and dance.

I remember with nostalgia and fondness the strenuous rehearsals, which often took place at Dr. Holtzman's house where we all felt at home. It was there that I met young Liz Holtzman, who later became a Congresswoman and has continued to serve her country in a variety of capacities. People often remember at least one outstanding teacher they have had. I was twice blessed. My first-grade teacher, Mrs. Zhupan, in Kustanovice, and Dr. Filia Holtzman at Brooklyn College. It was at the prompting of Dr. Holtzman that I decided to major in Russian, with a minor in romance languages.

By my fourth year of evening college, halfway to my B.A. degree, I was slowly but surely marching toward the realization of my dream of becoming a teacher. I felt that, barring some unexpected disaster, I was going to succeed. My intellectual curiosity was genuine; I had inherited Mother's love of learning. As difficult as my academic work was, I cherished every moment of it. Reading and studying English, Russian, French, and Italian classics in their original languages was an exciting and absorbing experience.

On the home front, things were going well too. Jason was a delightful baby and gave us much joy. Now that I was attending college only three nights a week, I had the opportunity to spend more time with him. And on the evenings that Shirley was teaching, I had him all to myself, engaging in make-believe cowboy fights and fencing that made him break into gleeful chuckles.

Also, I had switched to a new job. As a cutter in an automobile seat cover factory, I was earning more money. My increased salary combined with Shirley's enabled us to contemplate the possibility of our own apartment. Even under the best of circumstances, living with one's in-laws is not the most desirable arrangement, despite the fact that by now there was harmony in our house.

Through a personal connection, we were offered an apartment in a good neighborhood in the Bronx at a very low rent. This was an irresistible opportunity, even though it necessitated Shirley's switching from her school in Brooklyn. With small windows facing a dark courtyard, the rooms were rather gloomy, but Shirley decorated them in bright earth colors with her usual impeccable taste.

To avoid traveling so far to work, I decided to change jobs once more. Besides, with the equivalent of two years of college under my belt, I thought I should now look for the kind of work that would be not only more remunerative but also more prestigious, primarily for the sake of my family. I was of course still determined to start teaching as soon I finished college, but that was far in the future.

In response to an advertisement in *The New York Times*, I arranged for an interview with a Mr. Ehrlich, the owner of a Manhattan electronics plant that manufactured parts for military hardware. He was looking for a "production manager," and I figured that with my experience as a mechanic and electrician I could handle a position like that with minimal training.

As is often the case with advertisements, it turned out that the job description did not match the fancy title. Being a production manager there meant that I would perform manual work while at the same time supervising some fifty workers. When Mr. Ehrlich asked whether I knew any Spanish, my answer was a very confident "Yes"—I was sure I could rely on my knowledge of Italian to serve in place of the Spanish I had yet to learn.

Mr. Ehrlich, apparently impressed with my credentials, was prepared to hire me on the spot. For my part, of course, there was the question of salary for a job that sounded better on paper than in reality. To my happy surprise, I was to be paid $60 a week for forty hours, plus overtime, with a raise to follow should my work be satisfactory. That was almost twice the amount I was making cutting seat covers! I accepted the offer, no longer concerned with the prestige of my new position. I managed not to display my inner excitement to Mr. Ehrlich, but I couldn't wait to call Shirley and tell her the good news.

Chapter 18

A Dream Realized

In early July of 1954, I received a letter summoning me to the office of the U. S. Immigration and Naturalization Service. I was to appear on the 19th for my final citizenship papers. Imagine the excitement in the family, not to mention my nervousness! Although I knew I would be able to answer questions on American history and government, I was still apprehensive.

The impatiently awaited day finally came, and we took Jason with us for this singular event. The immigration official who interviewed me asked a few questions on American government that I was able to answer without much hesitation. Before dismissing me, however, he suggested politely that I Americanize my name from Yehudah to Jay. I was so happy about my new status that I would have taken any name he came up with.

At eleven o'clock some fifty men and women were assembled in a courtroom, where we were led in saying the Pledge of Allegiance. The solemnity with which it was recited made it sound almost like a prayer. Judge William V. Connell swore us in as a group, after which our names were called individually to come forward to receive our Certificates of Naturalization.

We all sat in reverent silence till the last name was called. The moment the judge left, the hall was filled with happy chatter and congratulations in a variety of accents and foreign tongues. Several people cried for joy as they hugged their relatives and loved ones.

I was overjoyed to have become at last a citizen of the United States. Though I had been fairly sure I would get my final papers, dealing with officialdom always carried with it some uncertainty. Now that I was securely clutching that piece of parchment, there were no more doubts in my mind. I was a full-fledged American with all the attendant privileges, including, for the first time in my life, the right to vote.

My wandering had definitely come to an end. I now had a safe and permanent home from which neither I nor my child would ever be dragged to a concentration camp. For most people lucky enough to have been born in America, it must be difficult to understand the elation that accompanies becoming a citizen of this precious country and, in my case, to have finally left behind the land of my oppressors.

Living in the Bronx was pleasant, but it was terribly inconvenient to have to travel back after classes in Brooklyn which often ran till 10:30 p.m. The registrar suggested that I consider transferring to City College, in Manhattan. Since this might have meant the loss of some hard-earned credits, I decided to stay and endure the difficulties—which I did for three more years.

My job at the factory was going well. Not only did I get my raise four weeks after I started, but there were other pluses I had not expected. For one, I was learning Spanish at a lightning rate. More important, supervising my floor and working with those delightful people was the most gratifying job I had had since my arrival in America. I have many wonderful memories of the generosity and affection of these honest, hard-working souls, most of them Puerto Rican women who often offered to share their lunch with me.

I was sorry to witness how poorly these workers were remunerated and how quickly they were laid off when business slowed down. I did everything I could to alleviate the indifference with which they were treated. I prevailed on Mr. Ehrlich to lengthen the lunch periods and to hire a couple of men for some of the more physically taxing jobs. I shifted the women around so they could take turns standing and sitting at their work. If a woman had to take some time off for a doctor's visit, I punched in for her so her pay would not be docked.

Time was literally flying, and I had just one more year of night school to finish my B.A. degree. Having decided to major in Russian, and hoping to teach it on the secondary level, I began to explore the market for such an eventuality. To my astonishment, I discovered that very few high schools offered Russian as part of the curriculum. Following the advice that taking a more popular language would increase the possibility of landing a position, I immediately registered for Spanish. The familiarity with the language which I had already acquired on the job made it easy for me to whiz through the elementary levels and start my work on advanced courses in literature.

February 1, 1956—the day for which I had yearned, the day I had often doubted would ever come—I received my Bachelor of Arts degree with my entire family rejoicing in my success, even those who had never believed I could achieve it. I was happy, of course, but in a subdued way, perhaps because I realized that there was so much more still to be done before I could fulfill my ultimate aspiration of becoming a teacher.

A month before graduation, I had filed an application at Hunter College for a Master's degree program in Spanish and Education. I requested a special dispensation because I did not have a sufficient number of electives in Spanish at the undergraduate level. Thanks to my outstanding record in the four foreign languages I had studied at Brooklyn College, I received notification that the elective requirement had been waived and that I was eligible for immediate registration.

I undertook a heavy program, attending evening classes in the regular sessions as well as summer school. By June 1957, I had a sufficient number of credits in both education and Spanish to be eligible for the New York City Substitute License examination. These were difficult and tense times for me. The New York City system was known for having one of the most stringent examinations in the country. In addition, I had to contend with the possibility that I might not pass the orals because of my foreign accent.

I found that the test was indeed very difficult, particularly the five questions on pedagogy for which we were given only five minutes each, hardly enough time to really show one's knowledge of the subject. Nevertheless, on June 26, I had my license and was ready to look for a teaching position as a permanent substitute!

On the very day that the list of eligible candidates was published, I received a call from Mrs. Lorge, the chairperson of the foreign language department at James Monroe High School in the Bronx inviting me for an interview. During the interview, I learned that a position was available for one semester, starting in September, to replace a teacher who was going on sabbatical. Despite the fact that it would mean a cut in pay—and that I might find myself without a job when the semester ended—I took a chance and accepted the offer.

Since my arrival in America, many wonderful things had happened to me and many aspirations had been realized. My success in getting an education, my marriage, the birth of Jason, and becoming a citizen were all happy, exciting events. Beginning my long-hoped-for entry into the teaching profession was certainly a dream come true.

Knowing ahead of time that I was going to teach three different levels of Spanish, I got hold of the texts I would be using in those courses. I began my preparations some six weeks before the semester was to start. During my lunch hour, and in the evenings that I did not attend classes at Hunter, I reviewed the books from cover to cover and made a number of lesson plans, even though I anticipated that they would have to be modified once I began teaching.

I informed Mr. Ehrlich that I was leaving, giving him a month's notice. He knew all along that I was determined to become a teacher and that sooner or later I was going to leave. It was difficult to leave behind so many kind people with whom I had enjoyed working, but I was sure that they understood. They all wished me luck.

My professional life began with a 9 a.m. faculty meeting the day after Labor Day. All the new teachers were escorted to the front row, where we sat together. I could tell from the nervous-looking faces of those around me that I was not the only one who was apprehensive about my debut. When we were introduced and welcomed by the principal, the applause further inspired in me a sense of pride in being part of this society of educators. Other than meeting my fellow teachers at a departmental gathering, nothing particularly eventful happened on that first day. It did, however, serve as a calming influence in preparation for the next morning, when I was actually going to face my Spanish classes.

Like most new teachers on the day before walking into a classroom of their own for the first time, I was filled with all sorts of trepidations. High on the list was the concern that I was not sufficiently prepared in my subject area. Beyond that, I imagined that I would not be able to control the class, and consequently be unable to teach. What I found was the very opposite. From the moment the bell rang, the sympathetic young people gave me their undivided attention. Perhaps it was because they were aware of my vulnerable state. It might also have been because I ignored much of what I had been taught in the methods courses, which were often conducted by college professors who had never worked with high school students. I began the class, not by holding tight authoritarian reins, but by interspersing my lesson with a message of affection for all my students as well as for the subject at hand.

This auspicious beginning set the tone for what was to become a continuing source of satisfaction and excitement at being in the company of youngsters who were eager to learn. The only worrisome days were those on which Mrs. Lorge was to observe my classes. But her laudatory reports on my teaching gave me confidence and I was no longer nervous in her presence. She was, to be sure, a demanding supervisor, but also an excellent coach from whom I learned many invaluable lessons.

Knowing that the teacher whose job I was taking was returning at the end of the semester, I began to look for another position, difficult to find in midyear. Once again the gods were with me. With an excellent final evaluation by Mrs. Lorge, and her recommendation, I was hired at Evander Childs High School, this time with the prospect of a permanent substitute assignment or even a tenured position. Although I had only one semester of experience, I started my teaching there with considerably more confidence, thanks in great part to the principal, Dr. Hyman Alpern, who took over where Mrs. Lorge left off. It was not long before I walked into my classes devoid of any nervousness, which in turn yielded even better results with my students. After the first year, my ability was appreciated enough that my new assignment included the most advanced course in Spanish.

Beyond the pleasure of being in the classroom, my professional life was enriched by my participation in several extracurricular activities. Among the most satisfying was coaching the soccer team, which twice won the Bronx championship and went on to gain second place in the five-borough playoffs. Working with those boys, who were for the most part immigrants themselves, gave me the opportunity to inspire many of them to become better students and to go on to college.

When the soccer season was over, I became faculty adviser to the drama club. I directed several plays, a rewarding experience and an excellent outlet for my passion for acting. Not only did this thorough involvement in the life of the school make me a more complete professional, but contact with the children both inside and outside the classroom was gratifying and delightful. The classroom was no longer just a place to teach a language, but a peaceful sanctuary, in a way, part of the process of healing the wounds of the past. As I had discovered in Cremona, being with children seemed to give me back the part of my own childhood that had been brutally taken from me by poverty and misfortune.

Although I was very happy to continue to teach Spanish, I felt all along that our children should be exposed to the Russian language. Despite the fact that during the Sputnik era much noise was being made by the Education Department about promoting the study of Russian, only a handful of high schools were offering such a course. Dr. Alpern agreed with me that something should be done, and wrote several letters to Dr. Hubner, the coordinator of foreign languages, to urge that Russian be introduced in our school. The fact that I was already available to teach it should certainly have been a favorable argument.

Dr. Alpern's correspondence bore no fruit other than a suggestion from Dr. Hubner that I offer an in-service course to teachers. Eager to teach the language on any terms, I agreed to do this though I was not at all satisfied with Dr. Hubner's decision to overlook the urgency of making it available to the students. Ironically, many of the teachers in my once-a-week class were not really interested in the language at all, but took the course for credit toward ascending a step in their pay scale.

I enjoyed working with them, but I was not ready to give up my aim of eventually teaching Russian at the high-school level. Given the Cold War and the fact that the Soviet Union was a superpower, I still believed that it was of paramount importance to prepare young men and women with the communication skills and cultural knowledge that would be necessary in order for them to relate to that country and its people.

Three happy years at Evander went by very quickly, but in the fall of 1961 I was faced with the possibility of losing my job. This was due, not to dissatisfaction with my work, but to procedures followed by the New York City Board of Education which published a list of people who had passed the license examination for regular teachers. This meant that it was more than likely that an appointment was going to be made for my substitute position. I learned from Dr. Alpern that he had refused to replace me the previous semester but doubted that he would be allowed to do so again. This despite the fact that I had by now completed my M.A. in Spanish and passed several parts of the examination for a permanent license.

Just as I was about to begin my search for a fall position, two of my colleagues, who lived in New Rochelle, informed me that the district was looking for a Spanish teacher to replace one who was retiring. Given my good reputation, they were willing to recommend me should I be interested in the job. In fact, one of them, who had several children in the system, was so excited about this prospect that she herself arranged an appointment for me with the chairperson of the foreign language department, Mrs. Schein.

Dr. Alpern—my ever-present mentor, who had so much to do with my growth as a teacher—briefed me for the meeting. He encouraged me not to sell myself short, not to accept a salary below what I was getting in the city, and assured me that if I was not hired at New Rochelle, he would help me find another position. He handed me a special letter of recommendation and copies of several of his complimentary observations to show Mrs. Schein in case that proved necessary. Believing that my ability to teach Russian would serve me well in getting the job, he reminded me to introduce the idea of starting a Russian class at New Rochelle High School.

The interview with Mrs. Schein went well. She was sufficiently impressed with my credentials to set up a meeting with the principal, Dr. Koons. Shortly after, I was hired for the fall term of 1961 with a raise over my salary at Evander. My schedule, in addition to four Spanish classes, would include a Russian class that was to be labeled a "terminal" course, that is, one offered only to seniors graduating in 1962. I was given to understand that it would be up to me to attract the next generation of students and build up this curriculum.

As glad as I was that I had a job for the fall, and one with a Russian program to boot, I was sorry to leave Evander, where I had so many good friends and where the students showed so much affection. The thought of my departure was made even more difficult to accept when I learned that long before I started looking for a new job, students and faculty advisers had voted to dedicate the 1961 Senior Yearbook to me. There is no greater honor in our profession than to be recognized by one's students and colleagues. At the graduation ceremony, with my family in attendance, I accepted this award with humility, knowing that there were many among the distinguished faculty who were just as deserving of the recognition. The inscriptions by members of the graduating class make this book one of my most valued possessions.

With the upcoming improvement in my salary, plus Shirley's income from a permanent teaching job at Morris High School, we could now afford to move into a brand new cooperative near Riverdale, in the upper Bronx. Our new apartment was lined with large windows that flooded all the rooms with sunlight throughout most of the day. From our balcony, which we decorated with plants, we had a panoramic view that included a small section of the Harlem River and a good portion of the impressive George Washington Bridge. What added to our contentment was the fact that, for the first time since our marriage, Shirley and I had our own bedroom rather than having to sleep on a couch in the living room.

People often say that time flies. It does indeed, and it is futile to try to stop it. It is important, however, to be able to account for its passage and have something tangible to show. I was very fortunate and grateful that America had given me the opportunity to achieve so many things that most people could only dream about. Since my arrival in America with so little formal education, I had achieved a B.A. and an M.A. from public institutions of learning, free of charge. I was about to begin work on a second Master's at Fordham University, this one in Russian, on a National Defense Education Act scholarship. I had a profession of which I was enormously proud. And we were blessed with a bright and handsome son who was enjoying all the privileges of a middle-class child, including summer camp in the Adirondack Mountains.

My job at New Rochelle High School was tremendously exciting. The students who registered for the so-called terminal Russian class were, with few exceptions, bright and eager to learn. Although the Spanish students needed more extrinsic motivation, they too were enjoyable to work with. My four years of teaching experience served me well. The fact that I was trained in the audiolingual method of language instruction, which stresses oral competence, made teaching a more stimulating and dynamic process. My students were very proud of the fact that they were able to use the language right away rather than be bogged down in the tedious process of learning grammar—a practice that was still prevalent among those who did not realize that grammar was an aid to learning rather than a substitute for the language itself. In addition, I was able to apply my familiarity with language laboratories, a technique that had come on the scene just a few years earlier, to make learning more effective for my students.

More than anything else, my constant search for those subtleties of the craft which could not be learned in teacher-preparation courses helped me to become a more effective teacher. In time, I understood with greater sensitivity the frustration that children experience when learning becomes difficult, and how important it is to come to their aid and not give up on them. At the very first meeting of each of my classes, I gave the students my telephone number and told them to feel free to call me if they experienced any difficulty with a homework assignment. Some of my colleagues thought I was crazy. They warned me that I was going to get obscene phone calls. I never did. The calls I got were from a few boys and girls who, in thin apologetic voices, asked for the very help I had offered. My students were also informed that every day at 7:30 a.m. and after school I would be in Room 104 waiting to review lessons they did not understand. Extra help to these kids was invariably the road to their success and, in a way, to mine. In the 1962 New York State Regents examination, out of over fifty students, only one did not pass.

There was of course a small price to be paid for my supposedly "eccentric ways" and "excessive devotion" to my students. A few of my colleagues occasionally accused me of setting new and undesired precedents. According to the established practice in our school, extra help was supposed to be given by the language department only on Thursday. Fortunately I was not alone in my "eccentricity"—there were other teachers who gave children help every day, for which we were rewarded with the respect and affection of our students.

As for the Russian program, things were going very well. Contrary to Mrs. Schein's doubts, I had no difficulty attracting students. As a matter of fact, so many sophomores and juniors wanted to participate that we were able to form two beginners classes. Even though the seniors would be leaving, I was sure that I would have a sufficient number of students left to form a second-level class for the fall of 1963. What was so encouraging to me was the fact that a good number of kids from various Spanish classes registered for the course. They were now willing to challenge themselves and undertake two languages. There were also several students in my 1962 class who gave up their lunch periods to take Russian as a sixth course instead of the usual five. The program became so successful that I had three Russian classes almost every year up to the very end of my stay at New Rochelle High School. Many wonderful students passed through my classes and a good number of them continued their studies in college and eventually pursued careers using their Russian knowledge.

In the summer of 1963, we felt we could afford the luxury of the trip to Europe that Shirley had dreamed about for a long time. With Jason safely in the camp where I had taught tennis since 1958, we sailed on the SS *France* to Le Havre. For me, the trip was more than a sightseeing tour. For one thing, I considered it important to expand my professional skills by spending as much time as I could in France, Spain, and Italy, steeping myself in their cultures and conversing with native speakers. Going to Europe at this point also served as a respite from hard work, a time away from the whirlwind activity of the last fifteen years, as well as a sentimental journey to some of the places where I had waited impatiently for the chance to come to my beloved America.

In those days the *France* was considered one of the grand vessels. I was taken by its imposing beauty, that was a far cry from the ship on which I had come over. On the deck of the *France*, unlike the *Marina Perch*, the strollers were elegantly dressed. They reflected a happy mood as opposed to the worry which sat on the faces of those Jewish and Italian immigrants on their way to a new land and uncertain futures. Instead of Pepino's accordion playing and the tarantellas on the

Marina Perch, the *France* had a colorfully dressed orchestra that played tangos and waltzes, to which fashionably dressed couples danced with rhythmic passion. In contrast to the virtually inedible food on the shabby *Perch,* the attractive fragrance of the delectable French cuisine wafted into the dining room as the eager-to-please waiters passed through the swinging doors.

One evening, I stood in a remote corner of the deck away from the noisy crowd. Looking at the sea, so much calmer now than the last time, I wondered what had happened to my fellow immigrants—to Rachel, who had survived Birkenau, and the two little girls who had been saved in a Romanian convent. Had fate been as kind to them as it had been to me? Had they managed to forget at least some of their earlier trauma? Was Perele, now twenty-two, reconciled to the reality that her "mommy and daddy" had perished in the Holocaust and had not met her in America? Were all immigrants as grateful to America as I was for opening such wide doors of opportunity?

From Le Havre we took a train to Paris. I could not wait to see the places I had read so much about, the country whose history, art, and literature had such a profound influence on my thinking. Most important, I was eager to use the French in which I was by now fluent, and which I hoped to be teaching soon. My expectations were more than realized. With abundant opportunity to speak the language, I received compliments on my ability, despite the rumor that the French are very critical if their language is not spoken to perfection.

Paris was indeed the center of impressive monuments of art, of beauty, a veritable feast for both sight and mind where one could be totally submerged in the cultural heritage of that historic city and its environs. Nôtre-Dame, the Louvre, Chartres, Versailles—all the places that had been accessible to me only pictorially or by description—were now tangible realities.

There were, of course, scattered reminders of the terror the Nazis had visited on the French people, both Jew and Gentile. As we walked on the lovely boulevards, we saw several commemorative plaques like one that read, **JEWISH CHILDREN WERE TAKEN FROM THIS BUILDING.** These children were among the approximately four thousand who were rounded up and deported from Paris.

Just behind Nôtre-Dame, hidden from prominence, we came across a structure resembling a crypt. It was underground, as though carved into a large hill, and over the entrance was an inscription that read, simply, **N'OUBLIE PAS!** (Don't forget!) This proved to be a memorial to the 200,000 who had been deported and lost their lives at the hands of the Nazis. Walking in, we faced a long, narrow corridor with cement walls that reached up to a black ceiling. On the black cement floor lay a cement coffin with the inscription, **ICI REPOSE UN DEPORTE INCONNU.** (Here lies an unknown deportee.) At the end of the corridor there were several little dark rooms resembling jail cells, inside of which were reminders of Nazi atrocities. A small pile of ashes lay in a corner of one of them. The somber silence and the oppressive atmosphere within this modest memorial reflected powerfully the tragedy that had befallen the French Jews and their fellow Christians. The poignant *"N'oublie pas!"* beckoned me to return to the place several times. For some inexplicable reason, while sitting in front of the memorial, I experienced a sense of sad calm, an urge to say a silent Kaddish.

We also met several Jewish families who told us of their personal losses and sufferings during the Nazi occupation. They recounted with sorrow how readily the French gendarmes had cooperated in the roundup of the Jews and their eventual deportation, while a few decent Christians tried to rescue some of them. I had read about those lamentable events, but it was more painful to hear about such atrocities from the lips of those who had endured the suffering. By now I realized that the reminders of those dark days would always be there, generated by my own memory or by the memory of others.

After six delightful days in Paris, we took a train to Madrid. The city was fascinating in its own right but without the elegance and charm of Paris, somewhat severe in its architecture as well as in the baroque statuary that filled its churches. The famous Escorial, a monastery constructed on the order of Philip II, is a perfect example of his austere medieval legacy—a far cry from Nôtre-Dame or Chartres, which illuminate rather than darken the places they stand in.

This austerity was well compensated for in many other ways. The naturally terraced Guadarrama mountains that loom high in the distance, as well as the pretty whitewashed houses perched on the hills that surround the city, display impressive beauty. I was also taken with the friendliness of the Spanish people, a characteristic not readily found in Paris. As for sightseeing, cultural activities, and entertainment, Madrid rivaled any of the great European cities. To see the richly endowed Prado Museum with the magnificent paintings of Velasquez, Goya, Picasso, El Greco, and other famous artists of the world was a truly remarkable experience.

On the train from Madrid to Seville, we traversed the barren elevated plateau of La Mancha. As I recalled with childlike excitement my reading of Don Quixote, it seemed as though nothing had changed in the past three hundred years. The arid landscape, the village of Toboso where Don Quixote found his beloved Dulcinea, the striking Sierra Morena mountains—from the train window they all faithfully lived up to Cervantes' description of them. Most likely for the purpose of attracting tourists to the area, there was even a stretch of windmills scattered through the fields, like those that Quixote took to be giants and fought with heroic bravery.

Seville possessed a softness typical of the southern province of Andalusia. The magnificent lacy cathedral, one of the largest in the world, was more akin to Chartres than those we had seen in the north. Delicate Mudejar architecture and decoration visible everywhere was an indelible reminder of the Muslim culture that had flourished in the city when it was the capital of Spain during some 700 years of Moorish occupation. On the recommendation of one of my fellow Spanish teachers, we attended a bullfight. The ceremonies that preceded the actual fight were indeed exciting—the procession of the bandilleros, the matadors, the music, and the happy crowd. That excitement did not foretell the bloody drama that was to follow once the bull entered the arena. When the picadors began the cruel job of enraging the poor animal with their goads, I realized that this brutality, which is touted as an exciting sport, was not for my sensibilities. My heart went out to that doomed creature. I identified with his helplessness and thought of all the people who had been herded into enclosures from which they would not come out alive. I could not understand why the crowd was so animated by this inhumane spectacle. We left after the first corrida and found more civilized entertainment. On my return to the States, I recommended to my colleague that he attend a performance of Flamenco dancing, for that turned out to be one of our most memorable experiences. This Gypsy art form runs the gamut of human feelings from unbridled gaiety to profound sorrow. The intensity and grace of the intricate songs and dances, performed by men and women in gorgeous costumes, engage the audience.

Our trip to Spain ended with brief visits to Granada and Toledo, a personal pleasure and a professional necessity. I felt that I would be returning to my classes with a renewed love for the Spanish culture. I hoped this would help me inspire my students to go beyond fulfilling the Regents requirement and eventually partake in that fascinating world of art and literature.

Quite happy with our visit to Spain, we moved on to my beloved Italy, where so much had happened to me in the two-and-a-half years I had spent there. Rome was first on our list. While visiting the city's impressive monuments, I made sure to point out to Shirley the streets that I had once walked, usually hungry and without a penny to my name. And, of course, I took her to the Trevi Fountain, where I had spent a lonely night lulled to sleep by the gentle murmur of the falling water.

In Rome, as in Paris, there were reminders of Hitler's horrors. In 1943, thousands of Jews were herded by the SS into a small area in the Jewish quarter for deportation to various concentration camps. When we visited there, we were encircled by the handful of survivors, who recounted some of the losses of Jewish life and the suffering they had endured during the war. An elderly lady, as though a spokesperson for her fellow Jews, concluded our encounter by raising her arms slightly, palms facing upward, and, with characteristically Italian gestures, saying despondently, "*Non capisco, perché hanno distrutto la nostra vita, come mai anche noi siamo italiani* [I don't understand why our lives were destroyed. After all, aren't we also Italians]?" Her bewilderment was well justified, because other than a little silver Star of David hanging on her neck there was nothing visibly Jewish about her, nor about the others. In fact, in terms of the usual and sometimes mistaken characterization of Italian physiognomy, language, and gestures, their behavior was typical of, and in cultural harmony with, that of many "real" Italians I had known.

After a few days in Rome we traveled to Cremona. Although there were other interesting sights there, I was eager to go first to the *caserma*, the site of the DP camp. I knew that seeing this place again was going to be an emotional experience, and so it proved. The camp had always been rundown, but while it was inhabited one could occasionally forget its shabby appearance. Now, without living souls, the *caserma* looked like a ghost town, overgrown with weeds and teeming with salamanders. As we mounted the stairs to the floor I had lived on, we met a derelict who occupied the very room I had shared with thirty-seven other people.

One particular sight moved me to tears—a faintly visible Hebrew inscription over a classroom that read **BET SAIFER AL SHAIM CH. N. BIALIK** (The School of Ch. N. Bialik), named after the great Hebrew poet. This was the room I had fixed up in order to have a place to meet with my children before the school was opened in camp. Shirley, too, was moved by this entire experience and could not imagine that at one time her teacher-husband had actually lived in this godforsaken place. Indeed, wandering through the ruins of the camp, I had the feeling that a much longer time span than fifteen years had passed since I left this place that was laden with so many memories.

I would have liked to see the Bruni family and once more thank Signora Bruni for the delicious soups she made for me when I was ill. In the place where their little house had stood there was now a new building occupied by another family who had no idea of the Brunis' whereabouts.

Had we had more time, I might have been able to get some information about Laura. It was just as well that I did not look for her. Although I had told Shirley a little about our relationship, I had the feeling that she would not appreciate meeting my dear friend. I also suspected that it would have been unsettling for me to see Laura, despite the fact that what had been a romance was by now a beautiful memory.

Returning to Arona, where I had recovered from my illness, was a far more pleasant experience than seeing the sad-looking *caserma*. I had no difficulty finding the villa where the convalescent home was located. It was now luxuriously redecorated and occupied by a private family who invited us to walk through the lovely gardens. Lago Maggiore retained its former beauty and the Swiss Alps appeared even more impressive than I recollected.

Once there, a trip to Isola Bella was a must. I hired a boat which was steered languidly and in total silence by a very old man. Despite the fact that it was a weekday, the sailboats and rowboats were out in huge numbers and the animated singing filled the air with melody just as in years past. At Isola Bella I selected a different restaurant and different points of interest than those I had visited with Laura, to be sure that Shirley and I would have our own exclusive memories.

We spent a lovely day at Isola Bella. When we danced to the romantic music, it was obvious from Shirley's radiant face that she was having a wonderful time. After spending the night in Stresa, we rented a car and drove through the awe-inspiring beauty of Switzerland on our way to Le Havre.

The return trip on the *France* was a pleasant one. The sailing conditions were more or less the same as when we were going to Europe, but there was one important difference. I was now heading for a place where I had a permanent anchor. I was going home to my own beautiful country, to my son, to my family. I remember from time to time nervously reaching for my passport to be sure that it was there. How wonderful it was to hear that reassuring "Welcome to America" from the customs officer!

Chapter 19

Teaching and Learning

We got back to the States in time to pick Jason up at camp with all his athletic and drama awards and unmatched socks. He looked wonderful and so much taller than when we had said good-bye to him. Jason, now thirteen, was to enter his last year of Junior High School by virtue of having gained a year in a special program for gifted children. Our reunion was a very happy one, and our articulate son, who had inherited his mother's superior capacity for the English language, gave us an amusing blow-by-blow description of the past seven weeks. The ten-day interval before we had to return to our respective schools afforded us the time to be together and do some sightseeing with Jason in the Adirondacks.

Thus came to an end a beautiful vacation, the kind I had never experienced in my life. Even in America, this was my first time away from work and from attending school for such an extended period. I was happy to return both to teaching and to the evening classes at Fordham University, where I had one more year to finish the course work for my M.A. in Russian.

At the high school, my first and second year classes were filled. There were also six students who would be eligible for a third year of Russian, but I knew that such a small class would never be granted. Not to disappoint these kids, who were eager to go on to the next level, I met with them three times a week during lunch period and taught them as we ate together though it was contrary to school regulations. I was not paid for this extra work.

My small trespassing on the rules notwithstanding, I was confident that I would receive tenure—not a small matter, given that suburban schools tend to be unreliable for permanent employment. Competence was not always the criterion for retaining a teacher, particularly during those years when school budgets were in question. Still, as a result of my dedication, and excellent evaluations by

Charles Blake, the new department chairman, I was in fact awarded tenure in 1964.

Along with teaching, there were yet a few other roles I was to play at New Rochelle High School. Charlie Blake, who all along had been a member of the foreign language department and a dear friend, knew a good deal about my past. He knew that I had been a mechanic before the Holocaust and that I had training in electronics. As our three language laboratories began to break down, there was an urgent need to have someone do the repairs. It was at his suggestion that I accepted this responsibility, in return for which my teaching load would be reduced to four classes—a real boon for anyone with five classes every day and, in my case, the additional work with the advanced Russian class and extra help for my other students.

When I began my duties in the language laboratories, I was quite surprised to discover how much of the mechanic remained in me, despite the many years that had passed. I felt proud that I was able to do the job, and enjoyed recapturing a skill that was once dear to me.

In the spring of 1965 I was hard at work preparing for my oral examinations in Russian, and within a few months had my M.A. degree in hand. I immediately applied to New York University for a Ph.D. program in comparative literature with a concentration in Russian, and was accepted for admission in the September term of the same year.

The second Master's degree brought with it a cherished compliment and reward. Dr. Holtzman, with whom I had remained in contact throughout these years, called me. After we exchanged the usual pleasantries, Dr. Holtzman told me that she left Brooklyn College to become chairperson of the Russian department at Hunter College. She offered me a teaching position at the Bronx campus (now Lehman College). My workload would consist of two weekly evening courses, one in Russian language and the other an introduction to literature. Imagine my excitement! The professor who had taught me these subjects years earlier showed enough trust in my knowledge, and in my suitability, to invite me to be on her staff. I accepted the job with pride. The main source of my elation was that I had the chance to transmit the rich heritage of Russian literature to a group of well-motivated students.

Not having taught at the college level before, I was concerned about what methods of language instruction I should use. It took only a few sessions for me to conclude that all learners, young children, teenagers, or adults, have similar needs and are sometimes daunted by similar fears of not being able to master the subject. The good college instructor, like the good high school teacher, tries to allay those fears. He runs an effective class by showing empathy, humanity, and love for the subject rather than by displaying his self-importance.

My decision to go on to Ph.D. work was not prompted primarily by a need to enhance my professional skills. Although additional education would undoubtedly strengthen them, I was more motivated this time by a love for learning and a desire to grow intellectually. I realized that America was laying before me the opportunity to go beyond my original dreams. Summer vacations and a hoped-for sabbatical were from now on to be devoted to the pursuit of knowledge unrelated to pecuniary considerations.

Given my Jewish background, I felt that Hebrew should also be part of my linguistic repertoire. Thus, while attending N.Y.U., I resumed studying Hebrew on my own. I had the additional incentive that if I acquired sufficient competence I might perhaps teach it some day. I spent the entire summer of 1966 poring over my Hebrew grammar books and listening to tapes. In addition, I recorded what must have been a hundred radio broadcasts of the daily Hebrew hour, to which I listened over and over at home and in my car as I drove to and from work. Within three years I was fluent, and prepared to teach a beginners' class.

I was now in my ninth year at New Rochelle High School. I was happy with my work and liked by the students. People in the community who appreciated my teaching exhorted their children to get into my classes for both Russian and Spanish. If Iona College or any other school in Westchester sent student teachers to the foreign language department, I was invariably selected as the supervising teacher. It appeared as though no better script could have been written for my professional life. I felt that I had reached maturity in my craft, but was cognizant at the same time that, as in the past, I must continue the search for new and perhaps better ways of doing the job. This was to remain a lifetime imperative.

I was particularly lucky in my efforts to add to my teaching arsenal. Charlie Blake was an outstanding chairman and a generous mentor. Despite his advanced years and over thirty years of teaching, he was an eternal innovator. Working with this consummate professional, I was able to experiment with new methods, always with his guidance and blessing. I never hesitated to invite him into my class or to discuss pedagogical ideas with him. This was a real privilege because, unfortunately, in the real world the connection between teacher and chairperson is usually based on periodic observations and departmental meetings where instructional issues are rarely discussed.

It was through Charlie's uniquely unselfish efforts that in 1970—along with a gifted science teacher, David Olney—I was named Teacher of the Year for the New Rochelle School District, which had a total of 450 teachers in its thirteen elementary schools, two junior highs, and high school. At a reception given us by the P.T.A., to which only a few faculty members came, Charlie was visibly proud of me. He showered me with compliments and extolled the virtues of my contributions to our school and community.

Mostly as a consequence of this recognition, in 1971 I was granted a half-year paid sabbatical for study, at a time when they were infrequently approved. Shirley, always ready to see the world and to fulfill her own intellectual curiosity, decided to take an unpaid leave and accompany me to Europe, this time on a learning mission. Jason, having just graduated from Brandeis University and eager to roam on his own, was glad to be rid of his doting parents. I now had the opportunity to satisfy a long-standing desire to take courses in the Soviet Union and in Spain. My desire to go to the Soviet Union was considerably stronger than my need to go to Spain. Aside from the fact that I was immersed in Russian literature, I was curious to see the country to which I had closely escaped being taken by force; I wanted to get some idea of what my life might have been had I not had the courage to desert from the Russian army. I wondered how large the lie was about the ideal Communist system as touted by Smirnov and the other Soviet faithful.

I also fantasized that somewhere in Odessa, Leningrad or Moscow I might, happily, run into Katya or Dinsky, both of whom I remembered with affection. The frightening but ludicrous thought that I might meet

Smirnov, with possibly disastrous consequences also crossed my mind. I reminded myself, however, that I was now a free man, an American citizen. My passport would surely shield me in the unlikely event that I was recognized as Nikolay, the volunteer who had gone AWOL.

First on the agenda was Spain. After briefly revisiting some of the cities we had been to the last time, we headed for the University of Malaga, where I was to spend the spring semester. I registered for two courses, one in contemporary Spanish literature and one in baroque art. The courses were fascinating and most instructive. Equally enlightening was living in an apartment, where I had contact with local citizens, and being exposed to the soft, melodious Andaluz language. No course of study can replace such a real-life experience.

At the end of May, Shirley and I flew from Spain to Moscow. Before leaving the United States, I had arranged, for reasons of safety, for us to join a group of university students who were going to spend about two months in the Soviet Union studying Russian language and literature. I wanted badly to visit my home town, which was now in Soviet hands, just to see my mother's grave, but tourists were not allowed to go there. I could not understand why the small city of Mukachevo, with no industry to speak of, was off limits to foreign visitors.

Despite my earlier feeling of being protected by my American passport, I felt nervous when we got to customs and saw military men parading with their rifles. Suddenly the memory of the many occasions of unease in the presence of those uniforms flashed before me. We were supposed to be met at the airport by Intourist representatives who were to take us to the school. Due to the usual Russian inefficiency, we were held up at the airport for four hours without any explanation and with our visas in the possession of the customs officials. The delay intensified my misgivings. I was convinced that something had gone wrong. Finally, however, the Intourist man arrived and we were cleared. The driver lost his way on primitive dirt roads that had no signs, and it was not until four in the morning that we reached Abramtzevo, fifty-seven kilometers from Moscow. Once there, in the company of the American students and the professor in charge of the group, I felt relieved of the distress I had experienced at the airport.

Abramtzevo, a country estate situated in the village of the same name, had originally belonged to Sergei Aksakov, a well-known writer. It was purchased in 1870 by a rich industrialist, Mamontov, a devoted patron of the arts, who turned the estate into a leading cultural center of nineteenth-century Russia. Mamontov attracted to Abramtzevo writers like Turgenev and Gogol, painters and musicians, and prominent figures from the theater and opera, like Stanislavsky and Chaliapin, who collaborated on cultural events to which the upper classes of Moscow flocked. In 1917, with the advent of the Bolshevik regime, Abramtzevo was turned into a museum displaying a rich heritage of Russian art.

Driving toward Abramtzevo in the pitch dark of the early morning, we did not realize that we would be surrounded by such natural splendor during our stay there. The lush rolling hills, dotted with small birch forests and a colorful profusion of wildflowers, were a perfect setting for those creative giants who had made such a superb contribution to world culture.

While abundant in physical beauty, Abramtzevo was lacking in the human spirit. The staff appeared listless, and even sad. It was as though robots were carrying out the commands given to them by the people in charge, who were, incidentally, quite rude to the workers and each other. This irritability could from time to time be observed among the Russian teachers themselves, though it was never shown toward the foreign students.

Shirley enrolled in a beginners' Russian class, while I took a class in linguistics, and two literature courses, one of them on Tolstoy. The lectures on Tolstoy smacked for the most part of Socialist Realism, the doctrine which mandates that all art forms must serve the State. From the professor's interpretation of the great writer, I had the impression that if Count Tolstoy were alive, he would surely be a Communist sympathizer, if not actually a member of the Party. I felt sorry for the poor professor. I suspected that he was compelled to toe the socialist line, living the lie that most of the intelligentsia of the day were obliged to live. I am sure that he was aware of Stalin's legacy of persecution and murder of intellectuals who refused to adhere to Communist doctrine. The gulags in Siberia and elsewhere in the Soviet Union were still operating, despite official denial of their existence.

I struck up a friendship later on with a former professor who, after serving several years in prison for his academic transgressions, had been demoted to doorman at a convalescent home. Then there was Sergei, one of the young instructors at Abramtzevo, who confided in me that he had been under intermittent scrutiny by the authorities, with occasional unexpected calls at his apartment by the KGB. He was never formally charged with any wrongdoing, but was told by the director of the school that he was excessively friendly with foreigners. When I was in Sergei's flat once with a few Italian students, the doorbell rang and he signaled to us to keep still. A few minutes later we looked out the window and saw three uniformed policemen leaving the building.

Abramtzevo was very limited in terms of my reasons for being in the Soviet Union. Although the courses were interesting, we did not really live in the kind of environment where I could have extensive contact with native people. Other than the dozen or so teachers who served more than three hundred foreign students, we were insulated from the outside world. We were taken to see the important sights in Moscow, but that, too, was in the company of our fellow students and Russian teachers.

The village itself was within walking distance and I visited it a few times, but the poor folk there had no time for inquisitive Americans during working days. They had to go on with their toil for survival. Another option temptingly advertised by the Intourist booklet was the accessibility to Moscow, but this turned out to be an overstatement. The only transportation available was a train called the *electrichka*, which had an unreliable schedule. One night, after Shirley and I had gone to see a play in Moscow, we waited almost two hours trying to get back to Abramtzevo. The *electrichka* never came, and we were obliged to hire a taxi. Not only did this prove quite expensive, but we did not make it back till after curfew, which earned us a reprimand from the director of the institute.

The four weeks at Abramtzevo drew to an end, and we prepared to leave for Leningrad. At a farewell luncheon on Sunday afternoon, we listened to endless speeches by the director and his innumerable assistants, in which frequent references were made to American, British, and Russian friendship. The students were excessively complimented, and the teachers were acknowledged for their dedicated hard work.

On Sunday evening the village of Abramtzevo hosted a picnic to which all the students were invited. A huge bonfire lit in a nearby meadow was already fully ablaze when we arrived. The organizers of the picnic and the people of Abramtzevo lived up to the Russian reputation for hospitality. Despite the general shortage of food in the Soviet Union, red and black caviar were included in the menu in honor of this special occasion. It was a bad day for chickens, for all around the bonfire the roasting fowl were strung up in a huge red necklace. Vodka and cheap Russian champagne flowed as freely as water from a tap.

Two accordionists, accompanied by a pretty young singer in colorful peasant costume, circled the fire and lured the listeners to join them in song. Soon animated dancing began. Young men and women were leaping in the air with impressive grace. Some of the dancers left their partners and invited a few of us to join them. "*Davaytye amerikantzy budiem tantzevat* [Come on Americans, let's dance]." Eager to try the skills I had acquired in Brooklyn College, I needed no special persuasion.

However, this last evening in Abramtzevo went beyond eating and entertainment. Shirley and I were approached by several people who, individually, never in the company of other Russians, were eager to confide their woes to us. We heard some heartrending tales, mostly from older people who still had vivid memories of personal tragedies suffered during the German invasion, and now the horrors imposed on them by the tyrannical system headed by Brezhnev.

Particularly moving was the story of Ana Savchenko, an elementary-school teacher in her late sixties, who had come to Abramtzevo from Kiev. Both her husband and a brother had died fighting in the Red army. As if that were not tragic enough, her father was arrested for "collaborating" with the Germans. His crime, according to the authorities, consisted of failing to drive out livestock from the collective farm as the German army was approaching, thus allowing food to fall into the hands of the enemy. The poor man spent three years in jail and was labeled for the rest of his short life as "an enemy of the people." Ana intermittently interrupted her story as tears rolled down her quivering, wrinkled face.

"I often visit the Eternal Light," she said, "that is located in the park on the side of the Kremlin. With hundreds of other mourners, I stand there and weep for my dead family. I ask myself, 'Why did some twenty million Russians perish? For what? So that Brezhnev and his cohorts,'" this she whispered almost inaudibly as she looked around fearfully, "'could live privileged lives while we struggle to survive under their oppression?' Can you believe it? They contaminated my only son with their ideologies to such a degree that I am afraid to talk to him, to tell him the truth about these hooligans, these liars." These and similar stories were told to us in hushed voices while the accordion played on, as though an accompaniment to the sadness that was pouring out of our narrators.

In contrast to the undulating hills and meadows in the area of Abramtzevo, on our way to Leningrad by train there were long stretches of flat land interspersed with occasional dense forests and fields of wildflowers. I was surprised by how much of that land was left uncultivated, as well as by the scarcity of grazing animals. The small villages dispersed on each side of the railroad appeared isolated from the rest of the world, and the little huts were in very poor repair. We made several stops at small towns which reeked of industrial pollutants. Workers loaded and unloaded the freight cars, but there were virtually no passengers getting on or off. It was as though travel to or from those places was prohibited.

In Leningrad we learned from Intourist that our school was not in the city proper but in a small town on the outskirts. Dyuni was situated on the bay of Finland, territory that the Soviets had taken in 1941 after the Russo-Finnish war. Unlike Abramtzevo, Dyuni was tailor-made for tourists like me, who went to the Soviet Union not only to learn more Russian but to dig into the realities of Russian life. Leningrad was easily accessible by bus, as well as by trains which actually ran on the hour. That was not what made our new location an ideal place for my purposes. In addition to housing a school for foreign students, Dyuni was also a vacation site for Russian workers and their families. It had a huge beach to which people from Leningrad and nearby towns flocked every day. This gave me the opportunity to be in a real Russian milieu. We ate in the same dining room as the Russian vacationers, and attended all kinds of cultural and social functions together. Once trusting friendships were established between us and a few brave Russians eager to tell their stories, it was easy to fathom the workings of this diabolical, oppressive system. There were indeed startling revelations. It was not as though what we saw and heard was completely new to us, but reading about Soviet life in *The New York Times* or some magazine is not the same as experiencing it in person and in a much broader context.

The most obvious aspect of the KGB-run tyranny was the people's pervasive fear that they were under constant surveillance. Rumor had it that tourists also were watched by the authorities and that our rooms were bugged with microphones in mirrors or in the ceiling lights. The dread of being watched was evident in a variety of ways, notably in the ambiguous language people used until they were sure they could trust us. One of the Russian teachers, who hesitantly revealed her Jewish identity, wanted to learn from us something about Israel but would not refer to it by name. She asked Shirley, "How is that little country?" It was amazing how distorted her information was about Israel. She told us that as far as she knew, "that little country" was the aggressor in that part of the world and had been the one to start the Yom Kippur war.

We also befriended a very handsome writer, Boris, and his wife, Tatyana, who had come from Siberia for a visit to Leningrad. Here, too, the fear of being followed and spied on was evident. Once he was sure that we were indeed Americans, he led us to an abandoned basketball court where he unloaded some of his frustrations and his unhappiness. To muffle our conversation he kept shooting baskets. As soon as he saw people approaching us, he would ask me to follow him into the water, away from the crowd, where we could continue our discussion.

"These are times of great disappointment, Jay," he told me. "We were hoping that Brezhnev would follow at least some aspects of Khrushchev's token liberal policy, but he reverted to Stalinism." He said that in order to eke out a living, he wrote trash that was acceptable to the regime but revolting to him. The only thing that saved him from total despair was publishing some of his writings in *samizdat* (underground literature that was distributed in defiance of the Soviet regime). He did this despite the constant fear that he might be denounced and arrested. He, too, echoed the sentiments of some of the intellectuals I had met in Abramtzevo. "Times, my friend, are not very different from the Stalin era. Thousands of writers and other innocent people are still being sent to the gulags. Under this police state we are completely cut off from the rest of the world. When I can no longer stand the lies we are fed, I risk the chance of being discovered and listen to the forbidden BBC program or read a few smuggled papers, my only connection to the West." Making me promise not to say anything to his wife, he told me that he had been contemplating suicide but could not bring himself do it because of his two young children. Our last encounter took place at six o'clock in the morning on a totally deserted beach. As we walked on the edge of the water, this time talking about his favorite American writers, among them Mark Twain, he noticed a uniformed man. "You see that fellow? Make no mistake about it, he is watching us." Without finishing his thoughts on Mark Twain, he left abruptly with a quick "*Do svidanya.*" I never saw Boris again.

The next person to confide in us was a professor of mathematics at the Leningrad University, who was vacationing at Dyuni with his wife and their baby boy. Edik Schwartz came from an observant Jewish family. His rise to the rank of professor virtually precluded his practice of Judaism. Since his wife did not know Yiddish at all, he had forgotten most of the mother tongue. To be sure that Shirley and I were indeed Jewish, as we claimed, he tested us by speaking to us in broken Yiddish before reverting to English, which he and his wife spoke fluently.

Unlike the others who revealed their troubles to us, Edik would not discuss politics while we were at Dyuni. He seemed more intimidated than those who dared to complain about their lot. It was not until we visited his summer dacha, really just a shack with two small rooms and no indoor kitchen facilities, that he spoke openly about his situation.

Edik, like the other people we spoke to, deplored the existing Soviet state and Brezhnev's reversion to Stalinism. In his case, there was the added dimension of rampant anti-Semitism, particularly at the university. He said in jest, "Too bad that my last name is not Nikolayev rather than Schwartz, perhaps then they would not have noticed that my nose was slightly hooked." He was especially concerned that through indoctrination, his son would lose all awareness of his Jewish origins. During one of our visits he asked me to sing some Yiddish songs to the baby, and teach them to him and his wife. He also apologized profusely for not inviting us to his apartment in Leningrad, making no secret of his fear that he might be accused of espionage or some other act that could cost him his job, or worse.

We did, however, have a few opportunities to visit Russian homes and see for ourselves the difficult lives that people had to suffer. Ira Ivanovna, whom we met at the beach, invited us to the apartment where she lived with her mother and her married sister in two tiny rooms, sharing a small centrally located kitchen with four other families who lived on the same floor in similarly crowded conditions. They had to stagger the use of the kitchen by allotting a certain time to each household. Ira's boyfriend, when he graduated from the university, had been obliged to take a position with an investigative unit of the KGB, a job he loathed. He told me that he had once had to arrest one of his friends on some trumped-up charge of being an "enemy of the people." Practically in tears, he said, "Can you imagine, Jay, how heavily that lies on my soul? I would give anything to be able to get rid of this work, this nightmare, but at least for the time being there is no way out." He knew for a fact that if he so much as made a reference to quitting, he would wind up in prison, probably for life.

In the ten weeks we spent in the Soviet Union, I spoke to many men and women who had similarly moving stories. I met a few of the faithful who, in contrast to the whispered accounts of the unhappy sufferers, vociferously boasted about the great glories of Soviet life. Most of the people we made contact with were numbed by their dismal condition or by vodka, which was easier to get than meat. They were resigned to their fate, to suffering in silence, to standing in long lines for the most basic necessities with the prospect of going home empty-handed. It seemed as though Gogol's and Dostoevski's meek men and women, whom I had met as fictional characters, had assumed a real life, destined to endure the tyranny that had plagued Russia throughout its history.

Not all of my reflections on Soviet life came from observation or conversations. I had a personal brush with the Russian iron hand. At Dyuni, even while people were on their vacation, they were subject to strict, almost military rule. No one was permitted to enter the dining room late. For all three meals, the vacationers gathered in front of the entrance to be sure that they were on time. At night there was a curfew. Every man, woman, and child had to be inside the building by ten o'clock, with lights out at eleven.

One evening I was visiting with a few of my Russian teachers. Around eleven o'clock they suggested that I return to my quarters. As I was leaving the building, two soldiers with rifles hanging on their shoulders stopped me, even though the foreign students were not subject to this rule. One of them confronted me demanding, "And where do you think you are going? Don't you know the curfew rules?"

"To my room," I answered.

"And what were you doing here? Don't you know that you must be in your building by ten o'clock?"

I explained that I was an American student and that I was visiting some friends.

"You lying son of a bitch," he shouted, infuriated. "Do you think that we are stupid? Americans don't speak Russian like you. Show me your documents."

Unfortunately, I did not have my passport with me. I asked him to accompany me to my room several buildings away, but he refused. Deciding that this was a very important case which required a higher authority, the soldiers sent for the man in charge of the resort. During the hour it took for the official to arrive, I was obliged to sit in a corner behind a desk, watched by both guards. I was petrified, thinking once more of my "volunteer" connection with the Russian army, and trying to persuade the fools that they had made a big mistake.

At last the chief came, the very man who had welcomed us on our arrival. This time, he was dressed in a military uniform with all his medals dangling from his chest. He recognized me instantly and burst out laughing. "You see, that is what you get for speaking Russian so well. These guys actually thought that you were Russian!" Turning to the soldiers, he showered them with insults and obscenities, reprimanding them for the way they had handled the situation. The poor souls apologized to me and we shook hands. To make me feel better, Lieutenant Griboyedov insisted that I join him in drinking a glass of vodka. My efforts to refuse were unsuccessful, and I returned home with stomach cramps.

The day before our semester was due to end, the foreign students were taken to *Dom Druzhbe* (the House of Friendship). In Leningrad, as in Abramtzevo, various dignitaries made farewell speeches about American and Russian friendship and treated us to a fine buffet. Were it not for one unfortunate incident, this visit to Leningrad would have been an appropriate way to say good-bye to the teachers and school officials who had tried hard to make our stay pleasant. Either somebody had goofed or had deliberately chosen to show an offensive anti-American propaganda film which featured scenes of American injustice toward minorities and the cruelty of the police toward citizens who demonstrated against government policies with which they disagreed. Though our teachers were embarrassed and tried to mollify us, Shirley and a few others were infuriated and walked out of the auditorium. It was on this sour note that we left Dyuni, where I had learned more on the beach, the deserted basketball court, and walking the streets of Leningrad than in the Russian classes.

A few of our teachers and several of our friends came to the airport to see us off. As we were about to board, I observed their sad Russian eyes, and I felt profound compassion for those people who, despite their difficult lives, had displayed toward us their hospitality. Notwithstanding the oppressive Soviet regime, our visit resulted in a permanent bond between us and these people of ill fortune. They, as well as their moving songs and their literature, will forever draw me to Russia. Yet I could not help thinking how lucky I was to live in a free country. I rejoiced in my good fortune that the Soviet army had not succeeded in hauling me to their "promised land."

We made one more stop before our return to the States. Shirley's brother, Col. Albert Kopp, was stationed with his family in Landstuhl, Germany, where he served as chief of psychiatry at the American hospital. Not having seen her brother for some years, Shirley was eager to visit him. Neither of us really wanted to set foot in the country which my wife referred to as a charnel house. I was particularly concerned with how it would affect me emotionally. Germany would not have just occasional reminders of the Holocaust such as I had encountered in other places; there I would be walking on the same streets as some of the murderers, and hearing the language that was still repugnant to me. In Germany, the horror would be omnipresent.

After some vacillation, we decided to go. The reunion with the family was very pleasant, and I was especially delighted to spend time with Albert's three lovely girls. Playing with them did provide some distraction, but not enough to prevent a vivid recollection of Hitler's carnage. The six days in Germany were anxiety-ridden. As I wandered the streets of Landstuhl, I saw angular-faced, middle-aged German men who, even without uniforms, resembled their Nazi brethren. The appearance of these men, the harsh-sounding language, and the air itself aroused fears and brought back memories I had been trying to suppress throughout the years.

In the center of nearby Kaiserslautern, I watched a parade of young scouts, boys and girls, marching to a band. Except for the absence of swastikas, the boys' uniforms looked almost identical to those worn by the Hitler youth the Nazis had groomed to carry out many of their assaults on the Jews. Had these children been contaminated by their country's atrocious history? Would their soft, attractive faces grow callous? Was their scout training a possible preparation for eventually killing Jews and other defenseless people? I wondered.

Chapter 20

The Road to the White House

Once we were in the air on our return trip, I managed with some difficulty to divert my thoughts from Landstuhl and Kaiserslautern and look forward to going home. When we approached Kennedy Airport, the pilot had to go into a holding pattern before we could land, and we flew over the Statue of Liberty several times. With both the Russian and the German experiences flashing through my mind, I was once again overwhelmed with gratitude for the privilege of living in my beloved America.

After this extended absence from school, I was eager to return to teaching. I felt that my sabbatical had served me well; distancing myself from the classroom for a semester had given me the opportunity to regenerate and assess my performance as a teacher.

With a few exceptions, my method of conducting my classes was going to follow the system I had evolved over the years, but there was one particular problem which nagged me throughout my teaching career. How could I effectively teach classes which contained a greater than usual diversity of abilities among the students? Even in a so-called homogeneous class of twenty students, there are as many personalities and abilities as there are students. I did, of course, apply as much as was possible, the individualized approach to teaching, but any good educator will tell you that it is easier said than done. I had to find a better way to deal with the very bright students who understood a point of grammar, or some other aspect of a language, at first explanation and even before. How could I keep them occupied and interested in a lesson, and prevent restlessness and possible discipline problems, while I made three more explanations to the rest of the class?

Although the value of going to teacher's conferences and workshops is sometimes overstated, I attended one at the New York State Foreign Language Association which eventually bore fruit. Discussed at this conference were ideas about new approaches to teaching foreign languages, among them "cooperative learning." Though there are probably as many versions of cooperative learning as there are teachers, it means that students teach their peers, or work together on projects in small groups under the teacher's supervision. Some forms of this technique have been used over the years, particularly in small rural areas where resourceful teachers—who had in their one-room schools three, sometimes four, different grade levels—assigned the more advanced students to work with the other children.

Still not quite clear how cooperative learning would solve my problem, it struck me as being a good idea and worth trying. It is rarely known outside of schools, but teachers are conservative and often reluctant to try new approaches, holding on for dear life to traditional models of instruction. In such an environment, it is difficult to be innovative without incurring the disapproval, and sometimes the wrath of colleagues. Nevertheless, I decided to go against the grain and evolve my own cooperative learning method.

I was lucky that Charlie Blake, unlike some other chairpersons, was amenable to change and willing to go along with my experimentation. Charlie and my students were included in the planning process. I explained to them the advantages of this new addition to my instruction, asked for their cooperation, and set our plan in motion.

I decided to start the experiment with my second year Russian class which contained seniors, who tend to be more mature. I selected my student assistants, with whom I spent several hours, preparing them for their function in the group. After presenting the lesson for that day, I divided the class into several sections and assigned to them two student leaders. The help provided by linguistically gifted students certainly improved the learning process of the class, but it also enhanced their own knowledge. Interestingly enough, I discovered that my helpers were occasionally better able to clarify for their peers aspects of the language which I found difficult to explain. Most importantly, on the occasions that the groups were working independently, I was free to give special attention to students who experienced particular difficulties with languages. My version of cooperative learning was not an instant success, but with time it developed into an effective teaching tool which eventually led to other changes in the language department's programming. It also led to changes in instruction that benefited many of our students at New Rochelle High School.

As long as I had been at the high school, students experienced difficulties with programming in the foreign language department. This was particularly so for those who were interested in studying two languages or those who wanted to go on to more advanced courses. If only one session of a given language course was offered and that conflicted with a class offered in another area during that period, the foreign language was usually dropped. We had to find a way not to lose these students who were genuinely interested in becoming proficient in a foreign language.

In one of my conversations with Charlie lamenting this situation, I, quite in jest, remarked, "Wouldn't it be wonderful if we could put all these students into one class and work with them on their respective languages?"

Charlie tilted his head to one side, as though mulling over my words, and very casually responded, "Not a bad idea, Jay, not a bad idea."

It was difficult to tell whether he meant that it was a good idea or was simply dismissing my offhand comment.

Our conversation was interrupted by the bell summoning me to my seventh-period Spanish class. With many other things on my mind, I gave no more thought to Charlie's reaction. I did, however, muse from time to time about such a possibility, never really believing that it could become a reality. Two weeks later, Charlie invited me into his office just as I was leaving the building. I could tell from his mischievous, proud smile that he had something exciting to tell me. "Sit down, sit down." He pushed me down on the chair. "I have some good news for you. That is, I hope you think it is good news. Your idea about teaching several languages in the same class would accommodate not only our Russian students but others from different language areas as well. I went to see Dr. Gaddy [the principal], and he would like us to experiment for one year to see whether it can work. We have to come up with a plan to run such a class. With your knowledge of all these languages, you are certainly more qualified than anyone else in the department to teach it."

With Charlie's professional know-how and guidance, I set out to design this multilingual class. As far as we knew, it had no precedent in modern language instruction. The first class was offered in the fall of 1973. It was Charlie's idea to dub our course "The Language Workshop" and limit the number of students to no more than sixteen.

As it happened, we had six students who were eligible for third year Russian but for whom no regular session would be scheduled due to underenrollment. I intended to work with them during my lunch period for a few days each week but that would not expose them to a full course of study. These boys and girls formed the base for the workshop. Charley decided to add to this group Hebrew, as a new offering, as well as Spanish and French students who would otherwise be left out because of conflicting schedules.

For the instructional model, I was going to rely heavily on the cooperative learning process which was perfectly suited for our Language Workshop. Part of the plan was for each language group to be allocated a separate corner of the room, where we put together the required number of desks. I would prepare the lessons for each cluster and be available for help as the students worked together or independently. At my request, the school purchased several portable eight-position recording and playback units. In addition to professional cassettes which were available in all the languages, I recorded some material for particular exercises that I thought would be essential.

Despite the skepticism of a few colleagues from our department, the Workshop turned out to be a huge success. I was particularly pleased that one of my students from the Language Workshop scored over 700 (out of 800) on the achievement test. He went on to study Russian at a university and was later invited to work for some time in the Soviet Union.

Our success brought us a measure of fame when the Westchester section of *The New York Times* gave us a favorable write-up. As a result, we began to get visitors from surrounding high schools and colleges who were interested in our method of foreign language instruction. Soon our reputation reached a few foreign language associations in the state and beyond, and I was invited to many professional meetings to speak on our new invention. Charlie and I were even featured speakers together at a conference of the Canadian Foreign Language Association in Toronto.

Adding to the satisfaction I was deriving from my work was the joy at my son's forthcoming marriage. In the midst of the pressures and pleasures of my professional life came this happy interlude in my personal life. Two years earlier, while traveling on his own in Europe, Jason had attended the Dublin Horse Show where he met his red-haired Irish bride-to-be, Bernardine Quinn. Our Tibbett Avenue apartment was filled with the excitement of the final preparations as dresses for the wedding were shortened, lengthened, or taken in by Bernardine and her sister, Mary, to the accompaniment of melodious Irish talk and occasional song.

On Sunday, September 8, a simple ceremony was performed at Temple Emanu-El in Yonkers, followed by dinner in the rabbi's library, an elegant room, with books lining one wall and a huge picture window in the wall opposite, looking out on a sunny garden. With an accordion, a room filled with lively guests, many of whom were Jason's friends, food, drink and dancing, it was, many people told us, one of the nicest weddings they had ever attended.

Jason's marriage, and the eventual birth of my three beautiful grandchildren—Matthias, Danielle, and Benjamin—belong to the category of miracles, because they are connected to my having survived the Holocaust. Even during this joyous occasion, I could not help thinking of the many parents and future brides and grooms who perished before they could stand together under the canopy.

The seventies ushered in an era of strong awareness of America's troubled schools; reports and assessments came out in profusion. We were told, among other things, that some of our students had been allowed to graduate with little or none of the basic knowledge and skills they needed to be productive citizens. Unfortunately, the critics were right in much of what they said. Although suburban schools were not faced with all of the ills that beset the inner cities, the New Rochelle school district had its share of dropouts and similar problems.

To the credit of Dr. Gaddy, as well as the teaching staff, there was a serious attempt to address some of these concerns. I wanted very much to be part of the team that was searching for solutions, rather than hide behind my successes in the foreign language department, which did not have many students at risk. As a member of the New Rochelle High School Committee for the Middle States Evaluation, I joined a group of educators who examined a variety of problems. I took a particular interest in the dropouts, since I too—albeit under very different circumstances—had suffered the consequences of being a dropout.

It was out of this involvement, however, that I realized there was a direct way in which I could help some of these lost souls, a number of whom were immigrants like me. I set out on a small personal crusade. From my room I could see the outside steps and the soccer field where some of these kids congregated. When I found time to speak to them, I learned that a good many were falling behind because they were English-language deficient, and therefore did not attend classes. Although we had ESL (English as a Second Language) courses, I decided to run my own little outreach program for both the foreign students and others who clearly needed, and were willing to accept, additional help.

Since my room was always open an hour before classes began, I persuaded some of these students to come there for tutoring. Besides working with them personally, I enlisted some of our bright kids to assist with subjects I could not handle. Of the many who promised to come for help, only two girls and two boys showed up for the first session. After that, attendance rose and fell from day to day, but our modest operation lasted for as long as I remained at New Rochelle High School. A good deal of credit for whatever success we had goes to my volunteer tutors who, in addition to teaching, served as new friends to these boys and girls and helped make them comfortable in our school. I wished more children had taken advantage of what we offered, but those who did were most appreciative.

In the fall of 1975, we were left without a faculty adviser for our student exchange program with La Rochelle, France, sister-city of New Rochelle—a connection which goes back to the coming of the first Huguenot settlers three hundred years ago. Charlie Blake used all his persuasive powers to get me to take over the program. Although somewhat reluctant, I realized that I could not refuse this man who had done so much for me. Besides, in the belief that our exchange with another culture was of salient educational value to our students, I had been involved with the program to some degree since its inception.

I accepted the additional responsibility with the condition that I would not have to accompany the groups of fifteen kids on the annual two-week trip to La Rochelle. One of the restrictions I had long ago imposed on myself was that no matter what extracurricular activity I participated in, it should never be at the expense of my classes. I was, in fact, very proud of my attendance record. I was one of few teachers who had not missed a day of school for six or seven straight years. Although the program had been well run before I took it over, I felt some changes were necessary. Most important, I wanted to make sure that all our academically deserving French students would have the opportunity to go abroad even if their families could not afford to send them. By organizing sales of various items, like chocolate, and putting on shows—which also allowed me to give vent to my acting and directing yearnings—I raised enough money to provide scholarships for two students and to cover all other expenses.

Other than the pleasure of working with so many charming youngsters from both New Rochelle and La Rochelle, running the exchange program had a very special meaning for me. I felt that these students were excellent ambassadors for their countries, and that through these personal contacts they learned lessons of respect for different cultures. It was always touching to see the warm good-byes among the kids when the time came for the French students to leave.

In 1977, my dear friend and mentor, Charlie Blake, decided to retire. I was disappointed, but still comforted by the knowledge that he would remain a loyal friend. I believe that it was at his prompting that in 1979, I was once more selected by the district as Teacher of the Year and my name was proposed to the New York State Department of Education as a candidate for State Teacher of the Year. I was asked to submit several supporting documents, including an autobiographical sketch, my philosophy of teaching, my professional development, and a list of extracurricular contributions to the school and community. All these were to be sent to Albany along with recommendations from the school superintendent, my principal, and other supervisory staff. Due to an oversight, the documents were mailed without the recommendations. These were later found, but too late to be forwarded to the selection committee.

To make up for the blunder, my name was submitted again in 1980, this time with all the necessary papers. Within a few months, the Board of Education was notified that I was one of four finalists out of 700 candidates nominated by school districts throughout the state. I was summoned to Albany with the other three candidates to be interviewed by four different selection committees, among them a group of high school students. Shirley accompanied me, but went shopping while the interviews were going on. By the time she returned, I had been declared the 1980 New York State Teacher of the Year, to be honored a few weeks later by the Board of Regents, the Governor, and the State Senate. Shirley and I looked at each other in disbelief. Indeed, who could have imagined on my arrival in America with so little formal education that such good fortune would come my way. Even before the official ceremony took place, letters of congratulation came from various educational associations, and with them invitations to receptions in my honor.

Now the hasty preparations began for filling out the necessary applications to compete with the other State Teachers for National Teacher of the Year which would entitle me to a year of travel to all parts of the country to speak to educators, children and civic groups. Mrs. Winifred Fairhall, our public relations officer, sent a wisely composed résumé to the Council of Chief State School Officers in Washington, where the applications are evaluated by representatives from at least a dozen educational associations. A few months later, our school district received word that I was one of the four finalists. We were to expect the prompt arrival of an educational supervisor who would spend two days in the district to assess not only my teaching but my overall worthiness.

The announcement was accompanied by information that described the other three finalists and their professional accomplishments. All of them were females, one from the elementary grades and two from high schools. When I saw their impressive credentials, I said to Shirley, "Well, my dear, with these ladies competing against me, I don't have the ghost of a chance. I am very grateful that I have gotten as far as being not only State Teacher of the Year but one of the finalists from among the 150,000 original nominees around the country."

In February 1981, a Mrs. Miller arrived from Washington. She was a member of the education staff of *Good Housekeeping* magazine (a sponsor of the award, along with the *Encyclopædia Britannica*), and it was her job as consultant to the Council to observe and report on each of the finalists on their home ground. Because I took it for granted that I would never make the cut, I felt at ease with my visitor and ready to follow Dr. Gaddy's helpful suggestion that, if I wanted to make a good impression, I should do exactly what I normally do during the course of the school day. Mrs. Miller came to my room an hour before classes began. After a few minutes of chatting, I excused myself and began working with both my students and the kids from my tutorial project. We "did our thing" the usual way, and I felt that we had gotten off to a good start.

The bell rang for the first period. Mrs. Miller had my teaching schedule and knew that it was the Language Workshop about which she had read in my résumé and which had been so highly praised by Dr. Gaddy in his recommendation. I felt particularly comfortable having guests in that class, for the Language Workshop had become a showcase to which visitors were often invited. As usual, the first part of the period was devoted to going over the homework assignments and introducing the new material, almost exclusively in the target language. Mrs. Miller accompanied me to the different groups, which consisted of Russian, Hebrew, French, and Spanish students. Once I had presented the lessons, she circulated among them on her own. Her affable manner made the students feel comfortable, and they went on with their work undaunted by her presence. From her exclamation, "This is quite an operation!" I concluded that she, like many other observers, was favorably impressed by what she saw.

The rest of the classes also went well, particularly third-year Spanish. The kids must have understood intuitively that Mrs. Miller was a special guest and that a bit of extra effort on their part would certainly make all of us look better. I soon realized that Mrs. Miller was going to spend the entire school day, and beyond, in my presence. This included my lunch period, where she apparently wanted to get a sense of my relationship with my colleagues. She also accompanied me to my library assignment, as well as to the language laboratory, where she watched me repair one of the broken machines while eliciting my opinion about the value of the lab in foreign language instruction.

After school was dismissed, we went to our TV studio, where a videotape was going to be made for the benefit of the judges who would be making the final selection. Mrs. Miller explained that the interview would deal with both my overall knowledge of educational issues and my pedagogical attitudes. The judges were also interested in how well the National Teacher would handle the media. The gods were with me. Mrs. Miller's gentle questioning, and my few previous experiences with radio and TV appearances, made for a successful interview.

The following day was slightly different. Mrs. Miller came to all of my language classes, but used the other three periods to speak to some of my colleagues as well as to my students. In addition, the PTA had arranged for her to meet with a few former students, parents of present and former students, and parents of children who were involved in the French Exchange program. This gathering was held in a large room where Mrs. Miller and some of her associates from *Good Housekeeping* met for informal conversations with various small groups. I couldn't believe my eyes when I peeked into the room and saw how many people had turned out after school that Friday to speak on my behalf.

There was one more meeting with Mrs. Miller, a Saturday evening dinner that included not only my wife but a former State Teacher of the Year and her husband. Mrs. Miller most likely wanted the opinion of her guests as to my fitness for this high honor.

I heard later from Dr. Gaddy that, during a short chat as they walked through the halls, Mrs. Miller had given him to understand that she was impressed with my teaching. I was pleased to hear that, but was not going to be obsessed by the idea of becoming National Teacher of the Year, attractive as it sounded. The recognition I had already received, plus my sincere belief that teaching was its own reward, motivated me enough to go on with my work in my usual way.

Still enjoying my status as State Teacher of the Year, however, I continued to receive invitations to address a variety of educational conferences, which gave me and Shirley the opportunity to spend weekends in interesting places and in grand style. With all that exciting activity going on, I almost forgot about Washington and gave little thought to what the outcome might be at the national level. One evening in late March, the telephone rang around ten o'clock. It was the New York State Commissioner, Gordon Ambach. "Jay," he asked, "are you standing or sitting?"

"Standing," I replied.

"Then sit down," he said, "because I have some news for you."

I honestly did not anticipate what he was going to say. A proud and very slow announcement came over the phone. "You are the 1981 National Teacher of the Year. Congratulations."

Commissioner Ambach swore me to secrecy, explaining that this could not become public till the day that I was to be honored in the White House. In the meantime, I should wait for instructions from the coordinator of the Council of Chief State School Officers, who would make arrangements for my going to Washington.

Imagine my excitement, as well as my frustration at not being able to tell anyone the incredible news except my wife, my son, who was now living in Ireland, and Dr. Gaddy, who was offended that he was not the first one to be informed by Commissioner Ambach. I must confess that I was no longer as dispassionate about becoming the National Teacher of the Year as I had been when I doubted the possibility of its happening. I was elated, proud, moved, and very grateful.

Ten days later, I received the call from the coordinator of the program, Mrs. Darlene Pierce. She gave me a general outline of my four-day stay in Washington, the appearances that would be scheduled for me, and the number of personal guests I could invite to the White House ceremony. All that remained now was four long weeks during which time seemed to be standing still.

Shirley, Jason, and I arrived in Washington on the evening of April 19. We were picked up by a special limousine and driven to the plush Watergate Hotel overlooking the Potomac River. Our accommodations consisted of a huge three-bedroom suite, with a long balcony almost hanging over the river, and phones in every room, including the three bathrooms. The living room was so large that on one afternoon, the *Encyclopædia Britannica* people gave a reception for us there that was attended by two hundred people.

The following morning my busy schedule began. Breakfast with the deputy Commissioner of Education and his staff and a tour of the

Education Department were followed by my address to the brass of
the department, which I had labored on nervously for days. Although I
was going to have a separate reception in Albany, the New York State
Department of Education gave a luncheon in my honor in Washington
as well. There were radio and newspaper interviews, to which I was
taken by John, our charming limousine driver. I was always accompanied by Mrs. Pierce, who wanted to make sure that all of America
became aware of this great event.

During the two days before my appearance at the White House I did
not have a moment to myself. I was interviewed by Richard Valeriani
on the *Today Show,* which was watched, as I learned later, by some of
my students and colleagues at New Rochelle High. On a visit to the
radio station of the Voice of America, I was informed that my interview was going to be broadcast to Eastern Europe. This broadcast included Czechoslovakia, which was still occupied by its Soviet
oppressors, despite the fact that the Czechs were allies who had fought
with them to help defeat Hitler. During my interview, I was able to tell

*At the White House, Secretary of Education Bell delivering a speech honoring
the author as the National Teacher of the Year. Standing to the right is Jay,
his wife and his son.*

my listeners, among other things, that I, once a Czech citizen, was now living in a free country and that they, too, should continue to fight for their freedom and rid themselves of the Soviet yoke.

In addition to the moving experience in the Rose Garden which I have described in the Prologue, there was yet one more event that would have a profound influence on my professional future. At a dinner reception to which leading educators and other guests were invited, T. H. Bell, Secretary of Education, turned to me and said, "How would you like to come to Washington more often? I am about to assemble a national commission of eighteen leading educators that will be charged with presenting a report on the quality of our schools. We must find solutions to some of the problems that plague us. My assistants have examined your record carefully, not only as a teacher but with respect to your contributions to education as a whole. I agree with them that you would make a fine commissioner. Would you like that?" I nodded my head in the affirmative, quite unaware of the ramifications of his proposal. "I have to make my speech now. You will probably hear from me in a few months." Secretary Bell delivered a most laudatory speech, at the end of which he asked me to join him at the podium and presented me with a Certificate of Appreciation for my significant contribution to education in the United States.

Considering the hectic round of activities, I was actually very glad that there was just one more day to be spent in Washington. One particular event stands out in my memory—a reception given me by Albert Shanker, president of the American Federation of Teachers. Generally speaking, union people are not in favor of programs that single out one individual for special recognition. It was clear that Mr. Shanker had a different opinion on the subject and possessed the courage to say so. In his short presentation to the invited guests, he pointed out that honoring an outstanding teacher on a local or national level was a demonstration of respect for the teaching profession as a whole, not just for the particular teacher. I agreed with Mr. Shanker's sentiments. I, too, felt that my awards were of symbolic value to the profession, which has yet to receive the recognition it deserves.

And so came to an end the four days filled with exhilarating, and sometimes fatiguing events, with just a few more to come on my return to New Rochelle. I was very glad to be back in my classes, where I felt far more comfortable than in some of the places I had been during my Washington stay.

My students, too, had a surprise for me—a beautifully decorated gold-colored T-shirt with a large inscription, NATL. TEACHER OF THE YEAR, on the front, and on the back, JAY BABY #1. The kids insisted that I model the gift, which was obviously designed with love, and responded with resounding applause. Making sure that the "ceremony" did not distract us for longer than five minutes, I called the class to order and began instruction. Since the public functions of the Teacher of the Year don't begin until September, I was able to enjoy two months of teaching without any major interruptions. The end of spring term seemed to arrive more quickly than in the past. I was looking forward to a year of traveling across America and addressing different audiences, but I also knew I was going to miss my students, and wished I could take them with me. The last day was particularly emotional. My room was crowded with kids from all my classes who came to bid me their affectionate farewells and wish me good luck.

Chapter 21

A Nation At Risk

In July 1981, Secretary Bell called to inform me that he had begun to put together the National Commission on Excellence in Education, and he formally invited me to be one of the members. He assured me that both he and David Gardner—President of the University of Utah, who would be the Commission's chairman—thought I could make a very important contribution. By now I had a better concept of what the Commission was going to be about than when the Secretary had broached the subject in Washington. I was overjoyed by the invitation, and felt privileged to serve my country in this vital effort. I was apprehensive about my role on the Commission, but I prepared myself during the summer by reviewing a number of previously published reports on the country's educational problems.

On October 9, the full Commission met in Washington for its first two-day session. In addition to the Commission and its staff, headed by Executive Director Milton Goldberg, over a hundred leading educators had been invited to this first gathering. Given the fact that this was a commission on education officially sanctioned by the President of the United States, the media coverage was extensive and the atmosphere charged with excitement.

The day began with Secretary Bell's introduction of the Commission members to President Reagan at the White House. When my turn came, Mr. Reagan told me that he was sorry he had been unable to preside at my ceremony and added jokingly that he had nevertheless sent his best ambassador, Nancy. As is the protocol for such receptions, we were all photographed with the President.

Afterward, the official proceedings began at the Rayburn Building. There I was, sitting nervously at a huge table, hoping to be worthy of the honor of serving on a panel that included distinguished educators with impressive credentials and accomplishments. To my right sat Glenn T. Seaborg, a Nobel Laureate, head of the Atomic Energy Commission during the Kennedy administration and now University Professor of Chemistry at Berkeley. At my left was Gerald Holton, Mallinckrodt Professor of Physics and Professor of the History of Science at Harvard University. Seated on either side of Secretary Bell were Anne Campbell, former Commissioner of Education of the State of Nebraska, and Yvonne Larsen, Past-President of the San Diego City School Board and now Vice-Chair of our Commission.

Among the other members, to ensure a diversity of viewpoints, were four college and university presidents, two high-school principals, a school superintendent, three members of professional associations and school boards, a retired board chairman of Bell Telephone Laboratories, and Albert Quie, former Governor of the State of Minnesota. I doubt whether anyone else was as insecure as I was to find myself in this company.

The Secretary delivered a moving and patriotic speech in which he pointed out the urgency of improving education in America and outlined to the media and the audience the goals to which the Commission was committed. He was followed by a few leading educators in the audience who underscored the importance of our undertaking and pledged their support of the Commission's effort.

Since the Commission's evaluation of the state of our schools was to be based to a great extent on reports from experts in the different fields of education, more than forty papers had been solicited. One of the most tedious and time-consuming responsibilities of serving on the Commission was to read these papers—which were often laden with educational jargon—and be prepared to report their essence to one's subcommittee or to the Commission as a whole. In addition, six hearings were held, in different cities across the country, on particular aspects of the curriculum. Educators, as well as the public at large, were invited to participate in person or to express their views in writing. The Commission embraced in its investigation all levels of education through high school, including colleges and universities primarily with regard to their involvement in teacher education training programs.

The first public hearing, on Mathematics and Technology Education, was chaired in March by Glenn Seaborg at Stanford University. Just a month later, I had the daunting task—preceded by a few restless nights—of following this world-renowned scientist in conducting the Language and Literacy hearing in Houston, Texas.

During the same period that I was participating in the functions of the Commission, I was touring the country as National Teacher of the Year. On the list of invitations there were states and cities I had hitherto only read or heard about—Kansas, Georgia, Colorado, Vermont, Texas, Baltimore, Seattle, San Francisco—never dreaming that I would visit so many of them in my lifetime.

The Teacher of the Year has to be prepared to speak on a large variety of topics that are not exactly within the realm of his expertise. I might be invited to be the keynote speaker at a conference that dealt with juvenile delinquency, or to discuss how to include moral values in the curriculum. In each case a great deal of hard work went into the preparation. It was nevertheless an interesting experience from which I was able to learn many things that were indeed relevant to the profession.

My audiences were as varied as were the locations I visited, but I was always happiest when I spoke to children about the importance of learning or about my own childhood experiences. It did not matter whether they were kindergarten kids or high school students; with them I was always in my natural element and never ill at ease. I felt that these kids were actually listening to me, and it was here that I was making an important contribution to the cause of learning.

Once I completed the bookings that Mrs. Pierce had arranged for me, I was free to accept engagements on my own. Those last four months proved particularly enjoyable. Totally unanticipated, this last leg of my tour abounded with recognition from a large variety of educational institutions and one more from President Reagan. On the occasion of his honoring some 140 outstanding students, I too was invited to the White House to receive a Presidential Scholar medal, plus one more kiss from the First Lady, who remembered me from our previous meeting. In Texas, Governor Clements hosted a reception at which he made me an honorary citizen of his state and gave me the key to the city of Austin.

Among the honors, the two I received at Brooklyn College—the Alumnus of 1982 and the Educational Leadership awards—were particularly precious. It was, after all, this treasured American public institution that had opened its doors to me and paved the road that I was now privileged to travel on. For the ceremony, the college invited a number of my former teachers, among them dear Dr. Filia Holtzman, who had played such a significant part in my education. Filia was overjoyed, and behaved as though her own son were being honored. I was more than ever aware, however, that among the family members who attended the reception, one person was missing—my beloved mother. As I accepted the plaque, her face flashed before me. She would have been so proud to hear me tell the gathering how much she had to do with the events of that evening.

Among the many cherished privileges of being the Teacher of the Year was the opportunity to see the length and breadth of our beautiful country. The mountains, the landscapes, and the rivers compare in beauty with any part of the world. What is especially wonderful is that you do not need a passport to see them, that they are all contained in one free nation. By the time my tour ended, I had been to some thirty states and to Mexico, where I was invited by Ambassador Gavin to represent America at the celebration of the sixtieth anniversary of public education there.

With my obligations as Teacher of the Year essentially over in June, I was able to devote all my time during the summer of 1982 to the Commission on Excellence in Education without missing a single meeting or responsibility. Although the Commission was chartered for a maximum of two years, by that September we were in possession of virtually all the data needed to begin the writing of our report.

Our major challenge was to decipher the huge amount of information and come up with a report that would offer viable recommendations to correct some of the shortcomings of our schools. As might be expected with a group of people who came from such diverse walks of life and with often conflicting political agendas, a Commission comprised of eighteen members was not going to be unanimous in its recommendations. There were widely differing views on every aspect of educational policy as well as on the length and language of the report itself.

The divergence of opinions became at times quite vociferous. What enabled us eventually to come to some consensus was that priceless attribute of civilization called compromise—something that can take place only in a country like America, where disagreement does not end in exile. I always refer to my serving on the Commission as my "most graphic and valuable lesson in the democratic process." In the final analysis we all understood that we were engaged in a very vital undertaking. Every voice was patiently listened to. There were no shrinking violets in our midst. We each had our personal causes that seemed crucial to education, either nationally or within our respective communities. We argued and fought on their behalf.

By early spring of 1983 we had a draft report. Despite the lack of unanimity on many points, the continuing process of compromise had forged a consensus for which much credit belongs to the collective wisdom and gentle hands of our chairpersons, David Gardner and Yvonne Larsen, as well as to the Executive Director of the Commission, Dr. Milton Goldberg.

The final version of our report, *A Nation at Risk: The Imperative for Educational Reform*, was designed to be succinct and unencumbered by excessive detail. The very first page carried that message:

> Our Nation is at risk. . . . the educational foundations of our society are presently being eroded by a rising tide of mediocrity. . .
>
> If an unfriendly foreign power had attempted to impose on America the mediocre educational performance that exists today, we might well have viewed it as an act of war. As it stands, we have allowed this to happen to ourselves. . . . We have, in effect, been committing an act of unthinking, unilateral educational disarmament.

The fundamental thrust of our recommendations was that our children be offered a strong academic curriculum devoid of irrelevance. We proposed that all our high-school students be required to take substantive courses in mathematics, the sciences, including computer science, and history. We were particularly emphatic about the development of a strong course of study in English that would combine literary essence with high-level communication and writing skills. This would provide a basis for all the other academic subjects and for life itself. We called on the Teacher Training Colleges to tighten their curricula and to produce better trained teachers for our

To Jay Sommer
With appreciation and best wishes,

Ronald Reagan

Jay Sommer at the White House receiving from President Reagan the National Commission's report, A Nation at Risk.

children. Although more controversial than some of the other provisions, we also urged higher teacher salaries and improved working conditions.

On April 26, 1983, at a White House ceremony, President Reagan give his official imprimatur to *A Nation at Risk* in the presence of the

Commission, invited guests, and the media. The President praised us for our contribution and awarded every member of the Commission a handsome plaque with a full-size reproduction of the report's cover. It was a proud and happy day for all of us who had contributed to the creation of this important document. Now we had to wait and hope that our report was not going to collect dust, that our work would prove to be of value to educators as well as to the public.

Notwithstanding some pessimism on the part of a few critics, the response to *A Nation at Risk* on the part of both the educational community and the public was favorable. Initially, 40,000 copies were printed for distribution by the Education Department and 2,000 for sale by the Government Printing Office. The demand was so great, however, that not only did the GPO issue several subsequent printings, but various educational organizations, periodicals, and newspapers duplicated the document. It is estimated that the final printing count ran to some 4 million copies.

The popularity of *A Nation at Risk* can be attributed to a number of reasons, among them its accurate assessment of the state of America's schools. It was indeed a clarion call that awakened our educational consciousness, dormant since the Sputnik era of the fifties. The report did not pretend to possess a magic wand that was going to cure all our educational ills. But it did inspire a national debate as well as additional studies on education on the national and local levels. It helped to launch a reform movement that attracted political as well as business leaders who were concerned with our troubled schools. That reform movement is still alive and well, as evidenced by the fact that as I write this in the spring of 1994, a landmark piece of legislation has been enacted. Called *Goals 2000: Educate America,* it provides, for the first time in the history of the jealously guarded state and local control of our schools, a set of uniform *national* educational standards and guidelines, with financial incentives to back them up.

As if the satisfaction of having served on the Commission were not enough, I received a call from Secretary Bell in May. After a minimum of small talk, he spoke of the urgency of getting the Commission's message across. "Jay," he said, "we think that you should be one of the ambassadors we send out to discuss the implications of *A Nation at Risk.* You were, after all, the only practicing teacher on the panel and surely one of its strongest patriotic voices. Would you like to undertake this for the 1983-84 school year?"

My answer was a resounding "Yes." The only thing that might stand in our way, I said, might be Dr. Gaddy's disapproval of my being away from school. But a call from the Secretary, plus the fact that the New Rochelle School District was going to be handsomely reimbursed for my absence, appeased my principal.

My year on the road on behalf of the Commission was yet another unforgettable experience that included a trip on Air Force One, accompanying President Reagan to endorse an effort on the part of Governor Lamar Alexander to improve education in the state of Tennessee. In addition to the fact that I had this unique opportunity to serve my country and discuss the report, was the added dimension of learning still more about my profession and getting a sharper sense of the state of American education.

My return to New Rochelle High School was a letdown. I had not expected a royal reception, but there were many indications that I was out of favor with the administration. I was cheered, however, by the warm reception I got from my students and some of my colleagues. Room 104 once more became a refuge for many kids who could always use some attention, even if it was not for help with their studies. Once more, many of the arrangements for the French Exchange program were my responsibility—I had in fact done some work on it during the year away—and invitations to speak to different classes were just as frequent as they were when I was State Teacher of the Year.

Although I was a tenured teacher with seniority over several colleagues in the language department, I became more and more aware of nuances that suggested the district wouldn't mind living without my services. This made for a rather unpleasant working atmosphere. As fate would have it, I was invited to become Visiting Professor at the Graduate School of Education of Long Island University, C. W. Post campus, for the 1984-85 school year. The prospect of being involved in the teacher training program, where I could impart some of my experience to future teachers, was most exhilarating. Much as I hated to leave my students, I decided to retire from secondary school teaching and accept the appointment. Thus I moved from the place where I seemed to have worn out my welcome to one where I was warmly received.

Due to the university's financial constraints, as well as the time that I needed to devote to this book, I switched after eight years as visiting professor (probably a national record in this category) to the status of adjunct professor. For the past two years, I have been teaching Spanish, serving as Director of Critical Languages, and maintaining contact with the Education Department.

The reduction in time spent at the university has made possible the fulfillment of one more wish. Ever since I started teaching, I hoped that one day I would be able to work with elementary school children in some capacity. This was out of the question in the New York State System because of my foreign accent. Well, that is no longer a problem. I am now a twice-weekly visiting scholar at the Montvale schools in New Jersey. Montvale is an exemplary district that has been recognized for its excellence by the Department of Education. I work with teachers on a variety of projects. I teach French to gifted and talented fourth-graders who give up part of their lunch period. I have taught a Russian minicourse to middle-school boys and girls. I read, teach songs, and tell stories to kindergartners. Just as I anticipated, working with these charming kids is a real delight, and the last remaining part of my dream has been realized.

Chapter 22

My Roots Revisited

In the last several chapters, I end the account of my professional life. I intend to remain a teacher until my last breath and to pay my debt to this country by continuing to speak on behalf of education.

The passage of time inevitably has softened the pain of the past. The nightmares and the black thoughts come less frequently. My life here, the opportunities afforded me, whatever success I have achieved in this great and good land have helped to heal some wounds. However, the past remains with me; my early life and the sorrows of the Holocaust cannot be erased. Like other survivors, I have chosen to be silent, to suppress certain memories so as not to make life more difficult for my family and myself. Writing this book has allowed me to give voice to feelings and recollections that have festered in me for too many years.

During this time, I have felt a growing need to return to my beginnings. I longed to see the places where my troubled childhood ran its course, where as a young man my dreams of a better life were abruptly shattered. I wanted to make sense of some of what I had endured, things which made no sense. Above all, I wanted to find my mother's grave.

In the summer of 1991, Shirley and I departed for Budapest. Although the city was teeming with people, the scars of World War II and the aftermath of the 1956 uprising by the Hungarians against their Soviet oppressors were still clearly visible. Many of the buildings which were riddled with shells and bombs by both the Germans and the Russians had not been repaired. Although Hungary finally had rid itself of Soviet domination, the Russians had left behind a drabness characteristic of all the places which they held hostage.

There were, though, signs that this city, once one of the jewels of Eastern Europe, was on the way to recovery. It was especially heartwarming to see that the Jewish community, which had been severely reduced in numbers by the Nazis and then oppressed by the

Jay standing in front of the Csepel plant from which he and Imre escaped.

Russians, was slowly returning to life. This revival was most apparent
in the places of worship, which had begun to attract a younger generation that earlier was at risk of losing its Jewish identity. In addition to
the smaller neighborhood synagogues that were now being refur-
bished, a monumental task was finally in progress to restore the
Dohány Street Synagogue, the Jewish religious and cultural center of
Hungary before the Nazi onslaught. The Jews of Budapest were
herded in there during the Holocaust, either to starve to death or to be
sent to Auschwitz.

First on the list of places that haunted my memory was Csepel, the
ammunition factory from which I escaped with my friend Imre
Neimann. Although Csepel, as far as I knew, was no longer a producer
of military goods, we were still not permitted to enter the plant. Even
from the outside, as we walked around part of the five-mile perimeter,
I could tell that the once busy smelting ovens and the deafening air
hammers were no longer at work.

With my wife at my side, it was easier to look once more at the unoccupied but still intimidating watchtowers above the high cement
walls on top of which was impenetrable barbed wire. How often I had
stood on the other side of that wall yearning to scale it and escape.
Now, other than the occasional squeak of a worn-out machine, Csepel
was silent and deserted, a graveyard for those who lost their lives
during the frightful bombings. Through a break in the wall I pointed
out to Shirley a dilapidated open railroad car like the one the inmates

and I used to load with scrap iron and push to the smelting area. As memories of that time flooded in, I broke down, mourning my fellow Jews, whose bodies were buried in a mass grave or simply thrown onto some deserted dump.

Back in Budapest, I showed Shirley the school where Harry and I were reunited, as well as the boiler room where I had spent the night despite Mr. Szécsényi's threats to denounce me to the Germans. I also located the printing shop where my supposed friend was to prepare false papers, but instead had two SS men waiting for me when I returned to pick them up. Evidently, the basement now served as lodging for a gypsy woman who, when I looked in, was telling a fortune. As I descended the stairs, I was filled with such anxiety that I turned and ran.

I made an attempt to find Imre, but could not trace him. Nor could I locate any members of the Hajdu family, who had sheltered me after my flight from the Russians.

In Budapest, we were guests of Éva Kelényi and her family. I had met Éva at a cousin's house in the United States, where I had learned that Malvinka, a neighbor of ours in Mukachevo, was her mother. I remember Malvinka affectionately as someone who had been very good to me, sometimes giving me food when I was hungry. This discovery gave birth to a close friendship with Éva, her sister Lilike, and their husbands, all of whom I came to regard as family.

Éva is one of those incredibly generous souls who runs around Budapest visiting sick people though she herself is not in the best of health. At least twice a year, she extends her charitable service to people living in her home town of Uzhgorod as well as in Mukachevo which was still under Soviet occupation when we visited her. Since she was due to make her pilgrimage about then, she decided to accompany us on our journey to Mukachevo and Kustanovice. Her presence would be extremely helpful because making the necessary arrangements was not an easy task, given the stupidity of the Russian bureaucracy.

With huge packages of clothing and food for her needy Jewish and Christian friends, we boarded the train for Chop, a town on the Russian border, where we were met by Volodya, a friend of Éva's, who had put himself and his car at our disposal. We stopped first in

Uzhgorod, at the house of Éva's childhood friend Nina, one of those rare Gentiles who was not contaminated by the anti-Semitism that prevailed in that part of the world.

All of us were to go to Mukachevo the next day where my first priority was to visit my mother's grave. I spent a long, sleepless night beset by anxieties. I recalled Mother's illness and her suffering before her death, and I was afraid that I would not be able to find her grave. My uncertainty came from the fact that, in 1969, a cousin had written, informing us that the cemetery where my mother was buried was soon to be bulldozed. For a handsome fee to the Russians, however, her remains could be transferred to a small plot designated for Jewish burial. Since money could not be forwarded legally, we sent packages of clothing which could be sold to raise the necessary sum. In 1970, barely in time, Mother's coffin was moved to another location. With nothing more than a picture of the gravestone sent by my cousin, who had since died, I had very little information about the new site.

Volodya, Nina, Éva, Shirley, and I drove to Mukachevo the next morning. We had been told that the new Jewish burial plots were located somewhere on the side of the large Christian cemetery. It took a while before we stumbled on a section that had no real entrance other than an opening in a broken fence. We had very nearly passed it. Except that the stones were the type generally used by Jews, there were no signs that identified the place as a Jewish cemetery. Only when we went in and saw the Hebrew inscriptions that had been hidden by dense growth, were we sure it was the right place. Compared with the two hundred year old cemetery which had been plowed under, the new burial place was small, only about a quarter of an acre in size.

The graveyard looked abandoned, as though it had had no visitors for years. It was so overgrown that some of the smaller tombstones were completely covered, and in some places it was impossible to tell where one grave ended and another began. We began our search. The five of us separated to cover different rows, with Volodya and Nina walking together. Because they did not know how to read Hebrew, I gave them the picture of Mother's tombstone to help identify it. We combed the place from end to end but could not find the grave. I was ready to leave, but Éva insisted that we not give up and we resumed our search. About five minutes into our second attempt, Éva cried out

Mr. and Mrs. Sommer at the grave of the author's mother.

from behind the tall grass where we could barely see her, "Here she is, here she is. I found her," as though speaking of my living mother.

All five of us, as if on command, began to pull the weeds from around the headstone. Within minutes the area was cleared. Éva, who knew all the proper rituals, had brought candles to place at the grave. We stood together, two Christians and three Jews, as one family, observing a Jewish tradition honoring one's parents. Together, in silence, we watched the candles melting quickly in the hot summer sun.

It was not until I was left alone that I was able to give vent to my feelings. My tears brought with them a sense of calm rather than emotional upheaval. I sat for a while embracing the gravestone and passing my fingers over Mother's name. At the last flicker of the candles, I said Kaddish and left the cemetery.

We were now on our way to the town itself, where Éva was going to visit one of the beneficiaries of her charitable work, Leah, a Holocaust survivor now living with her daughter in abject poverty. As a young girl of fifteen, Leah had been taken to Auschwitz from the Mukachevo ghetto in early May of 1944. Though she had survived Hitler's killing machine, she had experienced such severe cold during her captivity that she sustained frostbite over most of her body. Despite the health problems resulting from her imprisonment, Leah was able to marry and have a family. With the passage of time her physical condition had deteriorated to such a degree that she had been almost totally bedridden for the last ten years.

Éva asked me to accompany her and help carry the packages, containing canned foods as well as clothing. We entered a dark corridor in an old building and knocked on the door of an apartment on the ground floor. It took a few minutes before an emaciated woman in a tattered nightgown responded, and a few more minutes before she recognized Éva. She admitted us to a dreary one-room apartment. They embraced, and Éva asked Leah how she was. In a barely audible voice, she assured Éva that this was an especially good day because she had had enough strength to eat breakfast on her own and open the door for us. "Éva," she said haltingly with an angelic smile, "*die veist, heint hob ich afile gehert die feigelach singen* [You know, today I even heard the birds sing]." We spent about a half hour in the company of this heroic woman who, despite her terribly enfeebled state, clung to life and found consolation in things that others take for granted. Both Éva and I were overwhelmed with emotion, but tried to restrain ourselves in Leah's presence.

One might ask why I find it necessary to include Leah in my book. The answer is simple. For me she is the ultimate symbol of the survivors of Hitler's hell. We often hear about those who have overcome both their physical and mental pain and carved for themselves a normal and even successful existence. We very rarely hear of those who returned, not only with emotional scars, but with infirmities that doomed them to perpetual suffering.

As we strolled through the center of Mukachevo, it was clear that the once flourishing city was essentially dead. There was just a handful of shops open, most of them selling shabbily made trinkets for tourist consumption. The few food stores and bakeries were virtually empty. At different locations on the street people were selling farm products. We saw a woman carrying a basket with goat cheese wrapped in cheap brown paper. Before she had even placed herself, people descended on her like vultures. The cheese was sold in a moment.

It was painful to see that a city with such a large Jewish population at the beginning of World War II now had only about twenty families, most of whom came from the surrounding villages where life must have been totally impossible. The hundreds of Hebrew signs and inscriptions on Jewish establishments had vanished. Of the two large synagogues where I used to pray on the High Holy Days, and where I sought shelter from the cold, one was now a shabby-looking military storage depot; the other had been turned into a children's department store. The smaller places of worship, more than fifty of them, had met with similar fates.

Throughout the time of Russian occupation, clandestine prayer services had to be held in private homes. As a result of Gorbachev's liberalization, public houses of worship were slowly reforming. During the time that I visited Mukachevo and nearby Uzhgorod, I noted that even there a few tiny houses of worship were beginning to emerge. In fact, I attended a Saturday service in Uzhgorod. It was sad to see that the congregation was so small that they often could not gather the ten-man *minyan* required for a service. Even more depressing was the fact that they were for the most part only old Jews, who, for whatever reason, had not escaped the Russian noose and emigrated to Israel or the United States.

When we visited the old house in the Yiddishe Gass, now called Mayakovskaya where my poor mother had died, I met Menachem, a man who had also survived by escaping from a forced-labor camp. Like other survivors, he unburdened himself to me. Menachem, now in his early sixties was a retired academic and Hebrew scholar. He had a wife, two children, and sick old mother who had been at Auschwitz. Menachem's parents had been well-off before the war, but when he and his mother returned to Mukachevo they found their house confiscated by the Russians. They now lived in poverty, as did most people in that part of the world, Jew and Gentile.

Menachem told me of his own experiences and gave a long list of losses in his family. "It is very difficult to live in a place where so many sad memories haunt you. I would have liked to go to Israel or to America, but with my ailing mother and the Russian grip on us it was impossible." In a whisper he added, "What the Germans did not destroy of our Jewish religious and cultural life, the Soviets did. My two grown sons have very little sense of Jewishness. Our books were burned, and our Jewish schools closed, possibly forever. I only hope that my children will find a way out of this desert. Believe me, there is very little left in Mukachevo or in the Yiddishe Gass that is Yiddish. The Jewish homes that once reverberated with Hebrew prayer and with children's laughter have lost their Jewish character."

From the Yiddishe Gass we went to the neighborhood where we lived when we moved from Kustanovice. I was anxious to see those places where life had some happy moments along with the very hard times. The soccer field, where I spent many exciting hours playing with my brother Samuel, and the tennis courts, where Harry and I worked as ball boys, were still there. When we got to the shabby basement that was now unoccupied by humans and most likely a hiding place for rats, the sight made me angry rather than sad. How was it that fate had reduced us to such poverty that we had to live in such horrible conditions? Just before we left the courtyard, I spoke to a Ruthenian woman who now occupied part of the building. I was curious, did she know to whom this building had once belonged?

"Oh," she replied in a casual tone, "I think it belonged to a rich Zhid who was killed by the Germans a long time ago." The disgust I felt at that moment was also reflected in the disapproving expressions on the faces of both Nina and Volodya.

Despite the fact that we were told that the roads to Kustanovice were extremely bad, Volodya was determined to drive us there. As soon as we reached the outskirts of the village I felt as though nothing had changed since I had left as a child. The natural beauty of the countryside—the slender white birches that lined both sides of the forest, the rolling hills, and the meadows replete with wildflowers—all retained their former beauty. The huts and the tiny houses, though worn by time, had preserved their rustic charm. I knew at once that I was not going to have any difficulty finding the places that were at the same time precious and painful to me.

The first stop was at the elementary school, where I had learned from Mrs. Zhupan how inspiring to a child a good teacher could be. The school was in session, and I spent some time with the first-grade children in the same room where I had sat so many years ago. I told them a few stories about my childhood in the village and sang Carpatho-Ukrainian songs with them while Volodya videotaped our performance. The children were

Jay inside the entrance of the basement where poverty obliged them to live.

Jay Sommer meeting Ilona, his childhood friend, in Kustanovice after a fifty year separation.

enchanting and most responsive to all of us. My visit seemed more like a dream from the past than something real that was actually taking place in the company of my wife and my friends. As we waved good-bye, I silently wished that they would retain their natural love for people rather than become bullies and anti-Semites like the ones who threw stones at me on the way to school.

We continued on the familiar narrow dusty road, unchanged from the one on which I used to walk barefoot, that was littered with sharp pebbles that wounded my feet. As we drove, puzzled-looking children waved at us languidly. Within a few minutes we reached an area with a sharp decline on the right side of the road. "Stop, stop, Volodya!" I exclaimed excitedly. "We are here, we are here!" In the distance I saw the two wells from which I used to lug heavy buckets of water to the house. Since it was too steep for a car to descend, we parked on the side of the road. I darted down the hill as though carried by the wind, leaving everyone behind. Seconds later, I was approached by two curious children and a woman in her forties. With the help of my Russian and what I remembered of Ruthenian, I was able to tell her who I was and what I was looking for.

"Run," she urged one of her kids, "fetch *babushka* [grandma] from the fields; tell her to come right away." The woman introduced herself as Yulia, the daughter of Ilona, the *babushka* for whom she had sent her little boy. Ilona had been one of the children, other than my playmate Anya, who was friendly to me in those early years.

While we waited, I learned that the hut I so longed to see again, which should have stood quite near to where we were talking, had fallen apart some twenty years earlier. Even the rivulet by its side had disappeared under the mud which came down from the steep hills. The entire area was overgrown. I was deeply disappointed—somehow, we seem to want the scenes of our childhood to be preserved not only in our memory but in the real world as well.

When I saw Ilona in the distance, I began to run in her direction, not so much to meet her a few moments sooner, but to experience again the memory of having run in those beautiful meadows. As soon as I told Ilona who I was, she embraced me and called me by my Jewish name, which she used to mispronounce even when we were children. "So you are alive," she moaned as a few tears rolled down her wrinkled, weather-beaten face. "And how is Shmeelku [Samuel] and Hershel, and what happened to your mother? I remember how hard Feiga worked to earn a living." I told her very briefly what happened to Mother and Samuel. Obviously moved by my account, she shook her head from side to side repeatedly in sympathy, "*Shkoda* [What a pity]."

We walked hand in hand to join my companions and a host of other people who were now gathered around Shirley and my friends who spoke excellent Ruthenian. Ilona introduced us to her large family and her neighbors, all of whom were very curious about the strangers who had turned up in their remote, dormant little village. Yulia insisted that we celebrate the visit with a bite and a drink of their home-made vodka and wine.

All our protestations that we had just eaten and that we were in a hurry were of no consequence. We soon found ourselves seated in a courtyard around a table well-supplied with freshly-baked black bread, pastries filled with ground meat, and other farm delicacies rarely available to city folk. Much of the conversation was about life when my family lived there and how nothing had actually changed since we left. I was particularly pleased that many of the older folks spoke fondly about my mother. One of the unforgettable descriptions of her came from an eighty-six-year-old woman. "Your mother was a good person," she said. "She often made dresses for poor peasant women who could not pay her for months." Then she added, as though suddenly recalling something very important from the past, "Feiga always sang when she worked at her Singer machine or in the fields at harvest time."

While the others at the table continued chatting, I excused myself

Jay, standing on the spot where the little hut once stood.

and left the party. I wanted to be alone to roam for a while in those enchanting meadows that had so comforted me in my tender years. I walked into the tall corn fields where I used to hide mischievously from Mother, and gave in to the temptation to visit the hill where Anya's house had stood. It was no longer occupied by her family, but a neighbor told me that Anya had grown up to be *duzhe harna* (very pretty), had become a teacher, and now lived somewhere in Moravia.

As I walked back from Anya's house, my mind was crowded with thoughts about the distant past evoked by this visit to the village, happy memories and sad ones, each clamoring for attention: Mother's abiding love, Father's frequent beatings, Anya's faithful friendship, Samuel's tragic death.

The warm good-byes were accompanied by requests that we visit again. "Come every year," said a darling little blue-eyed girl who was passionately chewing on the gum that Éva had given her. If for no other reason than that my mother was remembered here with warmth and respect, the trip to this remote corner of the earth was more than worthwhile. To know that she was still remembered was a renewed source of happiness.

We spent two days in Uzhgorod before returning to Budapest. On the morning of our departure, I was invited to address a group of children in a tiny apartment that had recently been converted to a synagogue. These were children who had been attending Sunday school for the last year or so, led by the son of a rabbi who had died a few years after his return from Auschwitz. Having been brought up under the Soviet regime, the son himself was far removed from his father's piety and the practice of Jewish tradition. There was in him, perhaps, a vague childhood memory of Jewishness that beckoned him to help these children find their own identity.

It was heartwarming to spend several hours in the company of those little ones and try to respond to some very probing questions about my experience in the Holocaust. One little girl asked me, "Were all Germans as bad as Hitler?" And another, "Why didn't God help save the Jewish children?" For questions like these I had no answer, but I was glad that there was at least a small number of Jewish children in that part of the world who would continue to ask these questions when the rest of us would no longer be there.

Volodya and Nina drove us to the station on the Hungarian border, where we parted from these devoted people. On the train there was very little conversation among us about the events of the last few days, as though everything had been said just by our having been through them together. I had known all along that Shirley would be profoundly affected by the experience, and her silence confirmed it. Poor Éva appeared emotionally drained, for she too had many sad associations with some of the places we had seen; most of her family had perished in the Holocaust. Oddly enough, I was more unsettled as I sat on the train reliving what I had just experienced in Mukachevo and Kustanovice than I was when actually there. Not until we were flying back to New York did Shirley and I speak about our reactions to this visit.

Along with the pain, I felt a sense of peace, of completion on our return to New York. Yet there was one more trip that I felt compelled to make. In the spring of 1992, I arranged to go to Auschwitz. With the help of my dear friend Éva Kelényi, I hired a taxi in Budapest. Karcsi, the driver, was a Hungarian Jew who as a ten-year-old boy had been hidden by a Christian family during the Nazi occupation. We left Budapest early in the morning in the direction of Slovakia, where we would cross the border into Poland on our way to Cracow, some forty kilometers from Auschwitz. Alongside the highway that we traveled in Slovakia ran a railroad track and a winding river that was fed by the Low Tatra Mountains. Every time we crossed a bridge over that river, my heart stood still. I wondered whether it was here that Samuel jumped out of the train. Was it here in the midst of this serene beauty that the Nazis shot my brother? Is this the ground stained with the blood of that beautiful, gallant boy?

We arrived in Cracow in the evening, checked into our hotel, had some dinner, and went into town. As we roamed the streets, it was sadly visible that Hitler had achieved his goal of making Cracow *Jüdenrein* (cleansed of Jews). When the Germans invaded Poland in 1939, Cracow had 60,000 Jews; only 3,000 returned, and of these, most of the younger people eventually left for Israel or other places of refuge.

Back in the hotel, I became curious when I heard Italian being spoken by a number of teenagers. Who were they, and what were they doing in Cracow? I learned that they were Christian students from five different schools in Florence, and that the teachers and community leaders who accompanied them made a yearly pilgrimage to Auschwitz with a group of students to commemorate the Holocaust. With them was an Italian survivor, an elderly Jewish woman.

When the head of the group, Signora Pierelli, learned that I was going to Auschwitz, she invited me to join them on the bus the next morning which I did, while Karcsi followed in the car. On the way, Signora Pierelli made a speech bitterly condemning the Italian fascists who were responsible for sending Jews to the Auschwitz inferno. Then, in impeccable Tuscan Italian, the Jewish survivor gave a personal account of the horrors visited upon her people, stopping intermittently as emotion overcame her. Looking at their sad responsive faces, I felt great admiration for these young people whom I could not have met at a better time. Already feeling the distress that was to intensify once I saw the camp, I was greatly heartened by their empathy.

We passed through an entrance to Auschwitz One, established at the order of Himmler in 1940. Above the gate there was the inscription, well-known to Holocaust survivors, that reads, **ARBEIT MACHT FREI** (Work makes you free). The sign was meant to deceive the prisoners into believing that they were coming to a place of work rather than to one where most of them would die. This was a relatively small camp compared to the one adjacent, Birkenau, built a year later where the majority of Jews were held in wooden barracks.

We got off the bus in front of an information office, and the Italians began their preparations for a memorial march. Each of them put on a striped, triangular kerchief, their symbol for German atrocities. The marshal, who carried an Italian flag, was followed by a group with muffled drums, and behind them the rest of the contingent.

Karcsi and I followed the Italians as they marched solemnly through the camp, then separated from them to join a tour led by a young Polish woman. While we waited for the tour to begin, I looked at the barracks where untold human suffering had taken place and wept. But once we entered the rooms where the physical evidence of the Nazi atrocities was displayed, I felt so overwhelmed that I could not cry. The mute horror of the crematorium, the gas chamber, and the piles of human hair produced within me a devastating nausea and anguish such as I had never before experienced. I felt suffocated in those rooms and couldn't continue the tour. I needed to be outside and alone.

I separated from Karcsi and began to wander aimlessly, in a daze. Around noontime I went to Birkenau. Other than the barracks that showed the inhuman conditions under which the prisoners lived, there was no other evidence of Nazi villainy. Birkenau is, however, the largest cemetery in the world, lacking only the tombstones that would identify it as such.

It is a longstanding Jewish tradition to visit the burial place of members of one's family at least once a year and to hallow their memory. For the majority of survivors, the death camps are the only place one can observe that tradition. Auschwitz-Birkenau was the burial place of most of my family and friends. Once I entered Birkenau, I walked from barrack to barrack, reciting the first few lines from the memorial service and intoning the first names of as many members of my family as I could remember. I wanted to separate them from that abstract number, the six million. The list was long. Three half-brothers, four-half sisters, at least a dozen uncles and aunts, innumerable cousins and nephews: Ruchel, (Rachel) Tobi, Serl, Zlate Reisel, Chane, Oronka, Leib, Wolf, Yossel, Itzik, Magda, Moysele. The list went on.

By the time I visited all the barracks and walked the length and breadth of the camp it was evening. Karcsi, eager to begin the trip back to Budapest, came to look for me. I told him that I wanted to stay just a bit longer. He returned to the car. I sat down on the ground near a tiny stream, where I wept bitterly, a welcome release from the crushing weight on my heart.

We left Birkenau. Exhausted by my anguished emotions, I slept. When I awoke, we were back in Slovakia, driving through the towering Tatras.

Epilogue

Going back to Kustanovice, to Mukachevo, and to Budapest was essentially a sad experience. It neither alleviated the pain associated with those places, nor heightened the few pleasant memories of the past. But visiting Auschwitz sharpened the agony of the Holocaust for me and confirmed my sense that the Nazi abomination was beyond comprehension. To reduce to understandable terms what happened in Auschwitz and in other such places would necessitate a new set of human values. There is no precedent for such wholesale slaughter. The anguish endured by the victims of the Nazis defies imagination and stands outside of the human experience.

My ordeal cannot be compared to the horrors inflicted upon those imprisoned at Auschwitz. These I was spared by some unaccountable irony of fate. Although I escaped Hitler's death camps, I am destined nevertheless, always to live with the calamity that befell my murdered brethren. Furthermore, willingly or unwillingly, all of us survivors have transmitted some of this pain to our families.

Fortunately there is a chapter in the Holocaust story that did not totally destroy hope for mankind. That chapter belongs to the heroic souls, relatively few though they were, who opposed the evil of the Holocaust and did what they could to save Jews from the Nazi assault. These Christian rescuers, many of whom Israel honors as "The Righteous Among the Nations," were to be found in varying numbers in all of Nazi-occupied Europe. They were from all walks of life. The rescuers ranged from individuals, to religious groups, to virtually entire villages or countries. It is to these men and women that I dedicate the last pages of my book.

In Denmark, the government and the population cooperated in hiding some 8,000 Jews while arrangements were made with their neutral neighbor, Sweden, to take them in. With the exception of a few who died of natural causes all survived. The success of this effort tells us that perhaps there exists a collective sense of decency that can resist evil. In Denmark there were no individual idle bystanders.

Sweden, meanwhile, took further advantage of its neutral status and sent Raoul Wallenberg as a special envoy to Budapest, where he saved thousands of Hungarian Jews from the clutches of the Arrow Cross by issuing them false Swedish passports. Tragically, Wallenberg fell victim to Soviet savagery. When the Russians liberated Budapest, Wallenberg was arrested on some trumped-up charges of espionage and sent to a Gulag. His fate remains unknown.

In Italy, despite the country's alliance with Nazi Germany, many Jews were saved because a number of civilized human beings possessed by a sense of justice became involved in a rescue effort. In the forefront of this mission stands the clergy, headed by such men as the Archbishop of Florence, the Cardinal of Genoa, and a young priest, Don Repetto. They succeeded in hiding in their convents and churches men, women, and children who were destined to be deported. Lamentably, fascist evil was more potent than the benevolence of the rescuers. Out of 40,000 Jews living in Italy when the war began, 8,000 perished in Auschwitz and in other concentration camps.

Particularly impressive were the rescue efforts of the Italian military in the occupied zones of Croatia, Greece, and southern France. The army with the cooperation of some high-ranking members of the diplomatic corps went to great lengths to circumvent orders by the Germans to hand over the Jews of these countries. In this way the Italian Army saved some 25,000 Jews in the three occupied zones. The courage of these men in challenging Hitler and Mussolini sharply distinguishes them from those who "only obeyed orders."

Side by side with these collective efforts to rescue Jews stand the deeds of individual Gentiles who overcame fear and hid Jews in the face of possible imprisonment or even death. In Bulgaria, an unwilling ally of Germany, Dimeter Peshev, the president of the parliament had the moral courage to oppose his colleagues who were prepared to accede to German demands to deport Bulgaria's Jews, thus saving most of them.

In Poland, where anti-Semitism was deeply rooted, Jean Kowalyk, a seamstress, built a false wall in her house where she and her family hid several people, feeding them and caring for their sanitary needs. She held on to them despite periodic German surveillance of the house until liberation.

In Hungary, seventeen year old Malka Csizmadia from the small town of Sátoraljaújhely, the site of a labor camp holding some 300 Jewish men, performed her own rescue mission. What began on a small scale, sneaking out letters for the inmates, grew to a large operation involving her entire family. When Malka learned that the inmates were due to be taken to a concentration camp, the family arranged to smuggle twenty-five men, one at a time, to a nearby farm where they were eventually liberated by the Russians.

In Germany itself, a handful of civilians defied the Führer and saved their fellow citizens. Helen Jacobs hid Jews, created counterfeit ID's and raised money to buy food stamps on the black market. In 1943, the Gestapo tracked down her operation and she was sentenced to two-and-a half years in prison. The best-known of the rescuers today is Oskar Schindler, who successfully saved over 1,000 Polish Jews from almost certain death.

Since 1962, over 9,000 people have been honored at Yad Vashem, the Holocaust Memorial in Israel, with bronze medals bearing an inscription from the Talmud. It reads, "Whoever saves a single life is as one who has saved an entire world." There are many more rescuers whose courageous deeds have been recorded and still others who will never be recognized for their humanitarian deeds. These are people like the Hungarian workers at Csepel who surreptitiously shared their rations with us, and the young policeman at the agricultural school who quietly secured for me identification papers that helped me to remain in hiding.

It is perhaps because of such brave souls that we want to accept Anne Frank's view of mankind. As she expresses it in the play, *The Diary of Anne Frank*, "I think the world may be going through a phase. . . It'll pass, maybe not for hundreds of years, but some day. . . I still believe, in spite of everything, that people are really good at heart." I join Anne Frank in her childlike credo because her words help me to cope with my occasional despair and give me some hope for a better world.

Not just Jews, but civilized men and women everywhere should honor those who offered their humanity at a time when inhumanity reigned everywhere in Nazi Europe. They leave us a legacy of moral courage, a noble alternative to brutality that must be passed on to future generations.